To Paul
with much respect and
gratitude for his
very inspiring and
insightful scholarship!
          Best wishes,
          Gergana

          4/22/19

UNBINDING *THE PILLOW BOOK*

Unbinding *The Pillow Book*

The Many Lives of a Japanese Classic

Gergana Ivanova

Columbia University Press   *New York*

Columbia University Press wishes to express its appreciation for assistance given by the Wm. Theodore de Bary Fund in the publication of this book.

Columbia University Press
Publishers Since 1893
New York   Chichester, West Sussex
cup.columbia.edu

Library of Congress Cataloging-in-Publication Data
Names: Ivanova, Gergana E., author.
Title: Unbinding The Pillow Book : the many lives of a Japanese classic / Gergana E. Ivanova.
Description: New York : Columbia University Press, [2018] | Includes bibliographical
    references and index.
Identifiers: LCCN 2018014383 (print) | LCCN 2018020440 (ebook) | ISBN 9780231547604
    (electronic) | ISBN 9780231187985 (cloth : acid-free paper)
Subjects: LCSH: Sei Shonagon, approximately 967- Makura no soshi.
Classification: LCC PL788.6.M33 (ebook) | LCC PL788.6.M33 I88 2018 (print) |
    DDC 895.6/81—dc23
LC record available at https://lccn.loc.gov/2018014383

Cover design: Milenda Nan Ok Lee

Cover art credit: Collezione Marega. Università Pontificia Salesiana, Roma.

*На майка ми
с безкрайна благодарност и обич!*

Contents

Acknowledgments

My work on how *The Pillow Book* traveled across time and space turned into a long journey of its own. I was exceedingly fortunate that many inspiring, extraordinary, and greathearted people helped me along the way and made the journey even more rewarding.

I would like to express my deepest gratitude to Christina Laffin and Joshua S. Mostow, without whom I would never have dared to begin this study. Not only did they teach me how to write and ask meaningful questions about literature but also generously offered advice, feedback, and support whenever I needed their guidance during my graduate studies and beyond. I am grateful for every moment of working closely with them. At the University of British Columbia, I was also most fortunate to study with Sharalyn Orbaugh and Stefania Burk, who expanded my view of Japanese literature. I am sincerely thankful to Sonja Arntzen, whose mentorship and inspiration led me to enter the field of premodern Japanese literature.

Generous funding from the Social Sciences and Humanities Research Council of Canada, the Japan Foundation, and the University of British Columbia allowed me to spend two years in Japan to conduct essential research for this book. There, Mitamura Masako and Watanabe Kenji welcomed me warmly and generously taught me how to engage with premodern literary sources at Sophia University and Rikkyō University. Their continuing mentorship represents an incredible privilege. I wish to thank Aoki Shin'ichi, Komori Kiyoshi, Numajiri Toshimichi, Tsushima Tomoaki, and Uehara Sakukazu for allowing me to join their study group (Makura no Sōshi no Kai) and introducing me to significant and innovative research on *The Pillow Book*. I very much appreciate the insightful feedback and the support in accessing research-related material I received from Azuma Miho, Ellis Tinios, Gaye Rowley, Hayakawa Monta, Imanishi Shuichirō, Itō Moriyuki, Itō Nobuhiro, Kojima Naoko, Nakanishi Kenji, Shirakura Yoshihiko, Takahashi Tōru, and Yamamoto Tokurō. Thanks to Nishida Keiko at Sōai University I was able to comb through the largest collection of materials related to *The Pillow Book*, where I came upon many of the primary sources I discuss in this book. I am greatly indebted to my dear friends Miyuki and Jun Matsui for their hospitality and support over many years and for making every trip to Japan most enjoyable.

At the University of Cincinnati, I am grateful to the Taft Research Center and the University Research Council for their generous funding. I completed this monograph during the academic year 2016–2017, when I was a Taft Center research fellow. The Taft Center also provided me with a crucial opportunity to enhance my manuscript by inviting Jamie Newhard to serve as my interlocutor during the Taft Symposium. I wish to thank Jamie for her insightful reading of my work, astute advice, and stimulating questions that helped me refine my arguments. I would also like to express my gratitude to my colleagues and friends who offered generous editorial support, feedback, and encouragement at various stages: Sunnie Rucker-Chang, Ashley Currier, Ari Finkelstein, Mikiko Hirayama, Heidi Maibom, Junko Markovic, Michelle McCowan, Audrey Ostendorf, Michal Raucher, Carolette Norwood, Michèle Vialet, and Valerie Weinstein. Olga Hart kindly accommodated all my library needs such that I was never impeded by lack of resources, and Emmanuel Wilson helped me capture quality images. I am also thankful to Todd Herzog, the present department head, for his encouragement and for facilitating precious research time.

While completing this work, colleagues in the field of Japanese studies asked questions that encouraged me to think more deeply, offered constructive feedback, shared wisdom, and recommended material that allowed me to expand my pool of sources. I wish to thank Linda Chance, Rebecca Copeland, Torquil Duthie, Michael Emmerich, Asato Ikeda,

Ishigami Aki, Kazuko Kameda-Madar, Ewa Machotka, Laura Miller, Otilia Milutin, Satoko Naito, Yasuhara Makoto, and Marcia Yonemoto.

I am grateful to the staff at the Ajinomoto Center for Dietary Culture, the British Museum, Gentōsha Inc., the International Research Center for Japanese Studies (Nichibunken), the Museum of Fine Arts, Boston, the Nara Women's University Academic Information Center, the National Diet Library, the National Institute of Japanese Literature, Sōai University Library, and the Toyota City Library for providing me with images and granting me rights to reproduce them in this book. I also wish to thank the journal *Japanese Language and Literature* for allowing me to reprint portions of my article "Re-Gendering a Classic: *The Pillow Book* for Early Modern Female Readers" in chapter 4.

At Columbia University Press, I am greatly indebted to Jennifer Crewe and Christine Dunbar for their profound support and for making the publication process so pleasurable. Special thanks also go to Leslie Kriesel and Christian Winting. I am grateful to the anonymous readers, who offered extensive and highly valuable feedback that helped my manuscript reach its final form. This book has also benefited from Francesca Simkin's and Mike Ashby's remarkable editorial skills. Francesca undertook the first round of copyediting and worked with me on a tight schedule. Mike's meticulous copyediting contributed to the final shape of my manuscript. I wish to thank both of them for their highly professional work.

At home, I am always thankful to Preslava and Sawato for the contagious laughter and good cheer that they have lavished me with on a daily basis. It would be hard to imagine going through this whole process of completing and publishing a book without Masayuki's immense support, which words cannot describe. *Arigatō!*

UNBINDING *THE PILLOW BOOK*

CHAPTER ONE

What Is *The Pillow Book*?

The Pillow Book (*Makura no sōshi*, early eleventh century) is one of the texts that form the core of the Japanese literary canon as it is taught today within and outside Japan. Currently perceived as a masterpiece of world literature, it has become the most widely adapted Japanese literary work in English, as evident from the broad spectrum of novels, poems, and screenplays it has inspired. Despite the strong presence of this Heian-period (794–1185) text on the literary stage, its complex and multifaceted nature has defied categorization and definition. This study explores the multitude of views on *The Pillow Book* and its female author, Sei Shōnagon (964?–after 1027), that emerged beginning in the seventeenth century and into the early twentieth. My aim is to show that attempts to limit classical texts to a specific origin, definitive version, or singular meaning lead to misconceptions that suppress the many functions that such texts have performed over time. The complex reception history of *The Pillow Book*, in which the text was re-created in various forms, serves as a useful case study of how literary criticism, gender structures, and the status of women have changed over time. Historicizing and contextualizing some of the ways in which *The Pillow Book* was interpreted and Sei Shōnagon was imagined help us understand why specific perceptions of the text and its author emerged at the time they did and how different external factors infused life into the two, captivating readers' attention even centuries after the Heian period. This book is the first to offer an examination of the fluidity of *The Pillow Book* by placing it in the multiple contexts in which it was read and rewritten and showing how, even within the same historical setting, the text did not perform the same functions for audiences of differing genders.

The Pillow Book belongs to the large corpus of literary works by accomplished and highly educated women writers, including Ono no Komachi (mid-ninth century), Michitsuna's Mother (ca. 937–995), Murasaki Shikibu (ca. 973–1014), Izumi Shikibu (970s–after 1027), and Akazome Emon (960?–1040?), that emerged between the ninth and eleventh centuries in Japan and continue to inform present-day cultural production. Despite the seeming timelessness of these Heian-period texts, their assessment and the images of their authors have changed greatly over the centuries, both eliciting severe criticism and receiving fervent praise. Frequently referred to as classics, these works have been adapted into fictional tales, dramas, erotic parodies, illustrated narratives, didactic picture scrolls, and comic books to address such issues as the status of women, creativity, morality, sexuality, and national identity. Likewise, images of Heian women writers have been transformed multiple times, shaped as they have been by dominant ideologies rather than through reference to historical documents and direct interactions with their literary works. The vast number of appropriations produced over the course of a millennium is indicative of the significance these works have had for generations of readers. However, despite proliferating interpretations of Heian texts and representations of their female authors, readers are usually presented with only one view, shaped by a specific context and targeted at a particular audience.

For example, *The Pillow Book* is widely known in Japan as the work that opens with the words "In spring, the dawn" (*Haru wa akebono*), as the narrator of NHK's television series *History's Secret Stories* (*Rekishi hiwa hisutoria*) remarked in a 2014 episode that featured *The Pillow Book*.[1] The narrator wondered if the audience knew what was written in the remainder of the work, noting that the opening section "is familiar to anyone in Japan" because of its inclusion in school curricula. Titled "The Secrets of 'in spring, the dawn!' Sei Shōnagon's Sad Love Story" (*Haru wa akebono no himitsu! Sei Shōnagon kanashiki ai no monogatari*), the episode introduces *The Pillow Book* as a woman's blog about everyday life in the Heian imperial court. The narrator invites viewers to join her as she opens "this treasure bag of women's stories of tremulous excitement [written] a thousand years ago" that concerns "aristocrats' magnificent fashion, coveted sweets, and charming love tactics." This summary of *The Pillow Book* is not inaccurate, but it is just one view of the text, presumably targeted at an audience of modern-day Japanese women. It addresses what is commonly perceived as popular topics for women, notably fashion, food, and relationships, and presents *The Pillow Book* as a literary work that transcends time. To women in the Edo period (1603–1867), also known as the early modern period, *The Pillow Book* was recommended as reading material that offered instruction on how to cultivate literary erudition. Although the opening passage "In spring, the dawn," which imparts knowledge about Heian-period aesthetics associated with the four seasons, is today the most frequently reproduced part of the text in Japan, for early modern female audiences, *The Pillow Book* was condensed to a short episode about women's exceptional learnedness and quick-wittedness. In the same Edo period, readers of erotic literature viewed *The Pillow Book* as a collection of lists classifying various aspects of life into categories, such as "Long Things," "Short Things," and "Things That Make the Heart Beat Faster," because this mode of writing had inspired many guides to courtesans and manners in the "pleasure quarters."[2]

In addition to the playfully anachronistic view of *The Pillow Book* as a kind of Heian blog, readers today within and outside Japan are usually introduced to *The Pillow Book* as a miscellany (*zuihitsu*) of approximately three hundred disconnected lists, diary-like entries, and essay-type passages that reveal the refinement of the Heian imperial court and the strong character of its female author.[3] Although this may be a convenient way to describe Sei's heterogeneous writing, every aspect of this depiction is a product of later engagements with the text that aimed at shortening the distance between the context of the work's production and the setting in which it was read, interpreted, and assessed. Most interpretations of the text and representations of its author that linger in current scholarship and popular culture emerged in the years between the seventeenth century and the early twentieth—that is, the combined duration of the Edo and Meiji (1868–1912) periods. For instance, the first documented attempts to construct a definitive text of *The Pillow Book* out of the large number of textual variants and to section and rearrange it to make it more comprehensible can be traced back to the seventeenth century; the *zuihitsu* label was applied to the text in the eighteenth century, while the view of Sei Shōnagon's character as contrasting with that of Murasaki Shikibu, the author of *The Tale of Genji* (*Genji monogatari*, early eleventh century) also emerged in the eighteenth century and still held sway in the early twentieth.

Japan's unification after centuries of warfare at the end of the sixteenth century ushered in an era of unprecedented economic prosperity, a marked rise in literacy rates, and the cultural upheaval that would later come to be known as the Edo period. The establishment a few years later of the third military government, headed by the Tokugawa family, and the adoption of neo-Confucianism as the official state ideology led to a society divided into classes that had unequal access to power and privilege. Despite the rigid social hierarchy—with samurai occupying the top, followed by farmers, artisans, and merchants—the early modern Japanese of all social classes were equally entitled to the consumption of many informational and literary texts. The commercial publishing industry that developed in the early seventeenth century gradually expanded to include the publication of not only a wide range of literary texts but also renditions catering to diverse markets of readers in terms of gender, class, age, and literacy. Thus, scholarly editions of works from the Heian period came to be sold alongside adaptations for mass consumption, in a way reminiscent of present-day literary production. The trend continued into the Meiji period, when Japan was forced to open its borders to extensive exchange with the rest of the world and rapidly transformed into a modern nation-state. In this new context, women's education was no longer aimed at strengthening the family but focused instead on civilizing and advancing the Japanese nation.

The country's shifting position vis-à-vis the rest of the world further influenced the assessment and interpretation of literary works from the distant past. These texts continued to perform a vibrant role in debates about national and cultural identities, but in contrast to the earlier centuries when they were measured against Chinese writing, in the Meiji period Japan's literary heritage was discussed with regard to its commensurability with Western literature. In a similar way, the large number of editions of Heian literary works that have appeared in the book market in the past few decades, including reproductions accompanied by scholarly commentaries, extensively illustrated comics, and renditions in current slang, signals changes in Japanese society that have triggered revived interest in the classics. These recent publications not only transmit knowledge about Japan's past to younger generations but also instill in them a sense of cultural superiority in a West-dominated world order. Drawing from Edo- and Meiji-period sources enables us to identify precedents for reinventing ancient texts and the images of their authors to influence political contexts, affect sociocultural conditions, create readerships, and construct gender and thus comprehend the participation of literary works that have existed for at least a millennium in present-day cultural production.

THE ELEVENTH-CENTURY IMPERIAL COURT

Although Sei Shōnagon's image has been enriched by various anecdotes over the centuries, very little is known about her and *The Pillow Book*. Sei was born into a family of poets at a time when the aristocrats of the imperial court had developed a highly sophisticated culture. Her father, Kiyohara no Motosuke (908–990), served as one of the compilers of the *Later Collection of Japanese Poetry* (*Gosen wakashū*, commissioned 951) and is considered one of the Thirty-Six Poetry Immortals (Sanjūrokkasen).[4] Her great-grandfather was Kiyohara no Fukayabu (dates unknown), whose poems were included in the first and second imperially commissioned anthologies of poetry, *A Collection of Ancient and Modern Poems* (*Kokin wakashū*, ca. 905) and *Later Collection of Japanese Poetry*, respectively. In her thirties, Sei was recruited as an attendant to Empress Teishi (976–1000) and served at court from 993 until Teishi's death.

Fujiwara no Teishi was the daughter of Fujiwara no Michitaka (953–995). Teishi's entrance into the court of Emperor Ichijō (980–1011, r. 986–1011) in the year 990 at the age of fourteen coincided with the coming-of-age ceremony of the eleven-year-old emperor. During this same year, she was promoted to empress following her father's appointment as regent (*kanpaku*), which was the post of ultimate political power. Three years later, Sei Shōnagon joined Teishi's cultural salon.[5] Highly intelligent and talented midranking aristocratic women like Sei played an important role in the marriage politics of the Heian court, since their erudition and creativity were viewed as enhancing the cultural sophistication of their female patrons' salons. Being preferred by the emperor above his other consorts naturally increased a woman's chances of becoming the mother of a future sovereign. In 995, Michitaka's other daughter, Genshi, entered the court as a consort of the crown prince, indicating her father's growing power. However, in the same year, following Michitaka's death at age forty-three, the political situation began to change. Tragic events continued the following year, when Teishi's brothers Korechika and Takaie were exiled in the fifth month, and their mother, Kishi, died in the tenth. Also in 995, Teishi's uncle Fujiwara no Michinaga (966–1027), who had been her father's rival, became the head of the Fujiwara family and wielded uncontested political power from 996 to 1017. Left without political backing or close relatives at court for support, and threatened by the appointment of Michinaga's daughter Shōshi (988–1074) as another empress to Ichijō, Teishi lived for four more years undergoing hardship and humiliation.

Commissioned by her patron, as is evident from the epilogue that acknowledges the fact that she received the paper for it from Teishi, Sei Shōnagon produced a narrative that features her service at court and covers the years of her patron's tragic decline.[6] However, *The Pillow Book* is not a narrative permeated by lament but an account of the cultural and literary sophistication of the court that is imbued with humor and laughter. Touching on a wide range of issues, such as the status of women, subjectivity, aesthetic competence, and literacy, *The Pillow Book* depicts the court of Empress Teishi as triumphant and glamorous.[7]

It is unclear how *The Pillow Book* was received in the context of its creation. The fact that it was completed after the demise of Sei's patron, who had been a political rival to the reigning empress, raises the question of why its dissemination was not curtailed. One explanation could be that the work was regarded as an active "pacification" of angry spirits (*chinkon*) to Sei's patron and her immediate family, or, as Haruo Shirane has put it, "a literary prayer to the spirit of the deceased empress Teishi."[8]

Drawing from a wealth of literary works, *The Pillow Book* underscores the sophistication of Teishi's salon, whose members were likely its intended readership, and reveals the literary competence of its author. It is imbued with allusions to earlier literary works. Japanese literary sources include the *Collection of Ten Thousand Leaves* (*Man'yōshū*, late eighth century), *A Collection of Ancient and Modern Poems*, popular songs (*imayō*), and songs of celebration sung at court gatherings (*saibara*). Allusions to literary court romances (*monogatari*) and other works that have not survived may also be present in the text but are not evident to the modern reader. In addition to Japanese-language sources, *The Pillow Book* refers to many Chinese literary works, including Bo (also Bai) Juyi's (772–846) poetry anthology *Bai's Collected Works* (Ch. *Bai-shi wen ji*, J. *Hakushi monjū*, ca. 824); Chinese poems by Japanese poets that were included in Fujiwara no Kintō's *Collection of Japanese and Chinese Poems to Sing* (*Wakan rōeishū*, early eleventh century); a number of histories, compendia, and textbooks for young readers (known as *yōgakusho*), including *Records of the Historian* (Ch. *Shiji*, J. *Shiki*, 91 B.C.E.), *The History of the Former Han Dynasty* (Ch. *Han shu*, J. *Kanjo*, ca. 80) and *Beginner's Guide* (Ch. *Meng qiu*, J. *Mōgyū*, 746); and sutras, such as *The Lotus Sutra* (Sk. *Saddharma puṇḍarīka sūtra*, J. *Hokekyō*), *The Amida Sutra* (Sk. *Amitābha sūtra*, J. *Amidakyō*), and *The Contemplation Sutra* (Sk. *Amitāyurdhyāna sūtra*, J. *Kanmuryōjukyō*).[9] Women's knowledge of literary Sinitic in Heian Japan was a prerequisite for certain posts at court and was therefore highly encouraged by parents who hoped to position their daughters well for a court career.[10] In addition, Chinese poetry, and specifically that of Bo Juyi, dominated cultural life at court, as is clear from its inclusion in many texts of the time and its prominence in poetry contests.[11]

As recorded in the last passage of two textual variants of *The Pillow Book*, the *Nōinbon* and *Sankanbon* manuscripts, the text began to circulate within the court between 995 and 996, after the middle general of the left Tsunefusa (969–1023) had seized Sei's notebook and carried it off.[12] It was presumably after Sei had put the finishing touches on her manuscript, and most likely after the death of her patron, that the revised text joined the other copies of her narrative already in circulation. Its lack of a rigid textual structure, and the uncertainty about what exactly the text was, may have been part of encouraging scribes to freely copy, interpret, and modify it. Since the original manuscript was already lost by the late Heian period, various copies that were full of careless scribal errors and deliberate "improvements" continued to circulate, making the final intentions of the author unclear.[13] As early as the first years of the

Kamakura period (1185–1333), people were aware of the existence of different versions of *The Pillow Book*.[14]

HYBRIDITY OF *THE PILLOW BOOK*

The Pillow Book's textual multiplicity comprises various manuscript lineages, each bearing the traces of complex processes of splicing, collating, editing, and purposely altering preexisting manuscripts. It is frequently identified as the Japanese literary work with the largest number of textual variants.[15] Since the 1920s, when literary scholar Ikeda Kikan (1896–1956) grouped the numerous manuscripts of *The Pillow Book* based on similarities among them, Sei's work has been viewed as existing in the following four textual lines: *den Nōin shojihon* (the book in possession of Nōin), also known as the *Nōinbon*; *Sankanbon keitō shohon* (the books from the three-volume lineage), also known as *Antei ninen okugaki-bon* (the book with an afterword from the second year of Antei [1228]), frequently referred to as the *Sankanbon*; the *Maeda-ke-bon* (the book of the Maeda family); and the *Sakaibon* (the book from Sakai).[16] The work's exceedingly complicated textual history precludes any definitive conclusion about the authenticity of one textual line over the others because it is unclear what the text Sei Shōnagon wrote actually looked like. What has generally been considered the major difference among the textual variants was the sections into which the work was divided. Twentieth-century scholars classified the sections into three main categories: lists or catalogues (*ruijū-tekina shōdan*), essays (*zuisō-tekina shōdan*), and diary-like passages (*nikki-tekina shōdan*), and further drew a distinction between the manuscripts in which the sections are in a seemingly random order and those in which they are arranged by category.

Textual variants also differ from one another in terms of orthography, content, and number of passages, resulting in works with very divergent literary effects. For example, the intensity of authorial presence varies across manuscripts: in some texts the narrator seems passionately concerned with the topics she discusses, whereas in others she is presented as less outspoken. A close reading and comparison of some of the passages in the two randomly organized textual lines, the *Nōinbon* and the *Sankanbon*, give the impression that the *Nōinbon* consistently conveys a voice that is more intimate and closely connected with the social and historical specificities of the era in which the work was composed. The narrator's coquettish and self-conscious decorum reveals a strong awareness of the readers' gaze. The result is a narrative of immediacy and vitality. On the other hand, the *Sankanbon* textual line—the one currently considered the most authentic and used as a base text by mainstream modern scholars—contains passages that are more restrained and resemble impassive reportage.[17] The large number of textual variants of Sei Shōnagon's work challenges the assumption that there exists an authentic text that is definitive and remains stable through time.

Furthermore, *The Pillow Book* combines a wide range of literary genres, including diary, essay, lists, anecdotes, and poetry. As mentioned, it contains a vast number of Chinese expressions and is imbued with intertextual elements from both Japanese and Chinese sources. This hybridity of Sei Shōnagon's work has led to the text being characterized as dynamic (*dōtai*).[18]

However, despite *The Pillow Book*'s plurality of textual manifestations and voices, readers are usually offered only one representation of the text. For example, manuscripts that centuries later came to be categorized as belonging to the *Nōinbon* textual line were chosen as the preferred version of *The Pillow Book* in the Edo period and served as a base text for scholarly commentaries, adaptations, and parodies.[19] The situation shifted in postwar Japan when authoritative scholars, including Ikeda Kikan and Tanaka Jūtarō (1917–1987), popularized the *Sankanbon* textual line and hailed it as the most authentic *Pillow Book*, while acknowledging the lack of an extant manuscript written in Sei's hand.[20] In addition to shifts in the text's preferred manuscript lineage, Sei's work has frequently been "rewritten" by scholars, critics, writers, and translators whose engagements with it vary in scope and intention. Each interaction with the text has yielded its own version of *The Pillow Book*—intentionally or not—providing readers with yet another attempt at keeping Sei's narrative alive. Regardless of the transformations of the text, many of the versions among the vast number of works that claim a lineage to Sei's text have come to be recognized as *The Pillow Book*. In a similar way, Sei Shōnagon's image frequently shifted as her work was brought to new audiences.

THE PILLOW BOOK BEYOND THE COURT OF EMPRESS TEISHI

The Pillow Book's heterogeneity has influenced the work's journey over the centuries in multiple ways. On the one hand, it has resulted in a work amenable to transformations and multiple readings and allowed scholars and writers not only a site of contestation for literary and ideological authority but also a fruitful source for inspiring creative engagements with the past. On the other hand, however, a preoccupation with the formal features of the work and the difficulty of pinning down to one stable notion what *The Pillow Book* is have impeded attention to its rich content, resulting in marginalization of the work within the literary canon. As Mitamura Masako has observed, the scholarly focus on *The Pillow Book*'s textual multiplicity and categorization of the work as *zuihitsu* have led to literary devaluation of this Heian text. This is evident from the fact that scholarship on *The Tale of Genji* significantly exceeds that on *The Pillow Book*.[21] Mitamura's recollection of the prevalent attitude toward Sei's work in the 1970s and 1980s affirms Stanley Fish's concept of "interpretative communities"—that is, communities that provide training and membership to literary scholars—as governing and generating interpretation.[22] Citing Akiyama Ken's (1924–2015) view on *The Pillow Book* as a narcissistic (*jiko tōsui*) work unworthy of study, Mitamura offers an insight into one of the reasons why this eleventh-century text had drawn little scholarly attention.[23] Internationally known for his contribution to the study of *The Tale of Genji* and his faculty position at Tokyo University from the 1950s to the 1980s, Akiyama's disparagement of *The Pillow Book* must have curtailed for decades all attempts to go beyond an examination of Sei's character and the textual variants of her work. Fortunately, Mitamura's interest in the textual organization and linguistic expressions of *The Pillow Book* as a key to decode representations of actual historical events drew attention to the richness of the Heian text and paved the way for further research that burgeoned in the 1990s. Outside Japan, studies by Mark Morris, Tzvetana Kristeva, Naomi Fukumori, Edith Sarra, and Joshua S. Mostow examined the poetics and historicity of the work, representations of gender, and the political context in which *The Pillow Book* was produced.[24] Jennifer Guest's recent study of *kanbun* (Sino-Japanese) literacy in the

Heian period has provided new insights into the roles that the bountiful allusions to Chinese texts in Sei's work may have played in the social setting in which she wrote.[25]

An important aspect of *The Pillow Book*'s initial reception is that the text was most likely completed after Teishi had died and her salon had disappeared, unlike *The Tale of Genji*, which emerged as a literary work in a cultural salon related to the most politically powerful and influential family in the Heian period, whose fortunes flourished for almost a century.[26] Another factor, perhaps even more crucial, pertains to the work's formal features. The different styles that constitute Sei's narrative made the work resistant to generic categorization. As already mentioned, it was designated a *zuihitsu* (miscellany) in the late Edo period, following centuries of reception as a court romance, a work related to poetry (*kasho*), a diary (*nikki*), a collection of anecdotes (*setsuwashū*), and an instruction manual.[27] With the centrality of *waka* (and *renga*) in Japanese literature during the medieval period, the fact that *The Pillow Book* did not focus on poetry made the work less appealing to medieval readers than *The Ise Stories* (*Ise monogatari*, tenth century) and *The Tale of Genji*. Moreover, as Japanese scholars have noted, although *The Pillow Book* was referred to as one of the texts crucial to "understanding the meaning [*kokoro*] of Japanese poetry," the work's aesthetic of celebrating everything attractive, amusing, and interesting (*okashi*) did not appeal to the medieval masters of poetry.[28]

Sei Shōnagon's gender has also played a crucial role in the way readers have perceived the work. Sei's pairing with Murasaki Shikibu, which I discuss in chapter 5, is one of the discourses with a long history that has generated interpretations of the text and images of its author. Despite the fact that both *The Pillow Book* and *The Tale of Genji* discuss similar topics—including life in the imperial court during the Heian period, relationships between men and women, and courtly aesthetics—and that both writers share significant similarities in terms of gender, family background, education, and status within the court they served, *The Pillow Book* was considered to be inferior to *The Tale of Genji*. Emerging as a negative foil to the *Genji* writer, Sei was repeatedly reinvented as an exceedingly proud and conceited woman to underscore the superiority of Murasaki Shikibu and her text. Although *The Tale of Genji* has attained the status of most celebrated literary work in Japanese history, residues of the centuries-long pairing of the two Heian texts remain embedded in the ways *The Pillow Book* is perceived even today. This constructed rivalry between the two women writers also reveals male scholars' anxiety in the early years of the twentieth century about female creativity and literary talent. As Rebecca Copeland has noted, "The literary stage can only accommodate one [woman] writer at a time. We have Murasaki Shikibu—what need do we have of others? By prioritizing Murasaki in this way, critics also made her even less accessible to 'normal' women as a model."[29] Although male literary critics vilified Sei, in educational literature for "normal" women in the Meiji period and beyond, both Sei and Murasaki were upheld as models of literary erudition intended to empower female readers.

The marginalization of *The Pillow Book* has been further influenced by its pairing with Priest Kenkō's (1283?–1352?) *Essays in Idleness* (*Tsurezuregusa*, ca. 1330–1331). It was the poet Shōtetsu (1381–1459) who first suggested that *Essays in Idleness* imitated the style of *The Pillow Book*,[30] and in the subsequent centuries the questionable similarity of their formal features was frequently used to link the two works, leading to their being labeled as *zuihitsu* in the eighteenth century.[31] Removing Sei's work from the context of its creation, male scholars in the centuries that followed repeatedly construed it as one lacking in seriousness and depth. Despite the acknowledged status of Sei's text as the predecessor in this genre, within this dyad *The Pillow Book* was often viewed as inferior to the "mature" and "polished"[32] tone of the male recluse's writing.[33] The initial stage of the pairing of these texts occurred in the medieval period, when Buddhism was at its height. It is therefore not surprising that a female-authored text would be treated less sympathetically than a work composed by a male writer who was a Buddhist priest. This perception and assessment of the two narratives continued into the modern period and cast a shadow over later scholarship.

Despite *The Pillow Book*'s relegation to an inferior position in literary history, scholars have continuously asked fruitful questions of the work, such as, what does an original text imply? How, when, and why does a written work become literature? How is it affected by the absence of an original text? Why, despite the lack of a text traceable to the author's intentions, do some literary works continue to play important roles even a millennium after their production? As these questions show,

The Pillow Book continues to create ambiguity and disrupt dichotomies in the scholarly world by challenging the binaries of authenticity-imitation, homogeneity-heterogeneity, and stability-fluidity. The contested exegetical approaches, adaptations, and parodies, and works that have drawn inspiration from Sei's *Pillow Book* over the centuries, validate Hans R. Jauss's claim that "a literary work is not an object that stands by itself and that offers the same view to each reader in each period."[34] Scholarship on the reception history of *The Pillow Book* has developed only over the past two decades. In Japan, Tsushima Tomoaki, Numajiri Toshimichi, and Nakajima Wakako examined, respectively, the constructed nature of *zuihitsu*, early modern scholarly attempts to make the text "readable," and the shifts in the representation of Sei within medieval and early modern collections of anecdotes.[35] Outside Japan, R. Keller Kimbrough's pioneering study of the images of Sei in medieval narratives was followed by Valerie Henitiuk's work on the global circulation of the Heian text through translations of its opening passage, "In spring, the dawn," and Evelyne Lesigne-Audoly's examination of Kitamura Kigin's commentary.[36] Linda Chance's study of *zuihitsu* has provided important insights into the constructed nature of the genre and the history of the discourse that pairs *The Pillow Book* with *Essays in Idleness*.[37]

The terms "reception history" and "canon formation" in the Japanese context have been challenged recently by Michael Emmerich and Joshua S. Mostow through their explorations of the afterlives of *The Tale of Genji* and *The Ise Stories*, respectively. Advancing new concepts, the two scholars have offered highly productive tools for considering how texts that travel across time and space free us from preoccupation with the idea of the original text while drawing attention to the roles that gender, class, and political context play in shaping texts' meanings. More specifically, "replacement," as Emmerich defines it, refers to "all the varieties of books, . . . texts that are read instead of the (unknown) and (unknowable) original."[38] "(Cultural) appropriation," on the other hand, reflects the shifting place of a text across gender and class and how it "is employed for specific political and social ends," in Mostow's words.[39] Building upon Emmerich's and Mostow's work, I question why *The Pillow Book* and Sei Shōnagon have been presented over the years as transcending time and used to address various issues in completely new settings.

The history of rereading and rewriting *The Pillow Book* calls attention to a pattern that can further refine our understanding of the process of creating knowledge about literary texts. Over the centuries, there has been no common understanding of *The Pillow Book* as a unified work. Despite the stylistic and thematic richness of the text and the multifaceted personality of its narrator, *The Pillow Book* and Sei Shōnagon have frequently been presented through only one aspect that is so amplified that it comes to represent the whole while erasing all other features of the text or its author. The view of *The Pillow Book* and the image of Sei introduced as authoritative at any given moment take shape in a concrete context, convey a particular ideology, and are intended for a specific audience. My title, *Unbinding "The Pillow Book,"* is thus multivalent. I draw from the two main meanings of the verb "to unbind"—namely, "to unfasten, to loosen" and "to set free, to release from restraint." The former refers to the predominant tendency for later readers to focus on only one aspect of *The Pillow Book* and use it as representative of the whole work. This process of symbolically loosening the pages of *The Pillow Book* and picking only a few to serve as the entire work stands in sharp contrast to the manner in which the work was produced. Prompted by Sei's enthusiastic remark "Let's make it into a pillow!"[40] as recorded in the colophon, the earliest stage of composing *The Pillow Book* is usually identified with putting together the paper that Empress Teishi received from her brother Korechika. The practices of reading *The Pillow Book* in the subsequent centuries are analogous to the act of unbinding the work, be it through adaptation or interpretation based on selected parts of the text. *The Pillow Book Illustrated Scroll* (*Makura no sōshi emaki*, fourteenth century), which centers on diary-like passages; *Picture Book Mount Asahi* (*Ehon Asahiyama*, 1741), which features lists; and the early twentieth-century view of the work as a collection of self-praise episodes are only some examples of prioritizing certain aspects of the work as it is brought to new audiences.

My drawing on the latter meaning of "unbinding" reflects my desire in this study to release the work and its author from the fetters into which they have been forced, specifically the perception of *The Pillow Book* as a *zuihitsu* and the image of Sei as the boastful female writer. By showing how this Heian woman—who in medieval anecdotes was ridiculed for her wittiness and ability to outdo men—was hailed for her literary erudition in early modern instruction manuals for women and then transformed into a malicious female in modern literary histories, as well as how interpretation of *The Pillow Book* changed over time, I call attention to the constructed nature of Japanese women's literary works from the distant past and the simplified and stubbornly unchanging image of their authors. This study also reveals that *The Pillow Book* is too diverse to be captured in a single image, and that attempts to do so reflect our (deliberate or unintentional) blindness to its thematic, stylistic, and textual richness. Although *The Pillow Book* that Sei Shōnagon wrote is lost and irretrievable, its subsequent rewritings, though secondary to the text that first began to circulate, are equally important because they disclose how later readers "imagined" the literary past. Likewise, the copious accounts concerning Sei Shōnagon offer an insight into what it meant to be an accomplished woman at various junctures in Japan's history.

THE PILLOW BOOK IN MULTIPLE CONTEXTS

This book focuses on representations of *The Pillow Book* and Sei Shōnagon in discourses of women's education, the pleasure quarters, Confucian ideology, the formation of a modern nation-state, and literary criticism. Following this introductory chapter is an examination of scholarly attempts in early modern Japan to make the work easier to comprehend. The three complete commentaries produced in the Edo period by *haikai* (popular linked verse) poets reveal how scholars undertook to compile an authoritative text from the many manuscripts in circulation, divide it into sections that would facilitate reading of the work, and confine it to a single style or genre—namely, a collection of lists or playful random jottings. After centuries of reception of *The Pillow Book* as having similarities with works belonging to diverse modes of writing, eighteenth- and nineteenth-century national learning (*kokugaku*) scholars labeled it a *zuihitsu* after a Chinese genre that catalogued knowledge into categories. Although this categorization of *The Pillow Book* was used to underscore Japan's superiority over China in terms of literary heritage, it eventually led, in subsequent centuries, to the marginalization of the work.

Chapter 3 considers the eroticization of *The Pillow Book* in the Edo period, focusing on seventeen-syllable comic verses (*senryū*) and erotic adaptations. Popular writers constructed Sei's work as a collection of lists, as evident from the compilations of verses recorded during *haikai* poetry contests and the subversive guides to the pleasure quarters. These rewritings have been viewed as parodies of the eleventh-century text and have been dismissed as lesser works. However, delving more deeply into their contents reveals that they conveyed a specific gender ideology and functioned as a powerful tool to question established notions of identity and status. Using lists from *The Pillow Book*, early modern erotic parodies appropriated the Heian concepts of time and space and constructed an alternative version of Japan centered around the culture of pleasure seeking rather than the state ideology that fixed class and identity for life. These works recast the ancient aristocratic culture into new, contemporary contexts and presented Sei Shōnagon as a predecessor of early modern courtesans.

Chapter 4 examines three illustrated adaptations—specifically, a picture book that features women's work, a sex manual, and a letter-writing textbook, all of which seem to have been produced for female audiences, conveying knowledge that was seen as enhancing a woman's desirability as a wife. They present Sei Shōnagon as the embodiment of learning, quick-wittedness, and refinement. Expanding our pool of sources related to women's education in early modern Japan beyond the corpus of texts already labeled as letter-writing textbooks (*ōrai-mono*) or instruction manuals for girls (*jokunsho*), these illustrated texts reveal that a woman's sexual attractiveness was viewed as having the potential to improve her relationship with her husband and thus strengthen her position in the household.

Taking up the constructed rivalry between Sei Shōnagon and Murasaki Shikibu, which continues even today in popular culture and scholarly circles, chapter 5 provides an examination of contested representations of Sei from the eighteenth century to the early twentieth. Modern scholars transformed Sei Shōnagon into the antithesis of ideal femininity in discourses on national literature and gender construction. However, the negative image of Sei they construed did not automatically affect women's education. On the contrary, early modern popular texts with wide dissemination, state-sanctioned official textbooks, and popular journals, all of which were targeted at female audiences, hailed Sei as an exemplary woman and a talented and intelligent writer.

The concluding chapter considers rewritings of *The Pillow Book* in present-day popular culture within and outside Japan. The analysis of adaptations aimed at female readerships from the eighteenth century to the early twentieth in the preceding chapter is followed by a discussion of comic books and a translation into current girls' slang, produced in Japan in the past twenty years, to show how adaptations of *The Pillow Book* in the category of educational texts for young women have changed over the centuries. No longer intended to directly enhance a woman's marriageability or instill moral values, modern-day adaptations aimed as study guides for university entrance exams present the work as one that transcends time and use Sei as a tool to address the topic of feminine subjectivity. In addition, to draw parallels between diverse contexts of reception in the present, I examine how *The Pillow Book* has been transformed as it enters international contexts, considering Peter Greenaway's film *The Pillow Book* (1996) and historical novels produced for English-reading audiences. Many of these works construct *The Pillow Book* to depict a millennium-long tradition of Japanese women writers as amorous and sexually unrestrained and view Japanese literature as one that focuses entirely on carnal pleasures.

According to the colophon to *The Pillow Book*, when Sei heard comments on her writing, after the minister of the left had taken and circulated it, she exclaimed, "It is quite vexing, to have had my notes seen by others."[41] In this book, I invite readers to join me in reflecting on the significance that *The Pillow Book* has had for generations of readers and in imagining how Sei would have reacted to the multitude of diverse responses her work and image have elicited over the course of a millennium.

CHAPTER TWO

(Re)constructing the Text and Early Modern Scholarship

Given the rich content and diverse literary styles combined in *The Pillow Book* the categorization of the work as a *zuihitsu*, or miscellany, in modern literary histories seems befitting of the eleventh-century text.[1] Historically, however, at the time Sei Shōnagon was writing *zuihitsu* as a notion did not exist, and it was not until centuries later that this generic label became central to the way the work was perceived. Moreover, what scholars categorized as *zuihitsu* in the eighteenth century differed from *The Pillow Book* that Sei had created. The manuscript(s) in her own hand were lost by the end of the Heian period, and it was only through divergent copies that the text continued to reach later readers, mainly members of the aristocracy and the military elite. Although not completely replaced, this mode of literary consumption, reliant as it was on handwritten manuscripts, was largely eclipsed by commercial publishing, which developed in the seventeenth century and dramatically transformed Japanese society through the spread of information. The textual plurality of literary works from the past that had hitherto existed for centuries only as private manuscripts, or rather one-of-a-kind renditions of a given text, gave way to more unified or standardized versions that were to turn Japan's literary heritage into "common knowledge."[2] For the newly emerging mass readership to comprehend these centuries-old texts, it was necessary to update their archaic language to a more contemporary style and contextualize their contents by means of ample annotation. Although annotated versions of *The Pillow Book* were not published until the latter half of the seventeenth century, within less than a decade three commentaries suddenly appeared on the book market. These annotated editions of *The Pillow Book* differed significantly from one another and from the manuscripts that had circulated in medieval Japan. Regardless of the great alterations Sei's work had undergone in the process of creating a definitive text from the many extant versions, it was precisely these later renditions of *The Pillow Book* that prompted eighteenth-century scholars to describe the work as a *zuihitsu*. Despite the constructed nature of the text and its ahistorical genre categorization, the notion of *zuihitsu* has continued to affect the assessment and interpretation of *The Pillow Book* for more than three hundred years and persists as a generic label for the work both within and outside Japan.

This chapter examines the processes through which *The Pillow Book* came to be viewed as a miscellany in early modern Japan. Tracing the complex textual history of the work and the early scholarship about it, I stress the constructed nature of the text and the deliberate strategies used to imbue *The Pillow Book* with meaning. Specifically, my analysis shows that the text, which was classified as a miscellany in the latter half of the Edo period, was not the writing of Sei Shōnagon but a product of extensive manipulations at the hands of male scholars in the centuries following the completion of the work. I also cast doubt on the validity of the "miscellany" label by drawing attention to the fact that the attribution of *The Pillow Book* to the *zuihitsu* genre gained currency only among scholars and did not cross over into popular culture. I begin with a consideration of some of the textual variants that were in circulation before the seventeenth century and that played an important role in the construction of textual lineages of *The Pillow Book* in the early twentieth century. Next, I examine the strategies that the three complete commentaries published in the late seventeenth century used to produce an authoritative text, to make sense of the multiple styles combined in the work, and to describe Sei's writing based on its title. In the last section, I discuss the contexts in which *The Pillow Book* came to be classified as a *zuihitsu*. Considering the generic categorization of Sei's work, I begin my exploration of the intersections between literary production, gender, and ideology that continues through the remaining chapters of this book.

The Pillow Book began to circulate long before Sei Shōnagon had completed the text, as its famous colophon notes:[3] "While the minister of the left, still called 'governor of Ise,' was visiting my home, I offered a mat, and my notebook fell out on top of it. Panicking, I attempted to put it back, but he snatched it up and carried it off, just like that, and it was after a very long time that it was returned. It seems, the book says,[4] that it started to circulate from that time."[5]

According to the earliest extant annotation on *The Pillow Book*, known as "Notes on the *Sankanbon*" (Sankanbon kanmotsu), attached to the end of the *Sankanbon*-lineage manuscripts with a colophon dated 1228, the minister of the left refers to Minamoto no Tsunefusa (969–1023). Tsunefusa was Fujiwara no Michinaga's adopted son (*yūshi*) and served as a provincial governor in Ise from 995 to 996. He appears several times in *The Pillow Book* and is depicted as someone very close to Sei Shōnagon. Because of this friendship, Sei was rumored to have been from Michinaga's camp, which suggests that Tsunefusa was considered to be affiliated with Fujiwara no Michitaka's rival faction.[6] Although Tsunefusa carried off Sei's notebook sometime between 995 and 996, accounts of the events that took place over the next four or five years recorded in *The Pillow Book* suggest that the work continued to be written while versions or portions of its text were already in circulation.[7] As early as the latter half of the Heian period, at least two versions of *The Pillow Book* that belonged to people closely related to Sei Shōnagon and Empress Teishi were disseminated widely. These texts played an important role in the construction of two of the textual lineages of *The Pillow Book*, the *Nōinbon* and the *Sankanbon*. The postscript to the *Nōinbon* text suggests the existence of a version of *The Pillow Book* that belonged to the princess of the first order (*ippon no miya*). According to Ikeda Kikan, this princess was Fujiwara no Shūshi (997?–1049), also known as Princess Shūshi. Shūshi was the first child born to Emperor Ichijō and Empress Teishi. The proximity of Shūshi to Teishi's salon makes it possible that "the book of the princess of the first order" (*ippon no miya no hon*) may have significantly resembled the text that Sei wrote:

Everyone has a copy of *The Pillow Book*, but a truly good copy is difficult to find these days. This, [manuscript] too, is not that good, but since I heard that it had belonged to Nōin, I copied it, thinking that it would be no worse than others. The state of the paper and the handwriting are disappointing, but I intend not to lend it to many others. Among the many copies of *The Pillow Book*, this one is not too bad, but I do not find it extraordinary. I have seen the book of the princess of the first order of the Retired Emperor Ichijō of the past, which is superb. So says the book.[8]

This *Nōinbon* postscript juxtaposes two manuscripts—namely, Nōin's book (*Nōin ga hon*) and the book of the princess of the first order, the former being viewed as ordinary and without merits and the latter as superb (*medetaki*), although it is unclear on what standards these judgments were based.[9] Despite the copyist's assessment of Nōin's book as not outstanding, it does not preclude the possibility of the text's close association with Sei Shōnagon. In fact, Sei Shōnagon's son Tachibana no Norinaga was married to the sister of the famous poet Nōin (Tachibana no Nagayasu, 988–after 1048).[10] They had a son known as Tachibana no Norisue (dates unknown). Biographical information on Norisue can be found in "Notes on the *Sankanbon*" in the portion of the text next to Minamoto no Tsunefusa. It is unclear why Tsunefusa and Norisue have been included in the "Notes," but modern scholars have agreed that they were likely perceived as the people responsible for the circulation of the two main versions of *The Pillow Book*, the *Nōinbon* and the *Sankanbon*.[11] In other words, scholars conjecture that Nōin might have obtained *The Pillow Book* through Sei Shōnagon's grandson Norisue. The colophon and the postscript suggest that even in the eleventh century various versions of *The Pillow Book* were already in circulation, and although the two variants mentioned in the *Nōinbon* postscript—the book of the princess of the first order and Nōin's book—were associated with people close to Sei Shōnagon and Teishi, they were deemed as differing in quality and evaluated accordingly.

In addition to the *Sankanbon* and *Nōinbon*, whose contents seem to be in random order, Japanese scholars have identified, or rather constructed, two other textual lineages, the *Maeda-ke-bon* and the

Sakaibon. The text in both lineages is viewed as classified. The *Maeda-ke-bon* comes in four volumes presenting *wa*-type lists (catalogues of appellations of concrete entities, including places, deities, court positions, anthologies, plants, and robes) first, followed by *mono*-type lists (assortments of situations and deportment that evoke common emotions or invite similar assessment, such as "Embarrassing Things" and "Elegant Things"), then moving on to essays, and finally introducing diary-like passages. It does not have a postscript and is generally believed to have been produced during the late Heian period or early Kamakura period. The only extant copy entered the collection of the Maeda family in 1609, but its paper and handwriting suggest that it was made in the mid-Kamakura period.[12] Scholars such as Kusunoki Michitaka have argued for the strong influence of the *Nōinbon* and the *Sakaibon* on the *Maeda-ke-bon*.[13] The *Sakaibon*, on the other hand, consists of *wa*-type lists, *mono*-type lists, and essays presented in this order and does not include diary-like passages. Interestingly, this textual lineage contains essaylike passages that cannot be found in the other three manuscript lines, among which are sections with erotic overtones. Its postscript, dated 1570 and signed by Kiyohara no Edakata (1520–1590), presents the *Sakaibon* as a copy of the manuscript that belonged to the Kiyohara family, whose ancestor is Sei Shōnagon.[14]

The first attempts to create knowledge about *The Pillow Book* was the thirteenth-century annotation of the work attached to the *Sankanbon*-lineage manuscripts known as "Notes on the *Sankanbon*," as previously mentioned. Signed by Bōkyū Guō, it is a brief commentary that includes several notes mainly on historical figures and events. Since the 1960s, scholars have come to consider Bōkyū Guō as the influential poet, scholar, and editor Fujiwara no Teika (1162–1241). Recently, Sasaki Takahiro has questioned this theory because of the insufficient evidence on which it is based. Noting how dangerous it is to rely on general knowledge (*jōshiki*) and academic consensus (*teisetsu*), he has looked beyond the fictitious name Bōkyū Guō and considered the annotation, the main text, and the reception of the manuscript. Although Sasaki has concluded that the *Sankanbon* could be attributed to Teika or at least considered as a text Teika owned, he has raised important questions, such as why later copyists failed to identify Bōkyū

Guō as Teika and why medieval texts that cited *The Pillow Book* did not use what modern scholars consider Teika's text.[15]

The *Sankanbon* was copied several times, as the five postscripts suggest.[16] The earliest postscript reads, "The book says, Time had passed since I lost my own copy, which was carelessly made. Then I borrowed two manuscripts and made a copy. Since there is no authoritative text, it contains numerous ambiguities. Yet I looked at other sources and added notes regarding the dates as much as possible. I, too, might be wrong."[17]

Dated 1228, this manuscript appears to have been collated during the reign of Emperor Go-Horikawa (1212–1234, r. 1221–1232). In the fourteenth century, the *Sankanbon* became the base text for the *Pillow Book Illustrated Scroll* (*Makura no sōshi emaki*) that features seven of the diary-like passages from *The Pillow Book*. In the fifteenth century, the mention of a version of Sei's work consisting of three books (*sansatsu*) in *Conversations with Shōtetsu* (*Shōtetsu monogatari*) has led scholars to conclude that the author was referring to the *Sankanbon*.[18] However, this, too, is debatable since *kan* or *maki* is a quantifier for scrolls (*kansusō*), whereas *The Pillow Book* was written as a booklet (*sōshi*).[19]

Despite the fact that the *Sankanbon*-lineage manuscripts were copied multiple times, they were not necessarily the texts scholars and writers consulted. For example, Numajiri Toshimichi's analysis of the use of *The Pillow Book* in commentaries on *The Tale of Genji* has revealed that the *Sakaibon* functioned as a text that facilitated the reading of Murasaki Shikibu's work. Specifically, the Kamakura-period commentary *Variant Notes on Explicating Murasaki* (*Ihon Shimeishō*, 1252)[20] contains citations from four manuscripts of *The Pillow Book*.[21] Among them, the manuscript that belonged to the *Genji* scholar Saien (dates unknown) is deemed as being close to the *Sakaibon*, though not identical. This fact suggests that many more manuscripts of Sei Shōnagon's text were in circulation before the development of commercial printing in the seventeenth century, but the majority of them were later lost. Extant manuscripts of *The Pillow Book* provide us with a limited ability to reconstruct the versions of the text that circulated in the medieval period, thus blurring its textual history.[22]

Numajiri has further shown that the factions in the Kawachi school, which produced the majority of commentaries on *The Tale of Genji* in the late thirteenth century, cited from different texts of *The Pillow Book* in their *Genji* exegeses.[23] For instance, annotating his *Notes on Explicating Murasaki* (*Shimeishō*, 1267, 1294),[24] Priest Sojaku (dates unknown) quoted from a manuscript of *The Pillow Book* that he owned, whereas his brother Minamoto no Chikayuki (1188–after 1272), in his *Most Secret Teachings of The Tale of Genji* (*Genchū saihishō*, ca. 1364), cited the text secondhand by referring to quotations included in *Variant Notes on Explicating Murasaki*. The seemingly innumerable versions of *The Pillow Book* were used to mutually complement one another in order to reconstruct pieces of Sei's writing that had already been lost. The use of four different manuscripts of *The Pillow Book* in the compilation of *Variant Notes on Explicating Murasaki* reveals that in the thirteenth century Sei Shōnagon's work existed as an abstract notion that could be actualized through its various representations.

Unlike works such as the *Genji*, which attracted scholarly attention as early as the late twelfth century, and the *Ise*, which began to receive scholarly notice in the mid-thirteenth century,[25] it seems it was not until the second half of the seventeenth century that complete commentaries on *The Pillow Book* appeared on the book market; at any rate, there are no extant manuscripts or printed exegeses on *The Pillow Book* prior to that time. Moreover, unlike the *Ise* and the *Genji*, for which "definitive" texts, though multiple, were collated as early as the thirteenth century, the need to decide on an authoritative version of *The Pillow Book* was not of primary concern to scholars until the seventeenth century, when demand for printed commentaries on the work began to emerge.[26] The multiple textual variants of the eleventh-century work were unsuited to the new modes of disseminating literary knowledge of the classics that developed in the early Edo period. Since educating a broad audience required a unified text, selecting one manuscript over the others or constructing a stable text from the various representations of *The Pillow Book* became necessary for the first time.

THE THREE COMPLETE COMMENTARIES OF THE EDO PERIOD

The rapid development of printing technology and book markets in the early years of the seventeenth century made texts from the past easily accessible as physical objects. Literary works transmitted through a limited number of handwritten manuscripts among a circumscribed audience were put in print for the first time and made available to a readership beyond aristocrats, upper-class warriors, and Buddhist priests. Between 1596 and 1649, three texts from the *Nōinbon* lineage were published as "old movable-type editions" (*kokatsujiban*).[27] Scholars refer to them as the ten-line book (*jūgyō-hon*), twelve-line book (*jūnigyō-hon*), and thirteen-line book (*jūsangyō-hon*) based on the number of printed lines per page. Then in 1649, a new edition was printed using the woodblock technique (*seihan*)[28] and subsequently published several times.[29] To be able to grasp the contents of such texts, however, it was necessary for a reader to be not only equipped with knowledge of the archaic language in which they were composed but also familiar with the sociohistorical context. Beginning in the twelfth century, knowledge of literature from the past was transmitted as "a corpus of (more or less esoteric) teachings and a set of associated rules for their use."[30] This "secret teaching" (of how to read the canon) provided knowledge that was central to the "licensing of professional court" poets and as such was carefully guarded by conservative aristocrats.[31] This approach to the transmission of literary knowledge was not endorsed by all. For example, Matsunaga Teitoku (1571–1653), the founder of the Teimon school of *haikai* (comic linked verse), denounced this esoteric transmission of poetics and voiced his opposition, together with his disciples, by offering public lectures on the classics. Promoting the art of *haikai* as a form of poetry that was "accessible to a wide but not necessarily highly educated audience,"[32] they criticized the state of *waka*, or thirty-one syllable poems, which was a territory claimed by the aristocratic elite. Teitoku made literary works from the past available to a new readership, the majority of which was made up of wealthy townsmen. The notes of such public lectures were frequently published as commentaries, which, as Ii Haruki has noted, signaled the public acknowledgment of the work in question as a classic and showed the formation of a class of readers who necessitated such commentaries.[33]

During the entire early modern period, only three complete annotated editions of *The Pillow Book* emerged. Commonly referred to as the three commentaries of the Edo period (*Edo jidai no sanchū*),[34] each consists of an introductory section, reproduction of a complete text, and editorial comments on historical figures and vocabulary. It is unclear when exactly the first of these commentaries was completed, but it was printed in 1674. Even though the *Comprehensive Bibliographic Catalogue* (*Gunsho ichiran*, 1802) listed the author as unknown, modern scholars have reached the consensus that it was produced by Katō Bansai (1621–1674). A former disciple of the poet and scholar Matsunaga Teitoku's and a *haikai* master in his early years, Bansai was an influential figure in the literary circle of the Itakura family, whose members were appointed by the Tokugawa government to serve as Kyoto governors (*shoshidai*) for decades in the seventeenth century.[35] Titled *Commentary on Sei Shōnagon's "Pillow Book"* (*Sei Shōnagon Makura no sōshishō*), this commentary was preceded by Bansai's studies on other literary texts of the past such as *Essays in Idleness*, *The Ise Stories*, *An Account of My Hut* (*Hōjōki*, 1212), and *One Hundred Poets, One Poem Each* (*Hyakunin isshu*, thirteenth century), and was published in the year of his death.[36]

Two months after the publication of Bansai's commentary, the commentary of another former disciple of Teitoku's came onto the market. Titled *Sei Shōnagon's Spring Dawn Commentary* (*Sei Shōnagon Shunshoshō*), this commentary was produced by the *waka* and *haikai* poet Kitamura Kigin (1624–1705). The title originates from the opening of Sei's work, "In spring, the dawn" (*Haru wa akebono*). This commentary became the most widely read annotated edition of *The Pillow Book* from the late Edo period through the prewar Shōwa period (1926–1930), and all subsequent annotated editions of the text until 1931 were based on Kigin's work.[37] This was not unique for the many commentaries on classical texts he had produced; his commentary on *The Tale of Genji*, titled *The Moonlit Lake Commentary* (*Kogetsushō*) and published a year before his *Spring Dawn Commentary*, became the most widely used text by generations of scholars until the twentieth century. Presenting the text, commentary, and glosses on the same page, *The Moonlit Lake Commentary* made the work easily accessible to readers in a way that no other *Genji* commentary had done.[38] Kigin's *Spring Dawn Commentary* followed the same formatting and as a commentary on *The Pillow Book* was equally successful at least because of its usefulness and its association with Kigin.

The third commentary was published in 1681 by Okanishi Ichū (1639–1711), who belonged to Nishiyama Sōin's school of *haikai*, the main rival to Teitoku's school. Titled *Marginal Notes to "The Pillow Book"* (*Makura no sōshi bōchū*),[39] this annotated edition presents itself as relying heavily on Bansai's commentary, although a careful examination of the content has led scholars to detect significant influence from Kigin's work. There are various reasons why Ichū presented his reading of *The Pillow Book* as different from Kigin's. One was the tension between the two *haikai* schools; Kigin was a proponent of the Teimon school, while Ichū belonged to the Danrin. Located in Kyoto, the Teimon school maintained that knowledge of literary texts from the past, and especially those associated with the aristocracy, was essential for *haikai* composition. In contrast, the Danrin school, which catered to urban commoners in Osaka, opposed strict rules for *haikai* and focused on contemporary culture, including popular and vulgar themes, rather than looking back to the old elegant world.[40]

In the subsequent centuries, several other thematic and interpolated (*kaki-ire*) commentaries were produced.[41] For example, Tsuboi Yoshichika's *Digest to Clothing in Sei Shōnagon's "Pillow Book"* (*Sei Shōnagon Makura no sōshi shōzoku satsuyōshō*, 1729) offered a study of the attire and furniture that appear in the Heian text, and Tonomura Tsunehisa's *Roots of a Thousand Grasses* (*Chigusa no nezashi*, 1830) examines the plants to which Sei Shōnagon referred. In addition, many national learning (*kokugaku*) scholars produced interpolated commentaries in the eighteenth and nineteenth centuries, all based on Kigin's *Spring Dawn Commentary*. These commentaries circulated only in manuscript and were therefore not easily accessible. Their limited visibility has led modern scholars to conclude that *The Pillow Book* attracted scholarly attention only in the seventeenth century and was not regarded as an important text by later scholars.[42]

CONSTRUCTING AN AUTHORITATIVE TEXT

Unlike other classics for which Teika had already produced authoritative copies or "certified texts" (*shōhon*),[43] there was no manuscript generally recognized by scholars as Teika's copy of *The Pillow Book* at the time when Bansai, Kigin, and Ichū were writing their commentaries on Sei Shōnagon's text. As a result, copies of the text had continued to diverge during the subsequent four centuries, further expanding the textual multiplicity of the eleventh-century work. The main challenge that early modern scholars confronted was the extremely large number of manu-scripts from various textual lines, which resulted from multiple attempts at redaction and reconstruction of the text since the mid-Heian period. How did they then agree on an authoritative text?

Suzuki Tomotarō's extensive study of the textuality of the three Edo-period commentaries reveals that none of them was based on a single manuscript. Instead, commentators selected passages from various texts following a logic that remains obscure to later readers. Suzuki's analysis of the interrelations among the manuscripts, to which he refers as most likely influenced, certainly influenced, parent-child, and revised source text, is revealing of the varying degrees to which the commentators relied on specific versions of Sei's work. According to Suzuki, Bansai and Kigin drew from a common source unknown to us that had succeeded the 1649 edition, and as such their works can be viewed as "descendants" of this unidentified text. Bansai's commentary further included revised sections from the so-called Norihide postscript text (*Norihide okugakibon*, pres-ently classified as a text from the *Sankanbon* lineage). Kigin's commen-tary, on the other hand, was influenced by both the Norihide postscript text and the twelve-line text from the *Nōinbon* lineage, a distant prede-cessor of the 1649 edition.[44] Suzuki further argues that Ichū's commen-tary is a "descendant" of the 1649 edition, contains revised passages from both Bansai's and Hosokawa Yūsai's (1534–1610, preeminent authority on classical Japanese poetry) texts, and was influenced by Kigin's work.

Clearly, none of the three commentaries followed one particular tex-tual line. Each represents a medley of passages from manuscripts across textual lineages. These approaches also suggest that at the time the three commentaries were produced, scholars did not even view the manu-scripts of Sei's work as belonging to specific textual lines—which fur-ther affirms the constructed nature of the textual history of *The Pillow Book*.[45] Accordingly, the primary texts the three scholars produced are the results of collations and revisions, leading to the absence of a "pure" text (*junsuibon*), as Suzuki calls it.[46] "Pure" text here implies a version based on manuscript(s) within one textual lineage that modern scholars usually use for their commentaries.

The three early modern commentators, however, explain their approaches in different ways. First, Bansai addressed the textual multi-plicity of *The Pillow Book*, stating that the differences among the textual variants of Sei's work were numerous but owing mostly to scribal errors (*densha*). He further noted that he had collected a large number of old manuscripts (*kohon*) and printed books (*inpon*), examined them, and collated a text that he hoped would serve as the certified text (*shōhon*).[47] Among the old manuscripts he had gathered, he used "the book that has been handed down" (*denrai no hon*) as the base text. This manuscript belongs to the *Sankanbon* lineage, as becomes clear from the postscript signed by the high-ranking aristocrat Kajūji Norihide (1426–1496) that Bansai quotes.[48] In contrast, it is unclear whether *inpon* refers to printed versions of the text or to the five-volume *Nōinbon* copy made by Hosokawa Yūsai. *Inpon* 印本 in the case of the latter would mean "the priest's book," indicating Yūsai's entrance into Buddhist orders following the death of his patron, Oda Nobunaga (1534–1582), in 1582.[49]

Likewise, in his preface to the *Spring Dawn Commentary*, Kigin acknowledges the textual multiplicity of *The Pillow Book* and reflects on the difficulty of selecting one text as authoritative. He referred to the manuscripts according to the number of books of which they consisted, such as "two volumes" (*nisatsu*), "three volumes" (*sansatsu*), and "five volumes" (*gosatsu*), rather than "the old book," "the printed book," or "the book that has been handed down," as Bansai did in order to give an aura of authority to *The Pillow Book* he constructed. The different appellations suggest that Kigin paid attention to the physical format of the manuscripts, whereas Bansai distinguished the manuscripts by their extratextual characteristics. For Kigin, authority was related to the fact that a text had been read by his predecessors. The emphasis he placed on the postscripts shows that for him a textual variant's authority was manifested through a record of the copyist's name or the time of its production. In his commentary, Kigin acknowledges the fact that, unlike the *Collection of Ancient and Modern Poems*, *Later Collection of Japanese Poems* (*Gosen wakashū*, tenth century), and *The Tale of Genji*, no copy of *The Pillow Book* authorized by Teika exists, and so he has based his commentary on two manuscripts that stood out among the many other variants precisely because they contained postscripts.[50] For Kigin, postscripts in general signified that texts had been read in the past and, as such, were markers of authority. He describes one of the two manuscripts he obtained in 1653 from Bishū province as follows:[51] "As for this book, the paper is old and the handwriting style is from the past. Its meaning is clear, vermilion dots have been added, and even notes about people's lives and posts have been recorded."[52]

This manuscript belongs to the *Sankanbon* lineage, and as the postscripts signed by Bōkyū Guō and Kajūji Norihide suggest, it was a copy of a manuscript that served as the base text for the manuscript Bansai had used. The other manuscript that Kigin referenced comes from the *Sakaibon* lineage and bears a colophon by Kiyohara no Edakata, signed as Kunaikyō Kiyohara, as mentioned earlier. He described the *Sakaibon* as one that does not include "even one section of narrative [*monogatari*] that contains a poem by Sei Shōnagon"—in other words, a diary-like passage.[53] Kigin also noted that the order of the lists (*makura kotoba*) in this manuscript differs from the books commonly read (*yo no tsune no hon*).[54] He pointed out that later literary works had quoted from this manuscript, thus revealing that the *Sakaibon* had been widely read in the past.[55] He also acknowledged that he had compared variants from this textual lineage and selected the decent (*yoroshiki*) ones from among them.

Last, in his commentary *Marginal Notes to "The Pillow Book,"* Ichū ascribed the differences among the manuscripts of *The Pillow Book* to scribal errors and noted that he had used the five-volume manuscript and corrected its mistakes.[56] To underscore the value of his work, he stated that he had referenced a copy of Hosokawa Yūsai's manuscript, most likely the same one that Kigin mentioned in his work.[57] This manuscript by Yūsai was passed down to Miyagi Kōyō, a former student of Yūsai's and Ichū's teacher. Opening his commentary with the *Nōinbon* epilogue that was originally included in Yūsai's manuscript and was not cited in either Bansai's nor Kigin's annotated editions, Ichū thus imbued his commentary with greater authority. The colophon depicts the unfortunate fate of Sei in her later years.

Neither Bansai, Kigin, or Ichū describe in detail the sources they used for the compilation of their own texts of *The Pillow Book*. They avoided selecting a single text over the other available options but produced their own "primary" texts. Bansai referred to his final text as the correct text (*tadashiki*), Kigin called his the decent text (*yoroshiki*), while Ichū referenced a figure of authority from the past (Yūsai) to prove its authenticity. Each of these textual reconstructions of *The Pillow Book* laid claim to being the most authoritative version. Their multiplicity shows that Sei's work was a fluid text that allowed various approaches. Moreover, all three scholars relied heavily on a printed version of *The Pillow Book* rather than using manuscript copies, but they did not note this in their commentaries. This reveals that their remaking of *The Pillow Book* was based primarily on early modern technologies rather than on aristocratic connections that they would have needed to access old manuscripts.

SECTIONING THE TEXT

Central to the way *The Pillow Book* was perceived in the Edo period was Shōtetsu's pairing, in the fifteenth century, of Sei's work and *Essays in Idleness*, as recorded in his poetic treatise *Conversations with Shōtetsu*. Specifically, he wrote that *The Pillow Book* had been written in no particular order (*nan no sahō mo naku kakitaru mono*) and that *Essays in Idleness* imitated its style. Shōtetsu's evaluation was repeatedly taken up by later scholars and became central to discussions about the style and genre of *The Pillow Book* in the following centuries. A heterogeneous work like *The Pillow Book* required a division of the text into units whose content was comprehensible—the old handwritten manuscripts had contained uninterrupted text without punctuation or paragraphs. Modern annotated editions of *The Pillow Book* consist of more than three hundred sections, but how did seventeenth-century scholars divide the text? What were the effects of such divisions? And how did such division influence understanding of the text and perception of the work as a whole?

The earliest commentary—Bansai's *Commentary on Sei Shōnagon's "Pillow Book"*—comprises 157 sections, each with a heading that appears indented on a new line. Every section begins with a list and thus bears a title whose structure is either adjective or adjectival verb plus *mono* or a noun plus *wa*, such as "Susamajiki mono" (Dispiriting things) and "Yama wa" (Mountains).[58] The sections are divided into subsections (*setsu*), each starting on a new line and further broken into segments (*shō*). A note interpreting the text and an explanation about the text's thematic relation to the heading of the section follow each section. To make the text even more consistent, Bansai reordered some of the passages, grouping them into thematically related units.[59] He reworked *The Pillow Book* to construct a text in which the sections follow a certain

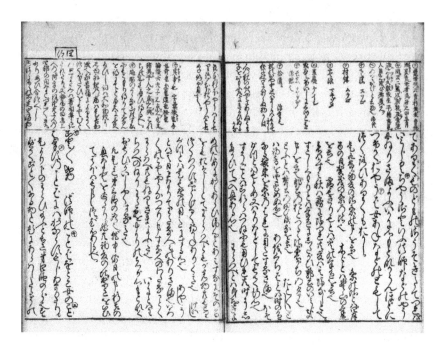

FIGURE 2.1 Two pages from the main body of Katō Bansai's *Commentary on Sei Shōnagon's "Pillow Book"* (*Sei Shōnagon Makura no sōshishō*, 1674). Courtesy of Shunsho Bunko, Sōai University Library, Osaka

order and logic, rather than being a collection of disconnected writings or random jottings (figure 2.1).

The fourth section in Bansai's commentary, which is the longest in the whole work, occupying two-thirds of book 1, serves as a good example of his approach. Under the heading "Things That Differ" (Kotogoto naru mono)[60] Bansai grouped a large portion of the text that modern editions of *The Pillow Book* present in seven sections.[61] These sections are titled "Things That Differ," "That Parents Should Bring Up Some Beloved Son" (Omowan ko o), "When the Empress Moved" (Daijin Narimasa ga ie ni), "The Cat That Lived in the Palace" (Ue ni saburō ōnneko wa), "On the First Day of the First Month" (Shōgatsu tsuitachi), "I Enjoy Watching the Officials" (Yorokobi sōsuru koso), and "The Eastern Wing of the Palace of Today" (Ima dairi no hingashi o ba).[62] Bansai further divided the section into twelve subsections.[63] It opens with examples of different ways of speaking and goes on to reflect on the miserable fate of young men who become priests and exorcists. The section further narrates an episode about the transfer of Empress Teishi and her female attendants to the residence of a midranking aristocrat, and another about the banishment of the dog Okinamaro from the palace in deference to the emperor's favorite cat. It continues with the narrator's musings about the weather on the days of the five annual ceremonies (*go-sekku*) that were traditionally held at the imperial court, and the ceremony upon the announcement of the new appointments at the beginning of the year. The section concludes with a vignette about banter between Sei and a high-ranking courtier named Narinobu. Clarifying the scope of the section, Bansai states that all the twelve subsections contain topics that express the general meaning (*omomuki*) of the phrase "things that differ."[64] According to him, the meaning of the text is hidden, remote, and profound—in other words, difficult to grasp on a first reading. Bansai tries to intuit what the logical connection may be between the different passages within the block of text he has made into a section. His approach is grounded in the concept of "the essence" (*kokoro*) of the phrase *kotogoto naru mono*. Tsushima Tomoaki views *kokoro* as the revised version of Bansai's idea of *rai-i* (来意), which Bansai had employed in 1661 in his commentary on *Essays in Idleness*, titled *Commentary on the Tsurezuregusa* (*Tsurezuregusashō*, or *Bansaishō*).[65] *Rai-i*, or the "meaning carried over theory," is "based on the intuition that each section 'seems independent, but the essence is the same,'"[66] in Linda Chance's words.

Having sectioned the text, Bansai, in a headnote, broadly defines the word *kotogoto*, including meanings such as unusual (*ki* 奇), different (*kotogoto* 異事), and strange (*kai* 怪).[67] Next, delineating the broad spectrum of meanings included in the section's heading, specifically "things that are not the same but are interchangeable," "things that are insufficient and unsophisticated," and "things that are unpredictable and suspicious,"[68] Bansai tries to fit each subsection within this long section 4 of his commentary. After each subsection he comments on its linkage to the whole section. In some cases the links seem plausible, whereas in others Bansai justifies his reorganization of the text in an evasive way. The first one is headed by what nowadays is known as the list titled "Things That Differ," which reads, "A priest's language. The speech of men and of women. The common people always tend to add extra syllables to their words."[69]

Bansai explains that each of these phrases exemplifies different ways of speaking. Specifically, that "the language of a priest" is "biased" (*katatsumuru*), "men's language" is "strong" (*tsuyoki*), "women's language" is "soft" (*yawara naru*), and that "commoners' language" is "improper" (*tadashikaranu*).[70] Another subsection, which describes how depressing it is for parents to bring a beloved son up to become a priest, Bansai links to the phrase "a priest's language" in the previous subsection. He notes that this subsection expands on the previous subsection by discussing young priests' ascetic practices.[71] The common topic of these subsections about priests, Bansai maintains, makes them related to one another. His justification of the positioning of another subsection within this section, however, is tenuous. Subsection 3 opens with the episode about the move of Teishi and her entourage into the residence of Taira no Narimasa. It tells of the small gate of Narimasa's residence, which forced the ladies-in-waiting to dismount from their carriages and walk in, thus exposing them to the gazes of male courtiers. According to Bansai, this episode extrapolates on the first subsection's phrase "men's language and women's language" and demonstrates the "thoughtful behavior" (*kokorozukai*) of men and women. He stresses that the episode teaches that one should not forget proper manners even when one becomes accustomed to a certain situation.[72] However, this episode in *The Pillow Book* does not include any verbal exchange between men and women. The mere fact that the subsection describes women's discomfort in the presence of men does not necessarily create a natural link to the preceding subsection. Even more ambiguous is Bansai's explanation of the logic regarding subsection 7. It depicts Narimasa's visit to the room in which Sei and the other ladies-in-waiting slept during the night and his being turned into a laughingstock by the female attendants. Bansai comments that Narimasa is "disgracefully laughed at" despite his intention to apologize for the earlier incident. He explains that the misunderstanding of Narimasa's intention makes this passage appropriate for the section "Things That Differ" and leaves it to the reader to decide which meaning of *kotogoto naru mono* applies to this episode. Having offered his view about the linkages of each subsection to the whole section, Bansai concludes by underscoring not only the organizational principle of the text but also the depth of its meaning as a series of interrelated episodes.[73]

In addition to combining passages into sections, Bansai rearranges the text so that thematically related sections appear one after the other. Thus, ordering the section titled "Mountains" (Yama wa) before the section "Peaks" (Mine wa), he comments, "This section is a continuation of the previous one regarding mountains. In the previous section, mountains that function as associated words [*yose*] in poetry have been recorded. This section includes peaks that do not appear in poems. Together with the previous section, it should be regarded as expressing contrasting meanings."[74]

Likewise, he arranges the sections titled "Pools" (Fuchi wa), "Seas" (Umi wa), and "Ferries" (Watari wa) one after the other since they are all related to water (*mizube*). Through a reorganization of the order in which sections appear, Bansai constructs a work where various forms of knowledge are catalogued into categories, which themselves are offered to the reader in a logical order. This approach made *The Pillow Book* amenable to being later categorized as a *zuihitsu*, or "logical ordering," the genre used by scholars in China and Chinese-studies scholars in Japan to encapsulate various kinds of knowledge.

Bansai's approach to the text, focusing on the logic by which topics and sections appear, and his division of the text into sections, subsections, and segments to demonstrate that the work has a well-organized structure, appears intended to challenge Shōtetsu's view of Sei's work as "written down in no particular order." In his preface, Bansai shows an awareness of the "unfair" treatment *The Pillow Book* had received among earlier scholars and of its small number of readers. He laments that Sei's work has been underappreciated, despite its being on par with the *Ise* and the *Genji*. Bansai notes,

> Speaking of the appreciation of our predecessors for this work, not only was it included in the category of "Scholarly Works" [Gakusho no hen] in *Yakumo mishō* but also its text was cited in various works. Kenkō wrote *Tzurezuregusa* based on it, and that fact began to be repeatedly quoted. As "Seigan chawa" notes, "*Makura no sōshi* was written down in no particular order.[75] It consists of three books. *Tsurezuregusa* was written in the tradition of *Makura no sōshi*."[76] These [works] were the first to appreciate this booklet. Is it even

slightly inferior to *Ise, Yamato, Genji, Sagoromo*, etc.? It is even less inferior to others such as *Taketori, Tsutsumi*, and *Hamamatsu*. However, the people who appreciate it are probably only one-tenth of those who [praise] the *Ise* [and] the *Genji*. It is shameful and regrettable. But there is a reason behind this, too.[77]

Although Bansai acknowledges that there is a reason for the marginalization of Sei's work, he does not explain it. He positions *The Pillow Book* as a Chinese studies–influenced compendium and presents it as a morally didactic work. Although Bansai does not describe the merits of the text itself, he hails the work as primarily edifying, stating that "the central point of it is not only to offer the pleasure of the leaves and flowers of words and to make clear old customs but also to teach the real meanings of things."[78] Frequently emphasizing the moral of a section or subsection, Bansai posits his view of *The Pillow Book* as a didactic work, similar to his approach to *Essays in Idleness*, which he deemed a Buddhist text.[79] To further emphasize the value of *The Pillow Book*, in his preface Bansai portrays the author Sei Shōnagon as an icon of intelligence and literary talent and stresses that her accomplishments have been praised for centuries.[80]

Kigin disagreed with Bansai regarding the thematically consistent and logically organized nature of Sei's work. In his *Spring Dawn Commentary*, the text is printed largely without any breaks and only the list-like passages' headings appear as indented titles. He keeps the headings of the lists and only adds a part alternation mark ⌒\ (*ioriten*) to indicate the beginning of a new passage (figure 2.2). Unlike Bansai, who explains why each of the episodes is included in its respective section, Kigin stresses the *unrelated* nature of the passages and sets them apart as independent of one another. In contrast to Bansai's multiple, large sections with thematically related subsections, Kigin uses comments such as "from here it is a different matter" (*koko yori mata betsu no koto nari*), "from here it is a separate section" (*koko yori mata betsu no dan nari*), or "from here it is again a different story" (*koko yori mata koto monogatari nari*)[81] to present *The Pillow Book* as a collection of disconnected passages. This approach led to the division of the text into almost twice as many sections as in Bansai's commentary. For example, the same section of the text that Bansai split into twelve subsections, Kigin

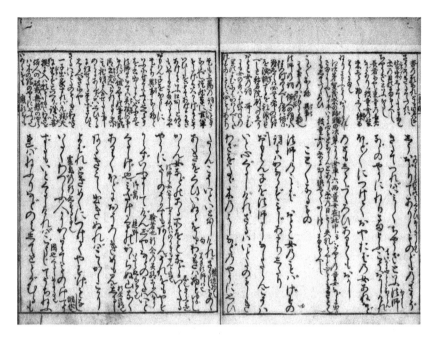

FIGURE 2.2 Two pages from the main body of *Sei Shōnagon's Spring Dawn Commentary* (*Sei Shōnagon Shunshoshō*, 1674) by Kitamura Kigin show how a part alternation mark divides the text. Courtesy of Shunsho Bunko, Sōai University Library, Osaka

treats as twelve completely independent sections. He explains that the passages were not written with the intent to make them match the *makura-kotoba*, or "pillow word," "Things That Differ." Although *makura-kotoba* as a poetic term is usually translated as "pillow word" or "fixed epithets 'on' which specific words lay,"[82] what Kigin refers to here are the section headings that Bansai constructs as themes unifying disparate notions. These passages are also called lists, and as a central style within the *zappai* (miscellaneous *haikai*) subgenre of *haikai* in the seventeenth century, they were known as *monohazuke* (detailing of things).[83] Kigin notes that instead of representing lists, the ordering of sections on completely different topics one after the other should be considered a "play of the brush" (*fudezusabi*, or *fude susabi*) and specifies that it is a way of writing that "depicts whatever comes to mind."[84] Kigin's idea of the playful movement of the brush refers to random jottings, and the phrase appears frequently in his commentary to indicate a change of topic in *The Pillow Book*. This is again an appeal to the idea of *zuihitsu* but understood differently from Bansai' interpretation. It is close to the writing of later scholars of national learning. As we shall see, such "play of the brush" in Sei Shōnagon's work would become central to the reception of *The Pillow Book* in the subsequent centuries.

Kigin emphasizes the primacy of *The Pillow Book* by presenting it on par with the *Genji*, and, unlike Bansai, he does not comment on its marginalized position. For him the value of Sei's work lies not in its textual organization but in its style. Kigin states, "Is it because of the exceptional style of this work that it has been discussed along with *Genji monogatari*, the utmost treasure of our country, and referred [together] as '*Genji* [and] *Makura no sōshi*'? Priest Yoshida Kenkō has quoted from this work many times. Its style, elegant language, and depth of meaning (I stop my praise here), are exceptional."[85]

He notes that the sole purpose of his commentary is to facilitate his disciples in their "study of poetry" (*kagaku*).[86] This pairing of *The Pillow Book* and *The Tale of Genji* dominates Kigin's writing on the study of *waka* and *haikai*. One example among the many references to the two works comes from his *Essential Style for Haikai* (*Haikai yōi fūtei*, 1673), written a year before the publication of his commentary: "If one does not read books of poetry like *The Tale of Genji* or *The Pillow Book*, if one does not soak one's spirit in the ancient style, if one does not use that language in various ways, how can one know true *haikai*?"[87]

Last, Okanishi Ichū's *Marginal Notes to "The Pillow Book"* offers relatively concise annotation to the one hundred and fifty sections into which it divides the text (figure 2.3). Following Bansai, Ichū views sections as blocks of thematically arranged passages, all united by the "essence" of the section. Unlike Bansai, however, Ichū narrows down the meaning of the headings of the sections and proposes more plausible linkages among the subsections within a large section. For instance, for the same section titled "Things That Differ," Ichū limits the meaning of the essence to "things that sound different, or things that were uttered in a different way."[88] After each passage within a large section he comments succinctly on how it is related to the essence of that section. Rather than justifying the position of a passage within the section, Ichū presents each passage as providing examples of various things that are viewed as different because of oral expression and aural perception. Accordingly, he explains that various ways of speaking sound different, and what

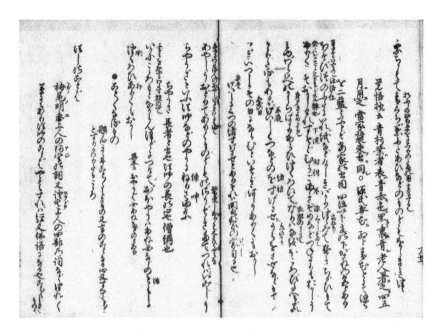

FIGURE 2.3 Two pages from the main body of Okanishi Ichū's *Marginal Notes to "The Pillow Book"* (*Makura no sōshi bōchū*, 1681), vol. 1, 11 *ura*–12 *omote*. Courtesy of Shunsho Bunko, Sōai University Library, Osaka

people heard about priests in the past differs from the present state. Moreover, differences in men's and women's speech turned Narimasa into a laughingstock when he approached Sei during the night, and later Narimasa's self-praise[89] communicated things in a different way. Ichū further asserts that things said about the dog and emperor's cat sound different and views the repartee between a courtier and a bishop as having sprung from misunderstanding.[90] Within his commentary Ichū shows that passages are grouped together to support the essence of a section, but although he quotes Shōtetsu's assertion on the lack of an organizational principle in the style of *The Pillow Book*, he does not comment on it. He closely follows Bansai's sectioning of the text but disagrees with the didactic approach of his predecessor. For Ichū, the overall meaning of *The Pillow Book* was to serve as a source of knowledge about poetry and old customs. The inclusion of twenty-five illustrations of Heian court architecture, attire, and people at the beginning of the commentary reinforces his perception of the historicity of Sei's work. Ichū's approach is an appropriation of the methodology of the earlier scholars. Like Bansai, he constructs *The Pillow Book* as a collection of lists, but like Kigin, he rejects its educational overtones.

As these examples show, Bansai, Kigin, and Ichū were concerned primarily with compiling and sectioning the text rather than regarding one preexisting manuscript as the best base text. Each scholar created his own version of *The Pillow Book* following his own organizational rubric, and thus three different "primary" editions went into circulation. Each version was an amalgam of textual lineages in accordance with the preferences of the editor. Among them, Kigin's commentaries became the standard text of *The Pillow Book* that later scholars used for their own commentaries. It was not until the mid-twentieth century that a complete commentary of *The Pillow Book* based entirely on a single textual line was produced.[91] With this publication of Tanaka Jūtarō's *Pillow Book* (*Makura no sōshi*, 1947), the *Sankanbon* textual line became the authoritative textual lineage of *The Pillow Book* and continues to be treated as such today. Since then, Japanese scholars have based their commentaries on the work on a single manuscript while supplying the missing parts using manuscripts within the same textual lineage.

SHAPING THE MEANING

The creation of knowledge about *The Pillow Book* in the Edo period began with the construction of a standard text and its sectioning and continued with attempts to make sense of the work as a whole. The three seventeenth-century commentators viewed the title of *The Pillow Book* as central in determining the nature of the text. Stating that later readers had assigned the title, Bansai interpreted it in two different ways, one focusing on its textual organization and the other on its content. One of the interpretations takes *makura* as referring to *uta-makura* (poem pillow), or words "on which the entire poem may depend, or rest as on a pillow."[92] Bansai further explains that "structurally, since this work first offers a concise statement whose essence [*kokoro*] later is revealed in depth, it is equal to *makura-kotoba* in poetry."[93] He likely referred to the lists of *The Pillow Book*, each of which included a heading and examples illustrating various aspects of the heading or topic. Thus he views the headings as segments, on which the lists "depend." Because Bansai has reorganized the work into sections, each beginning with a topic on which the whole section "rests," his view of *The Pillow Book* as a collection of *uta-makura* is plausible, but only for the version he produced. Another interpretation Bansai offers is based on what he views as Teika's comment in his collection of notes on poetry criticism titled *Mistaken Commentaries* (*Hekianshō*, 1226). Teika linked *makura* to the first-person plural pronoun "we" when written 臣等 *makura* and, accordingly, to the first-person singular pronoun when the word was written without the character 等 (*ra*). Looking for precedents in older texts, including *Records of Ancient Matters* (*Kojiki*, 712), *Record of Surnames* (*Shōjiroku*, 815), and *Procedures of the Engi Era* (*Engishiki*, 927) and applying Teika's comment to *The Pillow Book*, Bansai maintained that the work's title suggests "a personal diary notebook" (*warawa no nikki sōshi*). In a note, however, he explains that between the two possible interpretations of the title, "personal diary notebook" is what he believed was Sei Shōnagon's true intention (*hoi*). He supported this claim with a quotation from the colophon that recounts Sei's suggestion for the paper she received from Teishi—namely, "I will make it into a pillow." Bansai also explained the meaning of *sōshi* as a "draft" (*sōan*) or set of "notes" (*sōkō*). Accordingly, he regarded *The Pillow Book* as informal writing based on actual experience. Curiously, Bansai's interpretation of the title thus contradicts his view of the overall meaning of the work. Specifically, the logical organization of the content would have been hard to achieve through the casual style of Sei's autobiographical work as he views it. Yet Bansai's theory about the title was supported by Ichū, who simply restated it.[94]

Kigin also views the title of *The Pillow Book* as related to the fixed epithets used in poetry composition, but not because they were central to the structure of the work, as Bansai had noted. Instead, Kigin draws from the content of the work, specifically from an episode included in the colophon. According to this episode, Sei—having heard that the emperor commissioned the production of a copy of *Records of the Historian* (J. *Shiki*, Ch. *Shiji*, 91 B.C.E.)—suggested that she make the paper that Empress Teishi had received from her brother into a pillow (*makura*). Recognizing both *shiki* (spread) and *makura* as words associated with each other in Japanese poetry, as in the phrase *shikitae no makura* (hempen/spread-out pillow), Kigin asserts that *makura* in the title originated precisely from this reference to the pillow word *shiki*. He acknowledges that *sōshi* could be written using the characters for a "draft" version (草紙) or for a "book" (双紙). Noting that the former signified "the rough version of something" (*mono no shitagaki* or *sōkō* 草稿) and as such stressed the absence of a complete version (*seisho*) of a work, Kigin upholds the second meaning, "book" (双紙), as relevant to the title of *The Pillow Book* because it implies "to put together paper and exhaust in writing" and serves as the general term for narratives from the past.[95]

Bansai (and Ichū as his proponent) and Kigin took completely different approaches to *The Pillow Book*. Bansai's organization of the text and his view of it as a collection of sections focusing on a specific theme and comprising diverse examples were clearly related to the *monohazuke* style in miscellaneous *haikai*. In the next chapter, I discuss how collections of lists, or *monohazuke*, emerged as early as the last decade of the sixteenth century and continued to burgeon in the first and second centuries of the Edo period. By the time Bansai's commentary was published, several parodies of *The Pillow Book* imitating the lists of the eleventh-century work had been produced. Within them lists were labeled as *inu-makura* (*dog/fake pillows*), stressing the fact that they imitated the headings of the lists in Sei's work. It is intriguing that neither Bansai nor Ichū drew links between the lists in *The Pillow Book* and the texts that imitated the style of Sei's work, although the appellations of *inu-makura* and *monohazuke* would have been familiar to a wide readership from their inclusion in various erotic parodies of the text.[96] Instead, Bansai and Ichū referred to them as *uta-makura* and *makura-kotoba*. Their choice of terminology associated with the composition of *waka*, which had been a highly respected genre associated with Japanese aristocracy since ancient times, may have stemmed from a desire to avoid linking the work to a contemporary mode of poetry composition that had been gaining wide popularity and was perceived as vulgar. Likewise, Kigin's refusal to see *The Pillow Book* as a collection of lists, instead constructing it as an elegantly written compilation of disparate vignettes, may also be read as an attempt to avoid association of the work with the recently published erotic parodies imitating the lists of *The Pillow Book* (the focus of the next chapter). Until the late seventeenth century, the three commentaries were classified as "books on Japanese poetry and comic Japanese poetry" (*kasho narabi ni kyōka*) in publishers' catalogues, which suggests that they were read as texts facilitating poetry composition.[97] Thus, the three commentators' interpretations of the title of the work and its overall meaning reveal a desire to stress the antiquity and aristocratic nature of Sei's work and disengage it from popular literature and its themes related to sexuality and pleasure seeking.

NATIONAL LEARNING AND *THE PILLOW BOOK*

In the eighteenth and nineteenth centuries, the world of literary criticism was dominated by scholars of national learning, whose ideology opposed the "existing epistemological frameworks" of Tokugawa society.[98] These scholars criticized "the rigidly hierarchical and monolithic neo-Confucian worldview" and the traditional forms of transmission of knowledge.[99] They turned to literary works from Nara- and Heian-period Japan, and specifically poetry and poetics. Challenging the dominant tendency to reduce poetry to moral interpretations, they agreed that at the core of Japanese poetry lay human emotions (*ninjō*). Kada no Arimaro (1706–1751) asserted that the function of poetry was to "generate aesthetic enjoyment," while Kamo no Mabuchi (1697–1769) underscored its spontaneity and "pure expression of concrete human feelings," and Motoori Norinaga (1730–1801) defined poetry as "a social medium" of "affective essence and formal aesthetic."[100] Rejecting earlier Confucian and Buddhist readings of Japanese texts, Norinaga's interpretive approach to *The Tale of Genji* had a great impact on other scholars of national learning in the Edo period and continued to be used to define Japanese literature and culture into the modern period. Calling it *mono no aware* (to be moved with emotion),[101] or "poignancy of things," in his commentary *The Tale of Genji: A Little Jeweled Comb* (*Genji monogatari: Tama no ogushi*, 1799) he argued that "the main purpose of the tale is the depiction of the workings of the emotions."[102]

In this context, *The Pillow Book* entered the corpus of texts central to scholars' exploration of Japan's superiority over China, which was viewed as the source of "flawed forms of knowledge in the form of Confucianism and Buddhism" that their country had adopted.[103] National learning scholars did not themselves produce thorough, annotated editions of *The Pillow Book* but used Kigin's *Spring Dawn Commentary* as the base text and added their views on the work in the form of interpolated commentaries. These partial commentaries vary in length, but the most substantial ones were produced by Fujii Takanao (1764–1840), Iwasaki Yoshitaka (1804–1847), and Saitō Hikomaro (1768–1854). Interpolated commentaries were handwritten, never published during the Edo period, and reminiscent of the private and secret copies of classical texts that circulated in medieval Japan. As Hazama Tetsurō has insightfully noted, the lack of extensive scholarly engagements with *The Pillow Book* by the most influential practitioners of national learning, including Keichū (1640–1701), Norinaga, and Mabuchi, has greatly affected modern reception of the text.[104] Keichū's annotated editions of *The Ise Stories* and *The Tale of Genji*, titled *Conjectures about "The Ise Stories"* (*Seigo okudan*, 1693) and *Gleanings of Commentary on "Genji"* (*Genchū shūi*, 1696), respectively, marked the beginning of the era of the "new commentaries" on the works.[105] His philological approach was to replace the medieval tradition of didactic interpretations. The advent of the era of new commentaries on *The Pillow Book* was delayed until the late nineteenth century, which explains why the text was not broadly appreciated for its aesthetics and literary qualities in early modern Japan.

National learning scholars continued to debate the meaning of the title of Sei Shōnagon's work, and it was the three complete commentaries from the seventeenth century that acted as a springboard for ongoing discussions. Revising Kigin's *Spring Dawn Commentary* and using the text he had constructed as the authoritative version, they were less concerned with textual history than with organization of the content and the linguistic aspects of the work. Kigin's rejection of the work's perceived didacticism and his view of *The Pillow Book* as a book that would facilitate the study of poetry must have influenced the national learning scholars' preference for it over the other commentaries. Thus, for the remainder of the Edo period *The Pillow Book* was regarded within scholarly circles as randomly recorded musings. The problem scholars faced was how to classify the work.

In 1774 the poet and writer Ban Kōkei (1733–1806), lamenting the intense interest of his contemporaries in Chinese writing, produced the first historical study of Japanese literature. Titled *The Traces of Our National Literature* (*Kunitsufumi yoyo no ato*), the work examines texts written by Japanese writers from ancient times until the Edo period.[106]

Classifying Heian-period literary works as court romances (*monogatari*) and diaries (*nikki*), he stressed the fact that *The Pillow Book* did not fit into either of these categories. Kōkei did not explain how the work differed from *monogatari* and *nikki* and simply labeled it *zuihitsu*. His choice not to define *zuihitsu* makes it difficult for us to know why he viewed Sei's work as such. Although his categorization of *The Pillow Book* was not logically justified, Kōkei's singling the text out from among the other Heian-period literary works influenced its reception in the decades that followed.

What might Ban Kōkei have meant by *zuihitsu*? The term was imported from China, where it was first used for a work by the Song-period (960–1279) writer Hong Mai (1123–1202). Titled *Rongzhai's Miscellany* (Ch. *Rongzhai suibi*, J. *Yōsai zuihitsu*), this text contains observations on various topics, including literature, medicine, and astronomy, arranged in more than a thousand sections. The Japanese rendition of the Chinese term *suibi* appeared for the first time in *The Diary of the Courtier Sanetaka* (*Sanetaka kōki*, 1481). In his diary, the poet Sanjōnishi Sanetaka (1455–1537) used the term *zuihitsu* in the context of a Chinese-style compendium, referring to the work of the classical scholar Ichijō Kanera (1402–1481) as *Tōsai's Miscellany* (*Tōsai zuihitsu*, 1481).[107] The Confucian scholar Hayashi Razan (1583–1657) later used *zuihitsu* with regard to ten of the forty-seven volumes constituting his collection *Hayashi Razan's Collected Works* (*Hayashi Razan bunshū*). In the early seventeenth century, *zuihitsu* was a literary form employed primarily by scholars of Chinese studies in Japan, who modeled their works on earlier Chinese writing and included *zuihitsu* in their titles. In the eighteenth century, this form of writing was adopted by national learning scholars and writers of so-called playful prose (*gesaku*).[108] As Chance has noted, by including native writings with those influenced by their Chinese predecessors who catalogued knowledge into categories, scholars extended the limits of the genre to show that Japan had fostered a literary heritage of the same genre and was thus not inferior to China.[109] Thus, Kōkei situated *The Pillow Book* within a body of male-authored texts influenced by Chinese writing that were produced centuries after Sei's work.

Three decades later Kōkei cited Sei's text again in a work titled *Kanden's Essays Continued* (*Kanden jihitsu*, 1806). He praised *The Pillow Book* as interesting and noted that "since it is not fiction, its merit lies in its allowing a glimpse into the manners based on the ways of that era and relationships between various men and women."[110] He linked Sei Shōnagon's style to the notion of writing in a manner of "following the brush" (*fude ni makasete*) and defined it as "sporadic" (*hakanaki mono*). These remarks on *The Pillow Book* are part of Kōkei's discussion of fictional and historical (and as such nonfictional) works. He states that although fictional tales (*tsukuri monogatari*) like the *Genji* depict old customs and clothing, they do not represent the past accurately because they did not record actual events. According to him, *The Pillow Book* was a historical record written without a particular order. He juxtaposed it to court romances and noted that although fiction is inferior to real-life accounts, the style of the *Genji* had made the work attractive to readers, while the randomness of *The Pillow Book* had led to its marginalization.[111]

A definition of *zuihitsu* as a genre was first put forward by Ishihara Masaakira (1760–1821), a disciple of Motoori Norinaga's. In his *Year by Year Miscellany* (*Nennen zuihitsu*, 1801–1805), which also incorporated *zuihitsu* in its title, he stated,

> A *zuihitsu* is something in which you write down things you have seen and heard, said or thought, the useless and the serious alike as they come to you. This includes matters in which one is quite well versed, as well as shallow musings that one simply feels it would be a shame to forget. Unable to capture things in a subtle and delicate style, one is likely to include awkward or tasteless things that make it disappointing. But because a *zuihitsu* is not embellished, character, ability, and learning show, making it all the more interesting.[112]

Ishihara's definition underscored the spontaneity of the genre. He construed it as an "unembellished" (*tsukuroi no nai*) style of writing that exposed the writer's character and talent. In other words, Ishihara suggested that writers' personalities could be extrapolated from their works. His view was later developed by literary scholars in Meiji Japan who used the label *zuihitsu* to define Sei's personality, an approach that led to greater disdain for her work. Ishihara describes *The Pillow Book* as the most splendid *zuihitsu* since ancient times. Noting the theory that it was influenced by the collection of lists by the Tang poet Li Shangyin (813–858), he asserted that there was no evidence for such an argument.

Although he singled out *The Pillow Book* as the most superior miscellany in Japan, he devoted only a few lines to it. Instead, he commented extensively on other examples of *zuihitsu*—namely, *Essays in Idleness*, Amano Sadakage's (1663–1733) multivolume work *Salt Fields* (*Shiojiri*), and Motoori Norinaga's *The Beautiful Basket* (*Tamakatsuma*, 1793–1812). Among them, he first discussed *The Beautiful Basket* immediately after the definition of *zuihitsu*, asserting that all the mistakes for which his teacher's writing had been criticized were precisely because of the spontaneous nature of the work's genre.[113]

Ishihara's passage on *zuihitsu* includes a definition of this generic category and immediately precedes his defense of his teacher's work, thereby signaling a greater desire to justify the imperfection of Norinaga's *The Beautiful Basket* than to delineate the scope of the genre. His incorporation of *The Pillow Book* into this group of male-authored texts was likely motivated by the work's antiquity. Viewing it as a progenitor of *zuihitsu*, Ishihara used *The Pillow Book* to construct a literary tradition of the genre in Japan and situate the writing of his teacher within it. Chance's remark that "at this stage, *zuihitsu* was adopted as a catchall term for mostly large, loose collocations of any period, or any sort, and thus a genre that was not expected to have clear limits"[114] is revealing of the term's amenability to ideological manipulation. Presented as *zuihitsu*, *The Pillow Book* was thus frequently taken up to enhance the value of men's writing. The view of the eleventh-century work as anomalous led to its inclusion in various groups of texts and its construction as the pioneer of the genre that emerged in Japan even before Hong Mai's work in China. Accordingly, Edo-period scholars turned *The Pillow Book* into a *zuihitsu* not so much because an extensive analysis of its formal features or content revealed a natural link to this genre but because ideological concerns in various contexts necessitated the construction of *The Pillow Book* as the earliest *zuihitsu* within and outside Japan.

Since the eighteenth century the definition of *zuihitsu* has undergone significant changes, from a Chinese-inspired collection of classified knowledge and random jottings in the Edo period to a writing style reminiscent of impressionist painting (*inshōha*) at the beginning of the twentieth century.[115] In prewar Japan it came to signify "light, easy reading ranging from travelogues and semi-fictional stories to critical reviews and racy literati gossip,"[116] and in the postwar era it was adopted as a generic label for essays in which "writers seek consolation and identification of what is irreducibly Japanese in their world."[117] The publication of the eighty volumes of the *Collection of Japanese Miscellanies* (*Nihon zuihitsu taisei*) in the 1970s expanded the genre even further by adding a vast body of early modern works. The content within this spectrum of works varied greatly, from literature to politics, which shows that the modern genre of *zuihitsu* has been used as an all-embracing receptacle for works that are difficult to categorize.

Despite the constructed nature of the attribution of *The Pillow Book* to the genre of *zuihitsu* in the mid-Edo period, this view of the text continued into the modern period and persists to this day. As the definition of *zuihitsu* changed, so did the perception of Sei's work. Although *The Pillow Book* was used to underscore Japan's superiority over other countries by serving as a progenitor of a specific writing style that developed in Japan much earlier than in China and—as we will see in chapter 5—in Europe, its categorization as a miscellany led to the marginalization of the work within the Japanese literary canon. This stereotypical view of *The Pillow Book* that emphasizes only its style—described as random, spontaneous, and trivial—has frequently been used to present it as a lesser work. It creates a monolithic and ahistorical image of the eleventh-century text, rejects all other possible readings, and divorces the work from the context of its production. The focus on the form rather than on its content until the end of World War II reinforced the view of *The Pillow Book* as "anomalous," which in turn became central to the image of Sei Shōnagon. For example, in the *New History of National Literature* (*Shinkoku bungakushi*, 1912) Igarashi Chikara stated that regardless of her talent, Sei was "a drifter" (*hōrō shumi*), an "irresponsible unattached observer" (*musekinin naru takamimono*), and someone of "unstable personality" (*teichakusei no nai*).[118] These assessments were influenced not by historical records about Sei but by the understanding of the *zuihitsu* genre in the late nineteenth and early twentieth centuries. However, in attaching these attributes to her, he linked such personality traits to the genre of *zuihitsu* by discounting Sei as "the kind of person who would write a *zuihitsu*" (*zuihitsu o kaku beki hito*).[119] Thus, just as Sei came to be defined by the genre of *zuihitsu*, her image, too, influenced the genre. Igarashi's unfavorable assessment of Sei's text and personality set the tone for later evaluations of both the work and its author. Other scholars used the link between Sei's character and the style of her work to construct hierarchies among textual variants. For example, refuting the lack of a logical organization of the text in Kigin's *Spring Dawn Commentary* because of "the absence of chronological order, order of thought, and lack of associations," Ikeda Kikan stated that "[if] she [Sei] had written in this way, it would not have been a *zuihitsu* but the writing of a schizophrenic."[120]

The complex textual history of *The Pillow Book* shows how the absence of a definitive text deterred literary criticism from engaging with the work's content for centuries. Scholars in the early Edo period faced the challenge of reconstructing the text and deciding on its textual organization. Bansai, Kigin, and Ichū produced primary texts by collating versions from various textual lineages. Among the textual variants the commentators referenced, the recently printed *Nōinbon* version particularly influenced their commentaries. Thus the *Nōinbon* became the most widely read textual line in early modern Japan. Bansai (and Ichū) and Kigin further rearranged the text and presented *The Pillow Book* as a collection of lists and a collection of random jottings, respectively. Although these approaches to textual organization developed in contrast to each other, they were later amalgamated into the concept of *zuihitsu*. Scholars placed *The Pillow Book* within this broad category of writings dominated by male authors and treated the work either as a compendium of various forms of knowledge linked to works of Chinese literature or as a collection of musings recorded on the spot that bore similarities to Japanese writings from the late Edo period.

However, the view of *The Pillow Book* as a collection of random jottings that dominated scholarly circles, initially seen as "a play of the brush" and later as a miscellany, did not hold absolute sway. In popular culture, adaptations and texts inspired by *The Pillow Book* consistently presented it as a collection of lists (*monohazuke*) comprising disparate notions related to a unified thematic category, such as "Things That People Despise" or "Things That Make the Heart Beat Faster." Although scholars followed Kigin's approach to *The Pillow Book*, to writers of literature for mass consumption throughout the Edo period Sei's work was a compendium of catalogues, just as Bansai and Ichū had suggested. These popular texts are the focus of the next two chapters.

CHAPTER THREE

From a Guide to Court Life to a Guide to the Pleasure Quarters

The long-established tradition of reading *The Pillow Book* as a *zuihitsu*, or miscellany, persists into the present both within and outside Japan, despite the continuous debates surrounding the definition of *zuihitsu*. This labeling, which emerged eight hundred years after the completion of the text, reveals how shifting perceptions of literature and genre hierarchy, as well as scholars' familiarity with the work, have influenced views on the nature of Sei's writing over the centuries. Prior to being labeled *zuihitsu*, *The Pillow Book* was classified as a book of poems (*kasho*) alongside eleven poetry collections in Jōkaku's (1147–1226) *The ABCs of Waka* (*Waka iroha*, 1198) in the twelfth century.[1] In the thirteenth century, it appeared in a list of courtly romances (*monogatari*) in *The Sovereign's Eightfold Cloud Treatise* (*Yakumo mishō*, after 1221)[2] by the Retired Emperor Juntoku (1197–1242, r. 1210–1221).[3] To early modern readers *The Pillow Book* was a collection of lists, as the large number of adaptations in the Edo period suggests. Constituting one-third of the whole text of *The Pillow Book*, lists (*monozukushi* or *monohazuke*, literally "detailing of things") brought together disparate notions within categories, such as "Rare Things," "Flowering Plants," and "Ponds." The lists vary in length from a few lines to several pages. Consider two brief examples, a *mono*-type list and a *wa*-type list, respectively.

THINGS THAT GIVE A PATHETIC IMPRESSION (*MONO NO AWARE SHIRASEGAO NARU MONO*)

The voice of someone who blows his nose while he is speaking.
The expression of a woman plucking her eyebrows.[4]

GAMES (*ASOBIWAZA WA*)

The game of kick-ball is interesting, but it is not particularly attractive
    to watch.
Small-bow contests, covered rhymes, and go.[5]

Among the many literary styles *The Pillow Book* combines, lists became representative of the manner in which the work was written and became the basis for the majority of adaptations of the eleventh-century text in early modern Japan. Playful writings that imitated the cataloguing of knowledge in *The Pillow Book* preceded the publication of annotated editions of the work in the latter half of the seventeenth century and were the pioneers that offered a preview of Sei's text to a wide readership. Thus, *The Pillow Book* became known to early modern readers first for its style and later for its content.

Various factors contributed to the popularity of lists throughout the Edo period. In the seventeenth century, for example, taxonomies became a style of conveying information—specifically guides, primers, and rosters spanning various aspects of urban society. This vast body of informational texts that burgeoned in the era of commercial printing classified and transmitted social knowledge. Information, once available only to the elite, became "common property" as it was made accessible to a wide audience encompassing various levels of literacy.[6] In this new social context, lists were a style of knowledge transmission familiar to those who had read other informational texts. In the eighteenth century, lists continued to be popular because of their centrality within the *zappai* (miscellaneous *haikai*) subgenre of *haikai* (comic linked verses). *Zappai*, a term that was already in use in the Genroku period (1688–1704), referred to various forms of popular poetry that stood out for its novelty, wittiness, and playfulness. It comprised a large number of poetic forms, including *maeku-zuke* (verse capping), *nazo-zuke* (riddle capping), *kasa-zuke* (hat capping), *Ogura-zuke* (Ogura capping), and *Genji-zuke* (Genji capping). These practices did not usually take place independently and were often collectively labeled as *maeku-zuke*. Although adding a verse (*tsukeku*) to a foundation verse (*maeku*) had been practiced since the Heian period, *zappai* gradually became popular among commoners in the Kamigata region, and by the end of the seventeenth century it had taken over the city of Edo.

Zappai revived the appreciation for wittiness and repartee that had inspired aristocratic poetry circles in the past. Drawing from various old literary styles, including *waka* and *renga*, it emerged as a new kind of "dialogue poem" (*mondōka*) that stood out for its playfulness and novelty.[7] In this context, *The Pillow Book* inspired a style of poetry composition within the *zappai* subgenre known as lists, or *monohazuke*, which reached its peak during the Kanpō era (1741–1744). Poetry lists involved a short foundation verse consisting of an adjective or an adjectival verb and the noun *mono* (things), which was presented by a judge (*tenja*), and an added verse appropriate for the topic, which was given by each participant in a poetry gathering. Although there were no strict rules about the length of the foundation and added verses, it was common to assign a topic in the form of a five-syllable *maeku* and respond with a verse of either seven or five syllables or both. Lists composed during poetry contests were compiled in collections for later reference.[8]

The popularization of *The Pillow Book* in the Edo period took place as literary works of the past began to be adapted to contemporary life. The advent of commercial printing helped to democratize literacy by increasing the general public's access to classical texts, triggering the proliferation of parody in the seventeenth century. As Linda Hutcheon has shown, for a parody to be appreciated as such, producers retain specific aspects of the source work so that its targeted audience can decipher the parody.[9] For example, *Tales of a Phony* (*Nise monogatari*), a parody of *The Ise Stories* produced in the Kan'ei era (1624–1644), relied on readers' ability to recognize the slightly modified source text and interpret the already standardized iconography by the *Sagabon* editions of *The Ise Stories* in order to understand and enjoy the later rewriting.[10] Digests with a synopsis of the *Genji* chapters and representative poems also reveal that a certain degree of familiarity with the content of the Heian work was considered important.[11] Likewise, lists signaled association between later texts and *The Pillow Book* and acted as a code that bound producers and readers of early modern rewritings of Sei's work.[12]

The earliest readers of *The Pillow Book* in the Edo period, *haikai* poets and scholars of classical literature, must have appreciated the work for its form rather than its detailed accounts of life in the Heian court. The majority of adaptations of the text transformed it into a guidebook that included lists titled in the same way as in *The Pillow Book* while assigning them contents that focused on contemporary life and rarely referred to tenth-century court culture. Early modern rewritings of *The Pillow Book*, however, have attracted little scholarly attention, partly because of the marginalization of Sei Shōnagon's work vis-à-vis *The Tale of Genji* in modern scholarship, partly because of the overall neglect of Edo-period literature outside Japan until recently, and partly because of the prevalent view of parody as an inferior genre.[13] These texts are usually dismissed as being influenced by *The Pillow Book* and as lesser works. As Hutcheon contends, "multiple versions of a story in fact exist laterally, not vertically,"[14] and so their value should be gauged not through a comparison with Sei Shōnagon's text but through consideration of how and why *The Pillow Book* and the image of its author were brought into these later works. This and the next chapter consider the role that lists played in the popularization of *The Pillow Book* from the seventeenth to the nineteenth century. Here I focus on collections of lists that disclose a strong male perspective and reveal how the work was repackaged for male readers, whereas the next chapter examines rewritings intended for a female readership. Over the course of this chapter I analyze booklets in vernacular prose (*kana zōshi*), courtesan critiques (*yūjo hyōbanki*), and books of styles (*sharebon*), since they demonstrate how appropriations of women's writing for a gendered readership influenced later interpretation of the source text. These adaptations also elucidate why *The Pillow Book* was frequently rewritten into an erotic text and how Sei Shōnagon came to be perceived as a predecessor to early modern courtesans.

EARLY PLAYFUL REWRITINGS OF *THE PILLOW BOOK*

The earliest extant example of a *monohazuke* is a work titled *Dog/Fake Pillow and Mad Verses* (*Inu makura narabi ni kyōka*) (hereafter referred to as *Dog/Fake Pillow*). Published in 1600, it consists of seventy-three lists and nineteen comic verses (*kyōka*), organized under headings either taken from *The Pillow Book* or newly created.[15] The work imitates Sei Shōnagon's style but does not play upon the content of the source text. *Dog/Fake Pillow* is one of the works produced in the sixteenth and seventeenth centuries that contain the prefix *inu* (fake, sham, pseudo) in their titles.[16] Other texts include *Dog/Fake Tsukuba Collection* (*Inu Tsukuba-shū*, 1532), *Dog/Fake Essays in Idleness* (*Inu tsurezure*, 1619), and *Dog/Fake Hundred Poets, One Poem Each* (*Inu hyakunin isshu*, 1669), erotic parodies of the *Tsukuba Collection* (*Tsukubashū*, 1356), *Essays in Idleness* (*Tsurezuregusa*), and *One Hundred Poets, One Poem Each* (*Hyakunin isshu*), respectively.

Dog/Fake Pillow had long been associated with Hata Sōha (1550–1608), an active writer, poet, scholar, and physician to the imperial regent Toyotomi Hidetsugu (1568–1595) and the military leader Tokugawa Ieyasu (1542–1616), according to a note that appears in Matsudaira Tadaakira's nine-volume chronicle *A Contemporary Record* (*Tōdaiki*, seventeenth century).[17] Sōha also served the high-ranking aristocrat Konoe Nobutada (1565–1614) as an *otogishu*, or conversational partner and adviser.[18] Signing under various pen names, such as Jumyōin, Ryūan, and Ritsuan, Sōha authored the first printed commentary on *Essays in Idleness*, titled *Jumyōin's Commentary* (*Jumyōinshō*, 1604), and coauthored *The Hundred-Verse Sequence Composed by Jōha, Ryūan, and Others on the Second Day of the Seventh Month in 1593* (*Bunroku ni-nen shichigatsu futsuka Jōha Ryūan ra nani fune hyakuin*).[19] In the 1980s differences among *Dog/Fake Pillow*'s manuscripts and its old movable-type-printing edition led Noma Kōshin, an authority in early modern Japanese literature, to suggest that Sōha may have compiled the printed edition but that the earlier versions were most likely shaped at the hands of Nobutada's attendants.[20] A decade later Mutō Sadao contended that *Dog/Fake Pillow* was a record of *monohazuke* that had been composed by Nobutada and his men for amusement, which also suggests multiple authorship.[21]

This parody of *The Pillow Book* and Sōha's commentary on *Essays in Idleness* were published within the span of four years. The commentary was printed without the text of *Essays in Idleness*, which points to a readership consisting primarily of upper-class individuals who had access to manuscript copies of Kenkō's text, as Linda Chance has noted.[22] In a similar fashion, we can imagine that since *Dog/Fake Pillow* does not overtly refer to *The Pillow Book*, for it to work as a parody its intended audience must have comprised readers familiar with the eleventh-century work.

Dog/Fake Pillow covers a variety of topics, most of which related to the present. For example, the list titled "Delightful Things" (Ureshiki mono) features "a real bargain at a shop"; "Things That Discourage Conversation" (Hanashi ni shimanu mono) includes "rumors about the shogun"; and "military gear after the fighting has stopped" is listed as "Useful Things That Seem Useless" (Iranu yō de iru mono).[23] Moreover, many of the lists' headings and the topics within them in *Dog/Fake Pillow* pertain to gender and sexuality. According to Joshua S. Mostow's gender-sexuality paradigm in early seventeenth-century Edo, there existed an understanding of three genders: " 'pansexual' males (. . . proscribed from other adult men and children of either sex), . . . exclusively heterosexual females," and *wakashu* (adolescent males), who were appropriate objects of desire for both men and women.[24] *Dog/Fake Pillow* comments on the three genders, but *wakashu* receive the most attention among them. The work contains nineteen references to desirable youths, followed by twelve references to women, and only five to adult men. The focus on adolescent males is not unique to this parody of *The Pillow Book*. Other works in the genre of *kana zōshi* as well as later tales from the floating world (*ukiyo zōshi*) and seventeen-syllable comic verses (*senryū*) often took up images of desirable youths.

This literary fascination with *wakashu* can be traced to earlier medieval narratives, later categorized as "acolyte tales" (*chigo monogatari*), that revolve around love affairs between priests and boys.[25] The erotic relations seen in early modern fiction generally conform to the conventions of the "Way of Youngmen"[26] (*shudō*)—an asymmetrical dynamic within which each partner was assigned a different role, thus excluding the possibility of sameness between partners.[27] The older male, also known as *nenja* (person [implicitly male] who thinks of a particular youth),[28] was constructed as the superior partner, which granted him the prerogative to penetrate his younger beloved. Accordingly, the younger male, referred to as *wakashu*, was the junior and as such the receptive partner in the *shudō* dyad.[29] Sexual practices, however, were only one aspect of such male-male bonding structured around difference between the two partners in premodern Japan. Emotional attachment and pedagogical transmission of knowledge were also essential to the *shudō* followers. As a senior partner, the *nenja* acted as a role model and, ideally, a source of admiration and respect for the adolescent boy, who had embarked on training that would later provide him membership in the world of adult men. The relationship between the *nenja* and *wakashu* was described as being just as strong as one between a parent and a child.[30]

Dog/Fake Pillow embodies the perspective of a *nenja*. It presents adolescent males as objects of desire and classifies and evaluates their behavior and manners. There are several examples throughout the text illustrating a *nenja*'s desire to spend time with a *wakashu*. The literary practice of listing categorizes "the prospect of an evening tryst with one's *wakashu*" under a section titled "Things That Stand One's Hair on End" (Mi no kedachi no suru mono). "A flower-viewing walk with one's *wakashu*" appears in a section titled "Interesting Things" (Omoshiroki mono). "What follows evening stories/a tryst with a *wakashu*" is presented as one of the "Things One Would Like to Stop" (Tometaki mono) listed in the same section. "A *wakashu* who seems to be about to leave but stays" is classified in a section titled "Joyful Things When One Has Been Apprehensive" (Kizukai shite ureshiki mono). The text also evaluates various aspects of *wakashu* by presenting, for example, "imprudence of a fine *wakashu*" as "Bad Things in Good" (Yoki uchi ni mo nikuki mono), "nail dirt and nose hair of a *wakashu*" as "Unclean Things" (Kitanaki mono), "one's *wakashu* pretending romantic attraction to someone else" as "Things That Make One Angry" (Hara no tatsu mono), "pretense of love by a *wakashu*" as "Things of Mean Character" (Warukatagi naru mono), "a *wakashu* speaking well of one behind one's back" as "Things Joyful to the Heart" (Kikite ureshiki mono), and "the groundless jealousy of a *wakashu*" as "Joyful Things When One Has Been Apprehensive." Unlike the jealousy of men and women classified as "Fearsome Things" (Osoroshiki mono), a *wakashu*'s jealousy is listed among "joyful things." This juxtaposition with heterosexual fear of unfaithfulness reveals that the jealousy of an adolescent male who was sexually available to an elder man was not regarded as menacing, thus reinforcing the image of the *wakashu* as inferior, submissive, and controllable. Using various examples *Dog/Fake Pillow* encourages devotion, sincerity, faithfulness, and availability of a *wakashu* to his partner, while constructing grooming neglect, hypocrisy, and promiscuity as negative. In addition, it presents the notion of monogamy as essential for the ideal *wakashu*.

Depictions of women in *Dog/Fake Pillow* rely heavily on casting the female gender as contemptible. For instance, a woman's talent for writing is classified in the list heading of "Hateful Things" (Kokoro nikuki mono), "an intellectually pretentious woman" is included in "Things That Succeed Though Seeming Unlikely" (Narisō mo nōte naru mono), and "the jealousy of an aging woman" appears in the list of "Fearsome Things." Moreover, women who are disappointing in bed and women who have passed their prime are regarded as useless ("A woman who falls asleep on you after making love" and "an old wife" in "Things One Would Like to Send Away" [Inasetaki mono]), and women living alone or unmarried or widowed are construed as hateful ("a widow living alone" as "Things People Despise" [Hito ni anazuraruru mono]). The only positive reference among the twelve examples discussing women is the statement "One's only daughter giving birth to a son" in the list "Joyful Things When One Has Been Apprehensive" that comments on women as men's mothers.[31] The focus here, however, is on the "birth of a son," which is depicted as "a joyful thing."

Unlike the positive image of adolescent men, adult men are portrayed in a negative light. Examples include their fearsome jealousy and failed masculinity, recorded in the list "Things People Despise" and referring to an adopted husband and a masterless samurai, respectively. "The heart of the master's son" and "the sword of a strong man" as placed in the category of "Things the Bigger the Better" (Ōki de yoki mono) stand out as the only positive remarks on men.

Dog/Fake Pillow effectively transforms a work that depicts a female court of the past into a contemporary, male-dominated setting by representing *wakashu* as an object of desire and reducing women to their functions as mothers and sexual outlets for men. Unlike later erotic parodies, it does not use vulgar language, nor does it depict sexual acts explicitly. Rather, by imitating the classical style of *The Pillow Book*, the producers of *Dog/Fake Pillow* demonstrate knowledge of canonical literary sources associated with the aristocratic tradition. As Paul Gordon Schalow has noted, topics related to human experience were important for the composition of comic linked verses. Sexuality and gender were central among them, and in some *haikai* schools the incorporation of perspectives of male-male eroticism was considered a prerequisite for skillful poets.[32] In this context *The Pillow Book* offered male poets a useful resource for asserting masculinity and ownership of literary knowledge. Instead of taking up place-names of poetic associations (*uta-makura*) that were central to classical poetry composition or gauging the courtliness of appearances and behaviors of people in the capital in the tenth century, the practice of composing lists enabled writers to comment on life in early modern Japan. Thus Sei Shōnagon's taxonomies fueled what Haruo Shirane has called "haikai imagination," which dominated literary production in the Edo period and manifested itself in "taking pleasure in recontextualization: in defamiliarization, in dislocating habitual, conventionalized perceptions; and in refamiliarization, in recasting established poetic topics into new languages and material cultures."[33] In other words, by rewriting *The Pillow Book*, seventeenth-century writers incorporated the (imaginary) past into the present and fostered new horizons of expectations, thereby enriching the "present" for early modern readers.

Three decades after the publication of *Dog/Fake Pillow* another work that took inspiration from the lists of *The Pillow Book* appeared in print. Titled *Partial Pillow Book* (*Mottomo no sōshi*, 1632),[34] this two-volume work contains eighty lists that cite from ancient and contemporary literary sources, including Japanese poems (*waka*), anecdotes (*setsuwa*), Noh plays (*yōkyoku*), and *haikai*.[35] Because of its popularity, *Partial Pillow Book* had been reprinted five times by 1673. The inclusion of twenty-six *hokku* (seventeen-syllable beginning verses) that appear in Saitō Tokugen's (1559–1647) *haikai* collections led Noma Kōshin to conclude that *Partial Pillow Book*'s author was Tokugen.[36] Tokugen was an active *haikai* poet and the author of the first *haikai* treatise published in Edo, titled *A Primer for Haikai* (*Haikai shogakushō*, 1641). According to Noma, the rich poetic material in *Partial Pillow Book* suggests that its purpose was to educate the thirteen-year-old Prince Tomotada (1619–1662), a nephew and later an adopted son of Emperor Go-Mizunoo.[37] As such, it offers insight into what was considered to be important knowledge for Tomotada to acquire.

The work stands out for its encyclopedic coverage. A large number of lists have concrete headings containing an adjective and *mono*, such as "Long Things" (Nagaki mono), "Tall Things" (Takaki mono), "Large Things" (Hiroki mono), "Clean Things" (Kireinaru mono), and "Fast Things" (Hayaki mono), most of which consist of five or seven syllables. The contents of these lists encompass various aspects of life, such as classifying behaviors, objects, natural phenomena, and people. Other lists have more abstract headings, such as "Things/People That Wait" (Matsu mono) and "Things/People That Return" (Kaeru mono), and include several poems on a topic identical to the heading of the respective list. Moreover, there are lists that recount vignettes from literary works, such as *The Tale of Genji* and *The Ise Stories*. The cataloguing of literary knowledge into categories or under keywords introduced by the lists' headings implies that *Partial Pillow Book* was likely compiled to facilitate the impromptu production of poetry in the genre of *haikai*. In fact, *zappai* poets usually kept the foundation verse simple and clear, and it was the originality and freshness of the added verse that helped gauge the aptitude of the participants in a poetry gathering. The list of "White Things" (Shiroki mono) is a case in point.[38] It opens as follows: "In spring, the earliest plums that bloom, cherry blossoms, white camellia, white wisteria. In summer, white deutzia, the flower of the evening faces in full bloom, Princess Uriko/Melon. In fall, the moonlight, white bush clover, white chrysanthemum, dewdrops. In winter, the first snow, night frost, fallen leaves of a chinquapin tree, a spotted hawk."

The list continues with two poems, both by anonymous poets. The latter comes from *Collection of Japanese and Chinese Poems to Sing* (*Wakan rōeishū*). It reads,

> With white hair
> In the white of the moonlight
> Pushing through the white snow
> To break off a white plum[39]
> *shirajira shiraketaru yoru no tsukikage ni yuki fumiwakete ume no*
>   *hana oru*

A few personal belongings and animals associated with whiteness are mentioned after the poems, and the list concludes with the following *hokku*, or opening verse:

> snow—
> the white bag that contains
> the mountain this morning
> *yuki ya kesa yama o iretaru shirobukuro*[40]

This section is particularly reminiscent of *The Pillow Book*, and specifically its opening section, "In spring, the dawn," which details scenes associated with each season. In *Partial Pillow Book*, however, the author introduces new keywords that are all related to whiteness in each of the four seasons. The poems on the topic of snow provide actual examples of how "whiteness" can function in poetry. Similar to the other lists in this work, "White Things" compiles literary knowledge and topics related to everyday life and enhances the function of the text as a reference manual.

Both works, *Dog/Fake Pillow* and *Partial Pillow Book*, were pioneering rewritings of *The Pillow Book* in the early modern period and were either sponsored by or produced for members of the aristocracy. Although their titles are reminiscent of the eleventh-century work, they do not comment on its author. Images of Sei began to appear in rewritings of her work after the mid-seventeenth century, because diverse audiences in terms of class, gender, and literacy did not necessarily link *The Pillow Book* to Sei Shōnagon. No longer introduced as a lady-in-waiting to Empress Teishi, Sei emerged as a courtesan who had documented ancient courtiers' love lives in her work.

SEI SHŌNAGON'S *PILLOW BOOK* AND EROTIC "PILLOW BOOKS"

In the latter half of the seventeenth century, print technology, commercial gain, and the growing consumption of classical texts encouraged the production of highly eroticized rewritings of Heian texts. Woodblock prints of scenes from *The Ise Stories* and *The Tale of Genji* placed their protagonists in the newly established licensed pleasure quarters. Such scenes transformed the Heian works' elegant and subtle treatment of aristocratic eroticism as a form of courtship into sexually explicit scenes.[41] Woodblock prints related to *The Pillow Book* did not appear until the eighteenth century, but confusion about its content grew with the rise of salacious works referred to as "pillow books" (*makura zōshi*) in the latter half of the seventeenth century. Combining the characters for "pillow," "grass," and "paper," this new type of pillow book usually contained pornographic images that were called pillow pictures (*makura-e*). Although the exact pronunciation of the title of Sei Shōnagon's work before the seventeenth century is unclear, in many seventeenth-century texts, including *Partial Pillow Book* and the preface to Kigin's *Spring Dawn Commentary*, it appears as *makura sōshi* or *makura zōshi*.[42] By the end of the seventeenth century, the mass circulation of pillow books with pornographic content caused writers and scholars to draw a distinction between Sei Shōnagon's work and contemporary pillow books. As a result, the case particle *no* was inserted between *makura* and *sōshi*, functioning as an attributive marker, and beginning in the mid-Edo period Sei's text began to be called *Makura no sōshi* or *Sei Shōnagon Makura no sōshi*, whereas erotic works were referred to simply as *makura zōshi*.[43]

The existence of the two distinct pillow books in the eighteenth century is reflected in seventeen-syllable comic verses, or *senryū*. The following three poems point out differences between Sei Shōnagon's *Pillow Book* and pornographic works, despite the similarity of their appellations.

Nagon's is an unobjectionable pillow
Nagon no wa sashiai no nai makura nari[44]

Reading the clean Pillow in front of your parents
kiyorakana makura wa oya no mae de miru[45]

Madam Sei wrote a Pillow Book requiring annotation
chū no iru Makura no sōshi *o Seijo kaki*[46]

As the first two *senryū* show, in the eighteenth century Sei Shōnagon's *Pillow Book* was seen as a respectable literary work, in contrast to erotic pillow books, which were subject to censorship beginning in 1722. The third poem indicates that by the early modern period, Sei's work was comprehensible only when accompanied by commentary. This poem sets *The Pillow Book* apart from erotic books, which consisted primarily of images and minimal text and were thus easy to grasp.

Senryū also frequently linked the role of the hand in autoeroticism and sexual acts that erotic books encouraged to the act of writing Sei Shōnagon's *Pillow Book*. Thus, for example,

Raising the blind [rolling a tissue] with the hand that wrote *The Pillow Book*
 Makura sōshi o kaita te de misu o maki[47]

Traces of oil even when turning *The Pillow Book* [pillow book] pages
Makura no sōshi tsumami ni mo abura ato[48]

The first of these verses recalls the famous episode in *The Pillow Book* in which Sei Shōnagon raises the blind to show that she has guessed Empress Teishi's allusion to one of Bo Juyi's poems (discussed in chapter 5). *Misu* means both "blinds" used at a residence and "tissue paper" of the kind usually tucked inside the front of one's kimono. In referencing blinds, the author simultaneously alludes to the episode that had come to represent *The Pillow Book* in the Edo period and evokes the image of tissues used to wipe away bodily fluids after sexual activity. The oil (*abura*) in the second poem refers to lamp oil used when reading at night but also to lubricating oil for enhancing sexual intercourse. As these satiric poems reveal, the word *makura* (pillow) in the title of Sei Shōnagon's work would have suggested erotic connotations and thus invited parodic usage. Interestingly, it was the title rather than the content that was central to the way some readers and writers viewed *The Pillow Book* in the eighteenth century.

READING SEI'S TEXT THROUGH THE PLEASURE QUARTERS

The establishment of government-sanctioned brothel districts in the early seventeenth century and the development of a culture specific to them led to the production of a large number of written works that revealed the practices that took place in these quarters. Such literature provided a view into the pleasure districts for those who could not afford to visit or participate in their libidinal economy while also educating those who frequented them in proper comportment. A major genre within informational texts called courtesan critiques developed from the mid-seventeenth to the mid-eighteenth century. These works were targeted at an elite audience, specifically samurai and wealthy merchants who were regular customers of the pleasure quarter of Yoshiwara, as well as high-ranking courtesans.[49]

Seventeenth-century courtesan critiques were the earliest works that cited and adapted *The Pillow Book* in the context of the Yoshiwara brothel district, the only licensed pleasure quarter in Edo. The craze for cataloguing in the early Edo period was probably one of the reasons why *The Pillow Book* became popular in the context of pleasure seeking. Using the lists of *The Pillow Book*, the earliest courtesan critiques drawing from Sei's text, *Critique of the Drum Announcing the Time* (*Sanchōki toki no taiko*, 1667) and *Yoshiwara Cuckoo* (*Yoshiwara yobukodori*, 1668), provide vivid snapshots of life in the pleasure quarter. These courtesan ratings open with accounts of top-ranking women from various brothels in Yoshiwara, commenting on their merits and flaws. At first glance, it is not easy to identify the texts as adaptations of *The Pillow Book* because their titles do not signal any influence of Sei's work, but delving into the content of each work we find a section titled "Inu makura" (dog/fake pillows) following the women's profiles. *Inu makura* became the appellation for lists written in the style of *The Pillow Book* that were included in larger texts in the seventeenth century, although it is unclear whether or not this labeling was directly inspired by *The Pillow Book* or *Dog/Fake Pillow*, the first early modern rewriting of Sei's work. Lists in courtesan critiques evaluate various aspects of the appearance and manners of specific courtesans and the processes of courting as well as becoming intimate with them. Let us consider one example from *Critique of the Drum Announcing the Time* (figure 3.1).

SHORT THINGS

A night of intimate meeting
Yoshida's temper
Takayo's chin
The first letter one sends
Oribekagami's hair
Shamisen Tahē's fingers[50]

As this example shows, lists within courtesan critiques comment on specific, real people, the majority of whom were high-ranking courtesans.

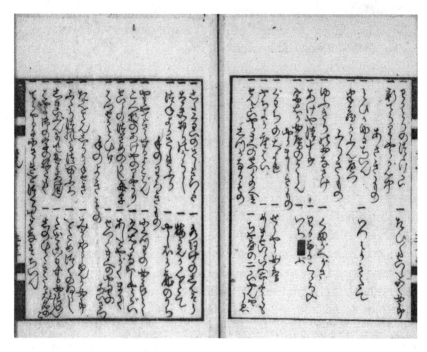

FIGURE 3.1 Two pages from *Critique of the Drum Announcing the Time* (*Sanchōki toki no taiko*, 1667), 32 *ura*–33 *omote*. Courtesy of Shunsho Bunko, Sōai University Library, Osaka

These works entertained those who frequented the pleasure quarter and were familiar with the names included in the lists while also attempting to entice customers.

Critique of the Drum Announcing the Time further classifies Katsuragi's procession (*dōchū*) as unsightly ("Migurushiki mono"), Karasaki's eyebrows as splendid ("Utsukushiki mono"), Ikuyo's temper as hateful ("Nikuki mono"), Matsugae's face as long ("Nagaki mono"), and Karumo and Kaseki's singing in unison as "Things One Wants to Hear" (Kikitaki mono). It is not difficult to discern entertaining and informational aspects of these passages. By promoting the aesthetics valued within Yoshiwara these taxonomies of human behavior and appearance create hierarchies at odds with the Tokugawa political system. Social stratification is no longer determined by birth but by standards of female attractiveness and desirability. Judged against such standards, courtesans are categorized in lists such as "Promising Things" (Tanomoshiki mono), "Splendid

Things" (Utsukushiki mono), "Charming Things" (Kawayurashiki mono), "Unsightly Things" (Migurushiki mono), "Unreliable Things" (Tanomoshigenaki mono), and "Hateful Things" (Nikuki mono). It is not merchants who occupy the bottom of the social hierarchy in the world of pleasure seeking but male entertainers (*taikomochi*) who talk too much ("Hateful Things") and courtesans who nap with their mouth open ("Unsightly Things") or frequently write pledges of love ("Unreliable Things"). Likewise, superiority is not associated with samurai status but with appealing facial features and manners. The lists in *Critique of the Drum Announcing the Time* present a worldview that centers on male sexual pleasure. The road leading to Yoshiwara along the embankment Nihon-zutsumi and a night when one has been rejected by a courtesan are classified as "Long Things"; a night spent with your darling is naturally seen as short; rumor about one's favorite courtesan is found in the list of "Things One Wants to Hear"; and the buying out of the contract of a beloved courtesan is described as a promising thing. Thus, this new order in literature surrounding Yoshiwara highlights the district's identity as an independent world of unique culture in which the strict four-class social system dissolves.

As patronage of the pleasure quarters expanded in the eighteenth century, detailed depictions of these districts, known as *saiken*, emerged. *Saiken* consisted of intricate maps of the pleasure quarters offering information about the names of the brothels and the courtesans associated with them, organized according to rank.[51] By the mid-eighteenth century, in addition to the detailed maps, a new genre came into circulation, the "books of styles."[52] As knowledge about social sensibilities became necessary because of an increase in patrons frequenting the pleasure districts, the accounts of specific women in courtesan critiques gave way to descriptions of the etiquette of brothels in a more general fashion. These texts usually presented two archetypes, the "tasteful and cultivated" patron (*tsū*), in contrast to the patron who was "loud, boorish, and with no sense of refined city manners" (*yabo*).[53]

Lists inspired by *The Pillow Book* were a convenient tool for cataloguing manners and behaviors in books of styles. *The Fool's Pillow Words* (*Ahō makura kotoba*, published in Kyoto in 1749) and *Gleanings of the Pillow Book and the Pleasure District* (*Shūi makura zōshi kagaishō*, published in Osaka in 1751; hereafter referred to as *Gleanings*) are revealing of how Sei's work took on a different function when incorporated into *sharebon* texts. *The Fool's Pillow Words* comments on various pleasure quarters throughout the country, whereas *Gleanings* introduces manners within the unlicensed brothel district of Shima-no-uchi in Osaka.[54] For example, the list of "Hateful Things" (Nikuki mono) in *Gleanings* comments on distasteful comportment by both courtesans and patrons as follows:

> A stingy patron who reprimands as if he himself knew brothel etiquette is hateful. It is really hateful when a courtesan called for the first time, or who has met a patron once or twice and does not yet know him well, fails to pick up the sake cup a maid [*nakai*] has filled or to turn toward the patron, but smoking a pipe only whispers secretly with the maid. When a courtesan wants to marry a man, if he is unable to buy out her contract even when she asks him to look after her, she goes to someone she dislikes and strategically flatters him.[55]

A desirable behavior, on the other hand, is illustrated in the list titled "Things That Make One's Heart Swell" (Omoi masari suru mono). It reads, "Needless to say, when you receive a beautifully written letter from a young woman, [but even more] when a letter from a loved one arrives though it is impossible to meet."[56] The episode underscores the importance of elegant handwriting by both courtesans and patrons and views correspondence as a way to reveal one's steadfastness. This reference to the significance of letters recalls *The Pillow Book* and its emphasis on flawless calligraphy and the choice of paper and presents aristocratic culture as a model for courtesan culture.[57]

In addition to *mono*-type lists, including the preceding passages, *wa*-type lists from Sei Shōnagon's work also populated the pages of *sharebon*. In *The Pillow Book*, the *wa*-type "poetic catalogues" classified topics similarly to *uta-makura* handbooks, which were designed to facilitate the composition of poetry. These poetic catalogues contained connotations with which the informed reader in the Heian period could engage. In contrast, *wa*-type lists in *sharebon* comprise names of entertainment districts, brothels, and courtesans. For example, the list titled

"Months" (Koro wa) in *Gleanings* imitates Sei Shōnagon's, which mentions all the months except for the second, sixth, and tenth, and concludes that since annual events (*nenjū gyōji*) are conducted in every month, all of them are interesting. The *Gleanings* list, however, comments on annual events in Shima-no-uchi and not the Heian court. It tells of the special atmosphere during the first and second months when new courtesans visit the teahouses to introduce themselves, the sightseeing excursions during the third and fourth months, burgeoning intimacy during the seventh and eighth months, the cold days during the eleventh month and the intermediaries' busy preparations for the end of the year, and finally the bustling atmosphere during the twelfth month. This section presents the brothel district as one that has its own culture, its own events, and its own calendar and shows how annual events get reapplied to a new context.

In a similar fashion, *The Fool's Pillow Words* opens with a list titled "Plains" (Hara wa). Rather than discussing plains as geographic regions, the text describes the pleasure quarters of Edo and Kyoto—namely, Yoshiwara and Shimabara, each containing the word "plain" (*hara*). The enumeration of pleasure quarters continues in the next list, titled "Mountains" (Yama wa)—namely, "Maroyama, Imoseyama."[58] Instead of place-names related to classical Japanese poetry as recorded in *The Pillow Book*, this list includes the names of the pleasure quarters of Maruyama in Nagasaki and Imoseyama in Kii. *The Pillow Book*'s list related to mountains contains names of mountains, many of which functioned as poetic place-names and had appeared in love poems in poetry collections, such as *Man'yōshū* (Mikasayama), *Goshūishū* (Sue no Matsuyama), and *Ise shū* (Itsuwa-matayama). The list reads,

Mounts Ogura, Mikasa, Konokure, Wasurezu, Iritachi, Kase, Hiwa, Katasari (I should be interested to know for whom it stood aside), Itsuwa, Nochise, Kasatori, Hira, Toko (I enjoy recalling the Emperor's poem that goes, "Nor ever dare reveal my name!"), Ibuki, Asakura (I like the idea that the lovers probably met again in another place), Iwata, Ōhire (its name also pleases me, for it brings to mind the envoys at the Extraordinary Festivals), Tamuke, Miwa (most delightful), Otowa, Machikane, Tamasaka,

Miminashi, Sue no Matsu, Katsuragi, the Sacred Mountain of Mino, Mounts Hahaso, Kurai, Kibi no Naka, Arashi, Sarashina, Obasute, Oshio, Asama, Katateme, Kaeru, Imose.[59]

The list with the same heading in *The Fool's Pillow Words* replaces the poetic names used to enhance courtship rituals in the Heian-period imperial court with places associated with commercialized sex in the eighteenth century. Likewise, the lists that follow seem at first glance related to topography and flora, but in fact they catalogue courtesans. Some examples include the sections "Rivers" (Kawa wa), "Provinces" (Kuni wa), "Flowers" (Hana wa), and "Trees" (Ki wa) and some of the entries within them, including Nokawa, Tsumagawa ("Rivers"); Izumi, Kawachi, ("Provinces"); Hatsuhana, Hanasato ("Flowers"); and Sakuragi, Matsukae ("Trees"), all of which were courtesans' names. Thus, *The Fool's Pillow Words* appropriates lists from *The Pillow Book* to comment on topics important to the culture of pleasure seeking, rather than on Japan's geography.

Marcia Yonemoto's study of early modern cartography has shown that written sources about the pleasure quarters, specifically *saiken* and *sharebon*, appropriated early modern mapping vocabulary to "redefine political and cultural space" in Edo-period Japan, thus echoing subversive sentiments.[60] Building on Yonemoto's argument, we can understand the focus on the knowledge of manners and etiquette in guides to the pleasure quarters as expressing a form of social criticism. These works project a society in which new identities and hierarchies emerge independent of the social divisions imposed by the shogunate. Indeed, the pleasure quarters allowed for an escape from a world in which class and identity were fixed for life. Despite the government's control, they came to function as independent communities with their own rules and manners. Through the development of a unique culture, these entertainment districts constructed their own identity that differed from the government's view of them as a marginal space. In this context, the lists of *The Pillow Book* were made use of to appropriate the concepts of time and space and construct an alternative version of Japan centered around the culture of pleasure seeking rather than state ideology. By shaping themselves as the "other" Japan, the licensed quarters imitated those in power and challenged the constructed nature of the symbolic expression of authority.

These two books of manners are a pastiche of quotations from and references to earlier texts, including *The Ise Stories, Tales of Saigyō (Saigyō monogatari*, twelfth century), *Stories Selected to Illustrate Ten Maxims (Jikkinshō*, 1252), *A Collection of Ancient and Modern Poems (Kokin wakashū), One Hundred Poets, One Poem Each*, and *The Life of an Amorous Man (Kōshoku ichidai otoko*, 1682). Alluding to these earlier works and adapting them to the context of the eighteenth-century pleasure quarters, the producers of books of styles also comment on the authoritative discourses of Confucianism and Buddhism. One example comes from *The Fool's Pillow Words* in which *The Pillow Book*'s section about a beloved son made to become a priest has been rewritten to describe the hardships of a daughter sold into prostitution: "It breaks my heart to think of parents selling a beloved daughter into prostitution. Besides, although it has been widely said that it is a promising thing since she may marry up, it is unfortunate precisely because she is regarded as mere merchandise for sale. The training period is extremely toilsome, and they say her sleep is restless. Needless to say, it seems irksome when she is transferred to another brothel."[61]

Unlike the episode titled "That Parents Should Bring Up Some Beloved Son" in *The Pillow Book* commenting on the miserable destiny of a young man who has taken holy vows, *The Fool's Pillow Words* is concerned with the destiny of a girl separated from her family. The narrator shows sympathy for young girls sold into prostitution by revealing the difficulty of their lives in brothels. The opening of the section brings *The Pillow Book* to mind in referencing a parent and child, but then the topic quickly changes, creating a sense of surprise and amusement for the reader. In discussing the style of works in the *sharebon* genre, J. Scott Miller has noted that these texts "have such a wide potential for subversion of reader expectations" with the use of satire.[62] However, drawing attention to the misfortune of young courtesans, the text provides criticism of the hegemonic discourse about filial piety and, specifically, of the selling of a daughter's body for the sake of her parents. This motif populates Edo-period fiction, one of the most famous examples coming from the play *The Treasury of Loyal Retainers (Chūshingura*, first performed in 1748). Specifically, in a scene that elicits sympathy and respect, Okaru, a dutiful daughter, agrees to be sold into prostitution by her father Yoichibei in order to raise money for a vendetta. *The Fool's Pillow Words*, however, does not present the heroine as exemplary but rather expresses pity for her state, and it can thus be viewed as offering a veiled criticism of neo-Confucian ideology.

Another aspect of this adaptation of Sei Shōnagon's *Pillow Book* is the inclusion of two stories from earlier texts dealing with courtesans and Buddhism. These narratives originate in *Tales of Saigyō* and *Stories Selected to Illustrate Ten Maxims*. One of the best-known episodes in the former describes the itinerant poet Saigyō's exchange of poems with a courtesan at Eguchi who refuses to offer him a place to stay when he is caught in a heavy rain. Before departing Saigyō composed the following poem:

> "Hard it must be, to tire completely, of the world's ways,
> if you are loath to offer, even a moment's lodging!"
> The courtesan replies:
> "I only thought, since I hear you're one, tired of the world,
> not to have your heart seek, a moment's lodging."[63]

The courtesan's rejoinder points to the hypocrisy of the request for accommodation from a courtesan by Saigyō, a Buddhist monk. Her refusal to provide "a moment's lodging" is doubled with the notion of this world being but a temporary abode. Thus her rejection of Saigyō is also a criticism of Buddhist views of sexuality and female roles as practitioners, since it is the courtesan (also known as Eguchi), rather than the monk, who displays a superior understanding of Buddhist tenets. Eguchi's response underscores the discrepancy between Buddhist ideology and the priest's conduct.[64]

In contrast, the episode from *Stories Selected to Illustrate Ten Maxims* tells a story about the holy man Shōkū and his desperate wish to see the incarnation of the Fugen bodhisattva.[65] In a dream he is instructed to visit a courtesan at Murotsu.[66] Soon after arriving at the port, he witnesses a courtesan entertaining others with the following song:

> At the Mitarai shores in Murozumi along the Suō sea
> the winds do not blow but little waves rise.[67]

The courtesan then transforms into Fugen and before long dies. Superficially, each story describes the unsuccessful proposition of a monk to a courtesan, with the account from the *Stories Selected to Illustrate Ten Maxims* portraying the woman as attractive but inaccessible. Thus these two famous episodes, which were later transmitted as popular stories and reenacted in Noh and Kabuki plays, reveal the tension between women's sexuality and Buddhist practice. Moreover, the agency granted to the female entertainers constructs them as superior to the monks, and this power relation is projected onto the institutions each of them represents—that is, the pleasure quarters and Buddhist clergy.

The texts further assert the link between the early modern pleasure quarters and the ancient Heian court. A section in *The Fool's Pillow Words* recounts the famous episode about the dog Okinamaro and the cat Myōbu that appear in *The Pillow Book* in the section titled "Things That Differ Though They Appear the Same" (Kotogoto naru mono). The quote from *The Pillow Book* introduces the emperor's cat and the dog, tells of the dog's attack on the cat and its subsequent exile to Dog Island, and concludes that "as the emperor held the cat close to his breast, [people] began to call courtesans 'cats.' "[68]

The author brings *The Pillow Book* into this later text but concludes with an unexpected ending that relates the Heian court to the pleasure quarters of early modern Japan. This sudden transformation is entertaining for the reader, but it also effectively rewrites *The Pillow Book* episode into a commentary related to courtesans. The text ties the emperor's love for his cat to the amorousness of Heian aristocracy and thus constructs an erotic image of the classical court that is linked to contemporary society.

Heian women are further associated with courtesans in the list titled "Deep Pools" (Fuchi) in *The Fool's Pillow Words*.[69] The heading is a pun based on homophones for "deep pools" and "remuneration," both pronounced *fuchi*. The latter alludes to episodes from *Stories Selected to Illustrate Ten Maxims* and Ihara Saikaku's *The Life of an Amorous Man* related to courtesans and money. The list reads,

> Tamabuchi, or remuneration for one, remuneration for two; having a concubine is so charming.
>
> In Shinmachi they say, "Meet with a Shimabara courtesan, dressed in a robe from Maruyama, with the independent spirit of Yoshiwara, in a house of assignation in Osaka. Hey, patrons, come this way!" In the collection of Lady Ise it says,

not a deep pool of
the Asuka River yet
my house has turned to
tumbling coins flowing like the
bubbling shallows of the stream[70]

The first reference is to Tamabuchi's daughter, a talented courtesan who impressed Emperor Uda in the ninth century, as recorded in *Stories Selected to Illustrate Ten Maxims*.[71] It is followed by a concise description of the ideal courtesan in the seventeenth century that appeared in various works, including *The Life of an Amorous Man*. Finally, Lady Ise's tenth-century poem recorded in *A Collection of Ancient and Modern Poems* reinforces the theme of courtesans and remuneration. The text has omitted the headnote to the poem, which reads, "Composed when she [Ise] sold her house."[72] Thus removing the poem from its context and focusing on money and pleasure seeking, *The Fool's Pillow Words* places a Heian woman poet among courtesans. This patchwork of citations of texts produced over a span of seven hundred years draws from diverse contexts to discuss women of pleasure in a timeless manner.

The Fool's Pillow Words and *Gleanings* reveal the appeal that Sei Shōnagon's work had for a readership related to or interested in the brothel districts. The playful usage of various literary works in lists modeled after those of Sei Shōnagon acted as a means of confirming readers' erudition when they recognized the source text. Knowledge of *The Pillow Book*, likewise, amplified the reader's pleasure at identifying excerpts from the Heian-period work that were adapted to the early modern culture of entertainment districts. The form and the content of Sei Shōnagon's text further enabled the production of a narrative with an underlying tone of criticism of the dominant structures of power and re-created a world at the core of which lay savviness related to pleasure seeking.

TYING THE TRADITION OF PROSTITUTION TO COURT CULTURE

Gleanings concludes with an epigraph that produces a highly sexualized image of Sei. It reads,

I have expressed Sei's feminine words through an entertaining story in erotic language [literally "bedroom words"], copying scenes of sexual intercourse and imitating the past of the heavenly floating bridge.[73] This whole work was omitted from the old *Pillow Book* because [Sei] feared that its secret would be revealed carelessly. Truly, [she] followed in the footsteps of Princess Kukuri,[74] became well versed in the way of love between men and women, and was naturally called a woman of elegance.[75]

This passage is reminiscent of the colophon of *The Pillow Book*, which claims that Sei Shōnagon's work was not originally intended for circulation. The relevant section reads,

As for these notes about things that struck my eyes and mind, I wrote them down and collected them together at home when I had nothing else to do, thinking to myself all the while, "Is anyone going to see this? Probably not." However, since there are places here and there where I have likely gone too far and said embarrassing things about others, I thought to hide them away carefully. Nonetheless, they leaked out, as they say, "like tears overflowing a dam."[76]

In this passage Sei expresses her concern over the fact that her notes, which she had hoped would not be read by others, have begun to circulate. According to the colophon, she is reluctant to have her writings read because of the criticisms she has made of others and the fact that they may take offense at what she has written. Drawing from this idea of Sei's hidden booklet, the narrator replaces the concern over disparaging comments about members of the aristocracy with anxiety over the erotic content of the work. Sei's *Pillow Book* is represented as a collection of "woman's words" (*onna kotoba*) and is transformed into one of "bedroom words" (*keigo*), implying erotic content. *Gleanings* also asserts that *The Pillow Book* contained scenes of sexual intercourse and constructs Sei as an exceedingly knowledgeable courtesan. The allusion to the deity Kukuri suggests that Sei was regarded as a matchmaker and her *Pillow Book* was intended to unite men and women. *Gleanings* projects an image of *The Pillow Book* as a manual of the manners associated with the Heian imperial court, which is construed as an ancient pleasure quarter. By modeling his work on the Heian predecessor, the author of the eighteenth-century text provides a contemporary version of the etiquette of pleasure seeking and situates his text within a literary tradition whose progenitor is Sei Shōnagon's *Pillow Book*.

This view of the Heian court as a pleasure quarter continues from the preface of *Gleanings*, which states,

> In the past, a lady-in-waiting named Sei Shōnagon was lonely every night and wrote in her work *The Pillow Book*, trying to convey ephemeral elegance and emotions to later readers. Once her writing was printed, these stories about the pleasure quarters were seen as vulgar, thus this single volume was omitted and not included in her book. Those who vaguely heard about it—perhaps because of the way it was circulated—would certainly call a "pillow book" a work portraying men and women of today naked in their bedrooms. Sei devoted herself solely to writing such accounts and was not concerned with the style. These sketches follow closely the style [of *The Pillow Book*] and are not concerned with its content, and eventually there is no one who knows what the omitted volume was.[77]

The preface tells readers that *Gleanings* was originally authored by Sei but that the erotic episodes were excluded from Sei's published work. It construes Sei Shōnagon as a courtesan from a pleasure quarter who recorded her experiences in order to transmit them to later generations of readers. The preface asserts the value of the work by stressing the fact that it is instructive reading for courtesans. This adaptation further plays on the idea of the absence of a definitive text of Sei's work because of its complex textual history. The significant differences among the extant manuscripts of *The Pillow Book* inspired early modern writers to claim that their works reflected the original version of Sei's text.

Similarly, the preface to *The Fool's Pillow Words* depicts Sei as a predecessor to early modern courtesans:

> The spring sun was gradually sinking, and the birds were heading to their nests. Having nothing else to do, [recalling the line in the poem] "how I would regret my name coming, pointlessly, to 'arm,"[78]

I drew my pillow closer, thinking only of the merrymaking in Naga-saki, which I have never seen, Tsu no Kuni, of which I have seen a great deal, Musashino, where I have never been, and the capital of pleasure seeking, where I have played around. As I fell asleep, a strange old woman appeared. "In the past I humbly served Princess Ahō, and while I mingled with others and entertained them, I did not lose my true self, and because of these secret acts of charity, I hopped from Chinese to Japanese pleasure quarters and unmis-takably learned their secrets.[79]

The preface further states that the woman quickly wrote a book and dis-appeared. When the narrator woke up, the book was still there, but since it had no title, he called it *The Fool's Pillow Words*. The image of the woman writer who served in the court alludes to Heian-period women writers. Here again, the act of writing *The Pillow Book* is viewed as closely related to prostitution. The mention of China and the woman's mastery of the ways of love in Chinese brothels further suggests that the old woman was most likely Sei Shōnagon. Her depiction as an experienced courtesan reveals a perception of female court attendants of the past as promiscuous women. The preface transforms the imperial court into a pleasure quarter and female attendants into prostitutes.

These two eighteenth-century works not only claim Sei Shōnagon's *Pillow Book* as their progenitor but also disclose a strong familiarity with Kigin's *The Spring Dawn Commentary* and imitate it in various ways. Both works provide notes accompanying the main text, reproducing some from Kigin's commentary and adding new ones. Thus, similar to Kigin's work, in *The Fool's Pillow Words* these notes demarcate bound-aries of sections, indicating, for example, "from here a new section begins" (*kore yori mata betsudan nari*),[80] as discussed in the previous chapter. Likewise, the notes in *Gleanings* reinforce the impression that this booklet is no different from the eleventh-century text (figure 3.2). The writer informs readers in a note that the passage that follows is Sei Shōnagon's well-known (*rei no*) "play of the brush" (*fudezusami*, an alternative reading for *fudezusabi*), an allusion to Kigin's commentary. A list of twelve works referred to in *Gleanings* immediately follows the table of contents. These texts include *Chronicles of Japan* (*Nihon shoki*, 720), Sugawara no Michizane's (845–903) *Classified National History*

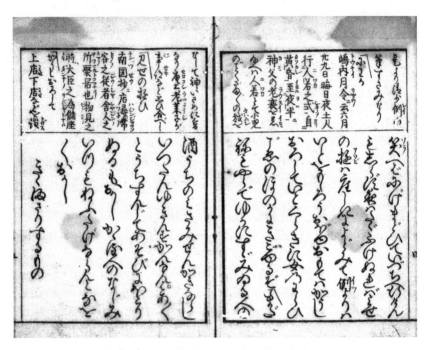

FIGURE 3.2 Two pages from *Gleanings of "The Pillow Book" and the Pleasure District* (*Shūi makura zōshi kagaishō*, 1751), 5 *ura*–6 *omote*, show how the text is shaped like a scholarly commentary and divides the notes accompanying the main text by means of a part alternation mark. Courtesy of Shunsho Bunko, Sōai University Library, Osaka

(*Ruijū kokushi*, 892), the collection of supplementary government regulations *Procedures of the Engi Era* (*Engishiki*, 905–927), Minamoto no Shitagō's *Topical Collection of Japanese Terms* (*Wamyōshō*, 934),[81] *The Tale of the Heike* (*Heike monogatari*, 1180–1185), *The Story of Yoshitsune* (*Gikeiki*, 1410), and the collection of songs *Fallen Leaves of Pines* (*Matsu no ochiba*, 1710). Most of these texts, which would have been understood as primarily classical histories, were referred to in the commentaries on *The Pillow Book* from the previous century. This presentation of historical works at the beginning of the text signals a narrative grounded in respected, canonical texts from the past. As was the case with annotations of *The Pillow Book*, the notes in *Gleanings* effectively guide readers through the work and highlight important aspects. Notes serve as an important tool for edifying a less-knowledgeable readership, and the annotated aspects of *Gleanings* are worth analyzing. The notes focus mainly on key concepts in the language of the pleasure district, including *jorō* (prostitute), *nakai* (intermediary between a patron and a prostitute), *miuke* (buying out a prostitute's contract), *taisetsu no kyaku* (a valued or regular patron). For example, the word "prostitute" (*jorō*) is defined as follows: "*Jorō*: An unlicensed prostitute in Shima-no-uchi. In *Kokushi* there is an episode about two beauties named Shima-no-senzai and Waka-no-mai during the time of Retired Emperor Toba, whom he summoned and watched dance. This is the origin of unlicensed prostitution."[82]

This definition of *jorō* is based on a classical episode about the *shirabyōshi* dancer Giō found in *The Tale of the Heike*. *Shirabyōshi* was a combination of dance and song performed by women dressed in male attire as part of court and temple celebrations during the twelfth and thirteenth centuries. The eighteenth-century *Gleanings* models its definition of current courtesans on a classical description of *shirabyōshi* performers found in an earlier, canonical text describing their activities at the imperial court.[83] It further provides a source for this definition by citing a work indicated as *Kokushi*, or *National History*. This likely refers not to Michizane's *Classified National History* but to some other text; however, the definition in fact draws from *The Tale of the Heike*. By citing an unknown history yet drawing from a famous example of entertainers associated with the imperial court of the past, the note presents prostitution outside the licensed quarters as having a long tradition and elevates the status of women engaged in this profession.

Despite being a newly written, mid-eighteenth-century text, *Gleanings* is annotated and formatted similarly to the earlier scholarly commentaries on *The Pillow Book*. The question therefore becomes why the author would present a contemporary text in the manner of an older one. By modeling *Gleanings* on *The Pillow Book* and its annotated editions, the author draws multiple parallels between court culture and that of the courtesans in Shima-no-uchi and uses Sei Shōnagon's work to introduce a different content using a familiar form. He construes the Heian court and the pleasure district as similar but not identical, as "almost the same but not quite."[84] On one hand, such representations stress the commonality between the cultures. On the other, by means of a content diverging from *The Pillow Book*, *Gleanings* depicts the world of Shima-no-uchi as self-contained, with its own order, customs, and festivities. The commentary form here also serves to elevate the pleasure quarters, if only playfully, by highlighting the necessity of special knowledge in order to understand them. By explaining the jargon used in the entertainment districts through annotation, the work allows the presumably ignorant reader to gain insights into the courtesans' world. Presented as such, the pleasure quarters emerge not as places for mere sexual transactions but as a realm of their own accessible only to sophisticates.

The view of Sei Shōnagon as a forerunner of early modern courtesans, as well as the perception of the Heian court as a pleasure quarter, did not emerge in a vacuum. By the dawn of the early modern period, the link between Japanese poetry and sexuality had existed for centuries. The passionate poems of Heian women encouraged views of them as prostitutes (*yūjo*), as medieval fictional narratives (*otogizōshi*) reveal.[85] Disseminated by traveling entertainers, some of whom offered sexual services, these fictional accounts often blurred the boundaries between the stories' characters and the storytellers, which resulted in misconceptions about Heian court women as prostitutes.[86] In the seventeenth century, the female gender of these writers, the focus on courtship and heterosexual relationships in their works, and the inclusion of Japanese poems led neo-Confucian scholars to allege that Heian literature was erotic and morally corrupting and therefore not appropriate for girls' education.[87] The classics were criticized not only for their lewd content but also for fostering female subjectivity through the mastery of aristocratic culture. As scholar Yamaga Sokō (1622–1685) pointed out, having read *The Tale of Genji*, *The Ise Stories*, and other works from the Heian period "girls then devote themselves to poetry composition, do painting and calligraphy, make artificial flowers, play the koto, and hold merry feasts, as a result of which ethics are forgotten, and the essential relationships between lord and retainer, father and son, husband and wife fall into disarray."[88] The official relegation of courtiers to a position of guardians of the arts, as a way to deprive them of political power, further fostered an understanding of the Heian period as effeminate.[89] Thus, seventeenth- and eighteenth-century military households associated images from *The Tale of Genji* with femininity and considered them as befitting women's trousseaux and the women's quarters (*ōoku*).[90] National learning scholars' debates over the nature of *waka* in the eighteenth century further shaped Heian literature as feminine.[91]

In seventeenth-century Japan, aristocratic culture served to create an imaginary world within the walled-in brothel districts that were established at the beginning of the Edo period all around the country. These pleasure quarters functioned "as an escape from and counterpart to the household."[92] However, these entertainment districts were not places for mere sexual services. As Watanabe Kenji has proposed, it would be more accurate to view the only licensed pleasure quarter of the city of Edo as containing two Yoshiwaras within itself, one functioning as a sexual outlet and the other offering a space for socialization and cultural production.[93] Elaborate brothel etiquette modeled upon the contemporary view of courtship and marriage practices of Heian court society governed interactions between courtesans and patrons.[94] Similar to the courtship ritual in tenth-century Japan, becoming intimate with a high-ranking courtesan required visits to Yoshiwara three nights in a row.[95] Moreover, courtesans' literary erudition was instrumental in attracting and keeping patrons through elegant letters, mastery of *waka*, and knowledge of classical literature, especially until the mid-Edo period.

The aura of sophisticated eroticism that Heian culture was perceived to carry was reinforced by the adoption of the so-called Genji names (*Genji-na*). Genji names were not restricted to female characters from *The Tale of Genji* but also included names of male figures and chapter titles. As Ejima Kiseki's *Courtesan's Amorous Shamisen* (*Keisei iro jamisen*, 1701), a collection of stories about courtesans from various pleasure districts in Japan, reveals, Yūgiri and Kashiwagi were names given to top-ranking courtesans (*tayū*) in Kyoto's Shimabara; Yoshiwara had Usugumo; and Osaka's Shinmachi was the home of Kashiwagi, Wakamurasaki, Kaoru, and Ukifune. Genji names were not restricted to courtesan rank and spread to the lower-ranking categories, such as *sancha* (powdered tea) and *umecha* (plum tea) in Yoshiwara and *kakoi* (locked up) and *hashi* (low ranking) in Shimabara and Shinmachi.[96]

Along with Genji names, woodblock prints depicting courtesans reading *The Tale of Genji* and various forms of entertainment linked to Murasaki's work, such as the games *Genji zake* and *Genji kō*, reveal the prevailing influence the eleventh-century text had on the culture of the pleasure quarters. The image of the Heian court as an erotic space led to a perception that women writers from the tenth and eleventh centuries were courtesans. One example of highly sexualized representations of

Heian writers is an erotic book titled *The Twin Mounds of Conjugality* (*Fūfu narabi no oka*, 1714).[97] Written by Hachimonjiya Jishō (d. 1745) and illustrated by Nishikawa Sukenobu (1671–1750), the book recounts sexually charged stories about twelve literary women from the Heian period, introduced in the preface as "truly amorous people from the past" (*irobukaki inishie no hito*). Profiling Princess Shokushi,[98] Ono no Komachi, Ise, Ukon, Izumi Shikibu, Koshikibu, Akazome Emon, Ise no Tayū, Murasaki Shikibu, Daini no Sanmi, Suō no Naishi, and Sei Shōnagon, the work consists of stories that open with a verse from the poem of the respective writer included in Fujiwara no Teika's *One Hundred Poets, One Poem Each* and depict the women trysting, pairing them with their actual husbands or imagined lovers. *The Twin Mounds of Conjugality* can be viewed as a parody of Confucian-inspired manuals for female readers that feature stories about exemplary women of the past. It is also reminiscent of the cataloguing of high-ranking courtesans in courtesan critiques. It is tempting to imagine that as *tayū* disappeared by the late eighteenth century, Heian women writers famed for their beauty and accomplishments took their place in erotic literature. As actual historical figures they held the power to stimulate men's imagination, while the lack of records about their lives facilitated the manipulation of their images.

The section that presents Sei is titled "Sei Shōnagon Who [Authored] *The Pillow Book* of Nightly Reality" (Yo o komete utsutsu no *Makura no sōshi* no Sei Shōnagon), alluding to her poem in Teika's collection.[99] The poem reads,

yo wo komete	Although, still wrapped in night,
tori no sora-ne ha	the cock's false cry
hakaru tomo	some may deceive,
yo ni afusaka no	never will the Barrier
seki ha yurusaji	of the Meeting Hill let you pass[100]

Introducing Sei as "a famous beauty whose literary talent was unparalleled," the text discloses to readers the context of the composition of *The Pillow Book*.[101] According to *The Twin Mounds of Conjugality*, Narimasa, who was deeply in love with Sei Shōnagon, pressed her older brother Kiyomi to arrange a tryst with his sister. Having been disowned by his parents because of his passion for *jōruri* (chanted narratives accompanying puppet plays), lack of interest in poetry, and various disagreements, Kiyomi plotted to sneak into the house and steal Sei during the night. When Kiyomi approached her chamber, Sei was practicing calligraphy (*tenarai*), facing the lamplight. The noted male calligrapher Yukinari, having been asked by her father to tutor her in handwriting, was visiting, and the two were discussing poetry. As he took her hand from behind, he became aroused and eventually embraced her. Sei pleaded, "Yukinari, if your heart is true, please do as you wish" (*Yukinari-san, jijitsu nara gojiyū ni*).[102] A detailed description of their sexual encounter follows, and the narrator explains that this was Sei's sexual initiation. She rejoiced at discovering the superiority of actual intercourse over masturbation with a dildo, which she had frequently practiced. As Yukinari was about to leave, she implored him to stay since her father was away for the night, a rare occurrence. The text tells readers that from then on, Yukinari instructed Sei regarding her *Pillow Book* and thus it began to circulate broadly.

The accompanying illustration (figure 3.3) depicts Sei and Yukinari in flagrante. Sei faces a writing table and holds a brush, while Yukinari embraces her from behind. Booklets are spread around the couple. Readers are allowed a peek by means of the *fuki-nuki yatai* (blown-off roof) technique that was commonly used in picture scrolls from the Heian and Kamakura periods. Beside the veranda, outside, Kiyomi is peeping

FIGURE 3.3 Sei Shōnagon and Yukinari engage in sexual intercourse, with Kiyomi watching from the left, as featured in *Twin Mounds of Conjugality* (*Fūfu narabi no oka*, 1714), vol. 3, 19 *ura*–20 *omote*. Courtesy of the International Research Center for Japanese Studies, Kyoto

through the raised blind and masturbating. A hen and a rooster are also included in the illustration sitting on a branch of a tree, though not actually mating. The reader and the masturbating male share their position as viewers observing the couple, which suggests that such an illustration was intended to sexually stimulate male readers. The image draws from editions of *One Hundred Poets, One Poem Each* that include a rooster in the illustration to Sei Shōnagon's poem.[103] The depiction of a rooster and a hen to parallel the trysting couple, however, is reminiscent of the illustration to episode 22 in the *Sagabon Ise monogatari*. This *Ise* episode presents an exchange of passionate poems between lovers. The allusion to this earlier work transposes the intense affection between the couple in the tenth-century text into the characters in the eighteenth-century *Twin Mound of Conjugality*. The image and the narrative characterize *The Pillow Book* as a work centering on sexuality, and unlike *senryū* that draw a distinction between the erotic "pillow pictures" and the eleventh-century *Pillow Book*, Sukenobu's work emphasizes their similarity.

The diverse audiences *The Pillow Book* reached in the Edo period viewed the work in a way that differed significantly from the perception of the text in tenth- and eleventh-century Japan. It was not the content of *The Pillow Book* but its anachronistically assigned title, the oversimplified perception of its rich style, and the salacious fabricated episodes about Sei's life that influenced interpretations of the work and the image of its author. The lists of *The Pillow Book* offered *zappai* practitioners and writers of erotic literature a convenient tool for projecting power in diverse contexts, including capping verses, asserting masculinity, demonstrating knowledge, and creating hierarchical rankings. In the early seventeenth century, lists included in *kana zōshi* expanded readers' worldview by cataloguing encyclopedic knowledge that facilitated the impromptu composition of comic linked verses. Lists of late seventeenth-century courtesan critiques presented Yoshiwara as an independent and self-contained world by rating courtesans and manners based on its own aesthetics. Eighteenth-century lists in *sharebon* further educated readers about the etiquette and rituals related to brothel districts, thus producing knowledge of the norms of these spaces. Along with courtesan critiques, books of styles challenged discourses of power by exposing their artificiality. Appropriating the style of a classical work, writers positioned their adaptations as offspring of a text associated with aristocratic circles and political power of earlier centuries and thus claimed ownership of cultural capital.

Confusion about the nature of Sei's work was further amplified with the popularization of erotic books that had a title identical to that of her eleventh-century text. While *senryū* drew a clear distinction between Sei's *Pillow Book* and the early modern pillow books, writers of popular literature constructed a highly sexualized image of Sei as a predecessor of early modern courtesans and viewed her writing as a compilation of erotic knowledge worth passing on to subsequent generations. No longer perceived as enhancing the cultural salons of their female patrons, the accomplishments of women writers from the Heian period were utilized to stimulate men's amorous fantasies. Shifting the focus from Heian court life to the world of courtesans, adaptations of *The Pillow Book* effectively transformed it from a record about ancient aristocratic society into a guide to the culture of pleasure and entertainment in early modern Japan.

CHAPTER FOUR

The Pillow Book
for Early Modern Female Readers

The rise in books specifically for women in the seventeenth century prompted the production of illustrated editions of *The Ise Stories, The Tale of Genji*, and *One Hundred Poets, One Poem Each* that were designed largely to promote women's moral and literary education. *The Pillow Book* was conspicuously absent from this list. Although scholars can offer only conjectures as to why this may be, *The Pillow Book*—in contrast to other classical texts, such as those noted previously—was not viewed as amenable to illustration. Although images of its author, Sei Shōnagon, were frequently included in texts for popular consumption, very few works present illustrations to accompany the text of *The Pillow Book*. Throughout the medieval and early modern periods only a few scholarly commentaries and adaptations of the work contain images, and there is no extant edition that presents the complete text of *The Pillow Book* with illustrations. The earliest surviving examples are *The Pillow Book Illustrated Scroll* (*Makura no sōshi emaki*, fourteenth century) and Okanishi Ichū's commentary *Marginal Notes to "The Pillow Book"* (*Makura no sōshi bōchū*, 1681), discussed in chapter 2.

The Pillow Book Illustrated Scroll is drawn in the monochrome (*hakubyō*) style with text by either Retired Emperor Fushimi (1265–1317, r. 1287–1298) or his daughter Princess Shinshi (dates unknown).[1] In its present form it consists of a single scroll featuring seven of the diary-like passages from *The Pillow Book*.[2] As Mitamura Masako has observed, five of the sections focus on Emperor Ichijō and Empress Teishi, depicting episodes between 995 and 999, when Teishi's salon was in decline. Mitamura also notes that the tension between Teishi's court and the faction of Fujiwara no Michinaga at the end of the tenth century parallels the rivalry between the so-called junior Daikakuji line of Emperor Kameyama (1249–1305, r. 1260–1274) and the "senior" Jimyōin line of Emperor Go-Fukakusa (1243–1304, r. 1246–1260) competing for the imperial throne three centuries later.[3] Mitamura argues that the production of a scroll focused on the splendor and harmony of the empress's court, despite the tragic consequences for Teishi and her entourage, reflected a desire to underscore and restore the imperial authority of the Jimyōin line.[4]

Unlike the fourteenth-century illustrated scroll, the images in Ichū's *Marginal Notes to "The Pillow Book"* function as visual annotations rather than featuring scenes from Sei's work. The twenty-five illustrations found at the beginning of Ichū's commentary introduce various aspects of Heian architecture and clothing, as well as concepts mentioned in *The Pillow Book*.[5] For example, the first picture features the gate of a four-pillared structure (*yotsuashi no mon*) and refers to the episode describing Empress Teishi's move to the residence of Narimasa.[6] The last two illustrations visualize "the paintings of the stormy sea and . . . the terrifying creatures with long arms and long legs" found in the northeast corner of Seiryō Palace, as mentioned in the section "The Sliding Screen in the Back of the Hall."[7]

It is notable that four centuries after the production of the picture scroll and approximately a century after the publication of the annotated edition of *The Pillow Book* that contained several images, between 1741 and 1818—that is, within the span of less than eighty years—three illustrated adaptations of *The Pillow Book* appeared in the book markets. These are *Picture Book Mount Asahi* (*Ehon Asahiyama*, 1741), *Erotic Book Spring Dawn* (*Ehon Haru no akebono*, 1772), and the seventeen-page "Sei Shōnagon's Unmatched Talent: Prodigious Words from Sei Shōnagon's *Pillow Book*" (Sei Shōnagon no kisai: Dō *Makura no sōshi* no kigo) that was included in *A Collection of Model Texts for Women* (*Onna yōbunshō yukikaiburi*, 1818), a compilation of exemplary texts for female readers.[8] The 1741 *Mount Asahi* consisted of an abridged *Pillow Book* constructed as a textbook for letter writing; the 1772 erotic book was a transformation of Sei Shōnagon's narrative into a manual for sex education and offered practical advice for improving spousal relations; the 1818 rewriting underscored the link between women's erudition and sexual allure. All three works are related in that the digest *Mount Asahi* served as the base text for *Spring Dawn* and "Sei Shōnagon's Unmatched Talent." In addition, the three adaptations focused on the listlike passages of *The Pillow Book*, claimed Sei Shōnagon as their author, and were composed and illustrated by men.

The selection of content and the accompanying illustrations in these three works, specifically the large number of images that are similar to pictures frequently appearing in early modern books for women, show that the three adaptations were produced for female audiences and conveyed knowledge that was viewed as able to enhance a woman's desirability as a wife.[9] Although each work focuses on different skills, all three emphasize the importance of female self-cultivation in their dealings with a prospective or current husband. Moreover, the image that the three texts construct of the writer Sei Shōnagon is not confined to traditional virtuous ideals, such as filial daughter, wise mother, or chaste wife. Instead, Sei is presented as the embodiment of learning, quick-wittedness, refinement, and in some cases sexual allure.

These adaptations have never been brought together and examined in the context of female education and readership. Moreover, having been categorized based on their titles rather than their contents, these works have until now attracted little scholarly attention.[10] Specifically, *Mount Asahi* has been referred to as a picture book (*ehon*), *Spring Dawn* has been categorized as erotica (*enpon*), and "Sei Shōnagon's Unmatched Talent" has been viewed as part of a letter-writing textbook (*ōraimono*).[11] But when we delve beneath the titles, we find that these rewritings of *The Pillow Book* enable us to expand our pool of sources related to women's education in early modern Japan beyond the corpus of texts already labeled as letter-writing textbooks for girls (*joshi yō ōraimono*) or instruction manuals for women (*jokunsho*). Indeed, as Marcia Yonemoto has argued, the inclusion of a large number of illustrations in texts that were intended for broad audiences reveals the way literacy in the latter half of the Edo period was measured—namely, by one's "familiarity with the dynamics of conveying information through the medium of print" and, specifically, the ability to recognize images and narratives that had circulated extensively.[12] Following Yonemoto's approach, we can interpret the inclusion of widely disseminated images from instruction manuals for women as well as the careful textual selection as suggesting that the three adaptations were geared toward a female readership. Bringing these three works into a discussion of books for female readers helps us consider the scope of knowledge that was viewed as desirable for a woman and the role that *The Pillow Book* played in female education in the eighteenth and into the early nineteenth century.

BOOKS FOR WOMEN

The second half of the seventeenth century saw the development of a genre referred to as books for women (*josho/nyosho*).[13] Because of their diverse subject matter, such books have been retrospectively divided into various categories by multiple scholars. Following the divisions established by Matsubara Hidee,[14] books for women fall into four categories, each centered around one of the following themes: Confucian values, including filial piety, kindness, faithfulness, education, tolerance, the three obediences (*sanjū*),[15] and the seven grounds for divorce (*shichikyo*);[16] details of everyday life such as clothing, food, dwellings, marriage, childbirth, annual events, female comportment, Shinto and Buddhist practices, and kimono sewing; the arts, such as flower arrangement, tea ceremony, music (koto and shamisen), calligraphy, painting, and games such as *sugoroku*; and literature, specifically the Japanese poetry recorded in the twenty-one imperial anthologies.[17] This final group owed its existence to the centrality of *waka* composition in young women's education. The knowledge books for women conveyed and the messages they communicated were aimed at educating and preparing women for their roles in the patriarchal family system.

Peter F. Kornicki has observed that the birth of the category of "books for women" signals "professional recognition of a new class of reader, if not of purchaser, and identification of certain types of books as appropriate for women."[18] This gendering of the book market and, by extension, of knowledge, reflects the gendered social order that the Tokugawa shogunate had imposed. The development of this genre also suggests that early modern women were expected to sustain a specifically gendered performance. The trend of repackaging Heian literary works for female audiences in the eighteenth century was preceded by a debate over the appropriateness of such texts as reading material for non-aristocratic women both young and old.[19] Japanese classics were criticized as immoral owing to a number of factors, including the association of literary creativity and composition with lewdness; the female gender of the Heian writers, which "naturally" implied a lack of knowledge of Chinese classics and virtues; the focus on *waka* in such texts, which was linked to lechery; and the perception of female learnedness as equal to conceitedness, as Kornicki has shown.[20]

Unlike the *Ise* and the *Genji*, which were thought to be inappropriately salacious, the three complete commentaries on *The Pillow Book* that emerged in the second half of the seventeenth century—precisely when these debates were most heated—did not criticize Sei Shōnagon's work for its perceived lewdness.[21] Although *The Pillow Book* contains a large number of passages focusing on encounters between a man and a woman, or on a woman's demonstration of the kind of knowledge and learning that put men to shame, the authors of these annotated editions did not express concern about the readings and interpretations of these sections. Why did the morality of *The Pillow Book* escape censure in the seventeenth century? Perhaps Sei Shōnagon's text was not included in the debates about the appropriateness of Heian classics as reading material for women because the work had already been relegated to the periphery of the literary canon. Moreover, the text's focus on Chinese classics rather than Japanese poetry might have elevated *The Pillow Book* in the eyes of Confucian scholars. Although *The Pillow Book* was not viewed as morally corrupting, the scant number of poems included in it likely made this Heian classic initially unappealing to the producers of instructional manuals for women. Since the main purpose of such textbooks was to cultivate poetry-composition skills, unlike poems from the *Ise* and the *Genji*, poems from Sei Shōnagon's work rarely appear in books related to women's conduct.

Furthermore, in the seventeenth century Kitamura Kigin elevated the status of *The Pillow Book* by asserting that it was in line with neo-Confucian didacticism and appropriate reading material for Tokugawa women. In his *Tales of the Maidenflower* (*Ominaeshi monogatari*, 1661) he demonstrates the moral value of the text by way of two episodes meant to represent the whole work. These passages include "a child full of filial piety" (*kō aru hito no ko*), an example of things that move the heart appearing in the section of the same name ("Aware naru mono"), and "the heart of a man" (*otoko no kokoro no uchi*), an entry in the list titled "Embarrassing Things" (Hazukashiki mono). In connection with the former section, the narrator expounds at length on filial piety, telling readers that it is the most essential human virtue. The text advises its female readers to serve their husbands and parents-in-law, raise and educate their children, and never neglect housework (specifically weaving and sewing); otherwise a woman will become estranged from her husband and hated by her mother-in-law, thus disappointing her parents and making her unfilial.[22] Although the topic of filial piety appears briefly and only in this section of *The Pillow Book, Tales of the Maidenflower* presents it as a fundamental issue in Sei's text. The narrator links the idea of love for one's parents to obedience to one's husband, thus constructing the relation of a woman to her husband as central to a woman's life. The latter section, about "the heart of a man," on the other hand, instructs women not to harbor resentment against their husbands.[23] The narrator goes on to illustrate this moral lesson with reference to the "Kawachigoe" episode (episode 23) of *The Ise Stories*, in which Narihira, though he visits a woman in the Takayasu district of Kawachi province, provokes in his first wife no signs of jealousy. The inclusion of the *Ise* episode, which had become an important anecdote in women's education, was aimed at imparting to readers that Heian texts featured common moral values. The reference to the *Ise* episode can also be viewed as a strategy to convey information via a narrative with wide circulation and was likely familiar to readers. Constructed in these ways as a work about woman's filial piety and lack of jealousy, *The Pillow Book* promoted feminine virtues that were perennial. In other words, *Tales of the Maidenflower* asserts that what was hailed as essential six hundred years ago, when *The Pillow Book* was composed, remained valid in the seventeenth century. Kigin's work was the first attempt to present a relatively detailed rendering of Sei Shōnagon's text to early modern readers, and specifically to women, since commentaries on *The Pillow Book* had yet to appear.

The production of editions of Heian literary works designed particularly for female audiences burgeoned after the end of the seventeenth century. As Joshua S. Mostow has suggested, the main reason for this development in the book market was the desire of "wealthy *chōnin*, rich farmer, and low-ranking samurai families . . . to place their daughters in service."[24]

In other words, mastery of courtly comportment and literary knowledge increased a woman's marriage prospects and offered an opportunity for social mobility, which was otherwise extremely limited during the Tokugawa regime. *One Hundred Poets, One Poem Each* was central to women's education beginning in the late seventeenth century, and *The Ise Stories* was favored as appropriate for women and included in their trousseaux from the end of the seventeenth to the end of the eighteenth century, whereas *The Tale of Genji* was represented by its chapter titles and the poems associated with them, there being no edition of the complete work particularly targeted at women, as Mostow has further shown.[25]

In her analysis of the social classes as presented in *Treasures for Women* (*Onna chōhōki*, 1692) and *Treasures for Men* (*Nan chōhōki*, 1693) Nakano Setsuko notes that the world of women (as depicted in genre scenes of women [*onna fūzokuzu*]) was less stratified than that of men. Although aristocrats and the imperial household were excluded from the four classes (warrior, artisan, farmer, and merchant), the courtly comportment conveyed through images of and narratives about aristocratic women of the past was upheld for emulation. Thus, the women in *onna fūzokuzu*—an aristocrat, a warrior, a commoner, a peasant, a mistress, a courtesan, a madam, and a widow—are depicted not as wives to men from their corresponding classes but with regard to virtues pertaining to courtliness (*yasashisa*) (figure 4.1).[26] Moreover, Yokota Fuyuhiko has pointed out that educational books for women, along with occupational encyclopedias and erotic literature, feature "an amazing variety of [women's] statuses and occupations."[27] Focusing on *Treasures for Women* and *A Treasure Chest of Greater Learning for Women* (*Onna daigaku takarabako*, 1716), he demonstrates that both works contain images of women engaged in various forms of socially productive labor. Rather than depicting women as representatives of a specific class, both works portray them performing a range of activities, including child-rearing, writing, sewing, picking cotton, hand-loom weaving, and doing laundry. As these two instruction manuals for female readers suggest, the inclusion of the word *onna* (woman) in their titles does not signal an intended readership limited to a specific class, status, or age group but centers around the notion of "woman's work," thus encompassing women who practiced more than a hundred occupations and activities, within and outside the household. Female readers from all walks of life could draw knowledge

FIGURE 4.1 Genre scene of women—an aristocrat, a warrior, a commoner, a peasant, a mistress, a courtesan, a madam, and a widow; *Treasures for Women* (*Onna chōhōki*, Edo period), vol. 1, 2 *ura*–3 *omote*. Courtesy of the National Diet Library, Tokyo

from common sources because both the centrality of a woman's relation to her husband in the patriarchal family system and the aristocratic ideal of femininity were hailed across the classes.

WOMEN'S WORK AND PASTIMES: *PICTURE BOOK MOUNT ASAHI*

In 1741 a Kyoto-based publisher released *Mount Asahi*, the aforementioned illustrated adaptation of *The Pillow Book*.[28] The work contained forty of the *mono*-type lists of *The Pillow Book* inscribed within pictures provided by Nishikawa Sukenobu (1671–1750).[29] The editor, signed in the preface as Minamoto Sekkō,[30] kept only six of the sections as they appear in *The Pillow Book* and significantly abridged the others, selecting no more than five entries for most of the lists from among the plentiful examples included in *The Pillow Book*.[31] Sekkō omitted all the diary-like and essaylike passages within the selected sections and many of the references to Heian culture and everyday life—such as festivals and actual historical figures—and descriptions of clothing and furniture. By removing the historical content of *The Pillow Book*, the editor shaped it into a work in which seemingly timeless topics related to women prevailed. For instance, readers are told that a frivolous woman is despicable ("Things People Despise" [Hito ni anazururu mono]), an unattractive woman who takes a nap is unsightly ("Things Unpleasant to See" [Migurushiki mono]), a son-in-law who neglects his wife is unpromising ("Situations One Has a Feeling Will Turn Out Badly" [Tanomoshigenaki mono]), and a young girl's voice should be soft and the hair of a woman from the lower classes should be short ("Things That Should Be Small" [Mijikakute arinu beki mono]).

The selections of entries from Sei Shōnagon's work suggest that an attempt was made to omit material that was perceived as morally inappropriate for girls and to include only innocuous cultural pastimes as well as references to motherhood. For example, the section titled "Distractions for Boring Times" (Tsurezure nagusamuru mono) features court romances (*monogatari*), the games of go and *sugoroku*, and small children's charming babbling, and its accompanying illustration depicts women caring for children and young women playing *sugoroku*. The same section has elided the statement about accepting a visitor during a period of abstinence, as recorded in *The Pillow Book*, which reads, "Even during a period of abstinence, if I receive a visit from a man who is witty and good at conversation, I let him come in."[32]

Such manipulation of the base text shows that the creators of this adaptation viewed the reference to a man's visit to a woman as irrelevant, or inappropriate, to girls' education.

The pictures accompanying the text abound in images of women, often in a group. There are many that show them engaged in daily activities such as combing their hair, sewing, playing go, holding and playing with children, reading, writing, playing the koto, and others focusing on travel and transportation (including images of carriages, boats, horses, and pilgrims). The pictures also feature the furniture that was part of a woman's trousseau, such as mirrors (*kyōdai*), wooden boxes for booklets and scrolls (*bunko*), tea sets, koto, *sugoroku* boards (*sugorokuban*), kimono stands (*ikō*), shell buckets (*kaioke*), comb boxes (*kushike*), and so on. In addition, one picture, contrary to its caption, which refers to "the objects used during the Doll Festival" (*hiina asobi no chōdo*), features a large shelf (*mizushi*) with books, scrolls, and wooden boxes (figure 4.2). Such shelves

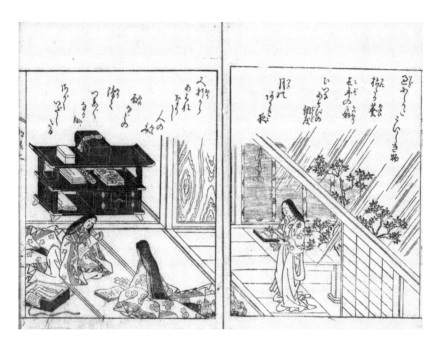

FIGURE 4.2 Section "Things That Stir Fond Memories of the Past" (Suginishi katakoishiki mono). The large shelf (*mizushi*) in the alcove behind the women was an important item in a woman's trousseau; *Picture Book Mount Asahi* (*Ehon Asahi-yama*, 1741), vol. 1, 18 *ura*–19 *omote*. Courtesy of Shunsho Bunko, Sōai University Library, Osaka

had been an important part of a woman's trousseau at least since the early seventeenth century, as evidenced in books for women, including *A Collection of Female Etiquette* (*Onna shoreishū*, 1660) and *Treasures for Women*. Despite the fact that there is no reference to this trousseau item in the text, its inclusion in the accompanying picture not only signals a desire to convey information to young female readers but also keeps the issue of marriage constantly in the forefront and in the reader's mind.

Items indispensable to a woman's trousseau appear also in pictures depicting couples. For example, the section "Pleasing Things" (Ureshiki mono) features a woman and a man facing each other with a book open in front of the man, as well as three women engaged in grooming in the next room (figure 4.3). The caption reads, "Pleasing things: A person in whose company one feels awkward asks one to supply the opening or closing line of a poem. If one happens to recall it, one is very pleased."[33]

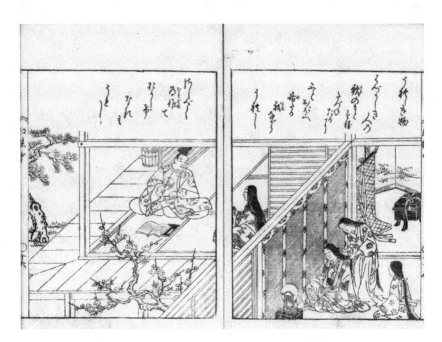

FIGURE 4.3 Section "Pleasing Things" (Ureshiki mono). In one room a man and woman face each other as a book lies open in front of the man, and in the next room three women are engaged in grooming; *Picture Book Mount Asahi* (*Ehon Asahi-yama*, 1741), vol. 2, 15 *ura*–16 *omote*. Courtesy of Shunsho Bunko, Sōai University Library, Osaka

The caption and the picture, which portrays court women, are reminiscent of the scenes in which a woman caps a verse when challenged by a man. There are several such scenes depicted in *The Pillow Book*, in all of which men praise women for their ability to complete the poems.[34] The most exemplary of these scenes is the one recounting the episode about Emperor Murakami (r. 946–967) and the Sen'yōden Consort (d. 967), whom he asked to recite all the poems in the *Collection of Ancient and Modern Poems* upon providing the headnote and the poet's name.[35] Such a visual allusion suggests that *Mount Asahi* was intended to foster women's education, specifically women's mastery of poetry. The picture portrays women in the next room surrounded by particularly feminine furniture, including a mirror stand, a kimono stand, and a shell bucket, used for storing the shells of the shell-matching game. Shell buckets were included in a woman's trousseau because the shells symbolized conjugal fidelity owing to the fact that there was only one match for each shell. Although shell buckets are usually depicted as hexagonal or octagonal, in earlier books for women they often appear as cuboids, as in the illustrations in *A Collection of Female Etiquette* and *Treasures for Women* (figures 4.4, 4.5).[36] The symbolism of shell buckets is explained in a whole section of *Treasures for Women* drawing on episodes in *Records of Ancient Matters* (*Kojiki*, 712) and *Chronicles of Japan* (*Nihon Shoki*, 720) related to shells, concluding, "Since there are millions of shells, but they do not match any others, so [a woman] learns the way of chastity, [according to which] she never exchanges vows with a man other than her husband until the end of her life."[37]

The illustration to the section "Pleasing Things" featuring trousseau items extends the content of *Mount Asahi* and joins the notion of female erudition with dowry, thus suggesting that a woman's learnedness was viewed as a desirable trait in a bride.

Another feature of this digest of *The Pillow Book* implying that the work was targeted at a female readership is the catalogue of published

FIGURE 4.4 Cuboid shell buckets featured as part of a woman's trousseau; *A Collection of Female Etiquette* (*Onna shoreishū*, 1660), vol. 2. Courtesy of Nara Women's University Academic Information Center, Nara

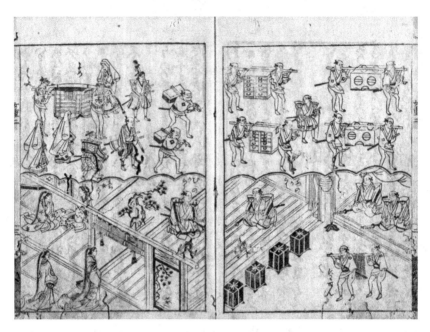

FIGURE 4.5 Cuboid shell buckets featured as part of a woman's trousseau; *Treasures for Women* (*Onna chōhōki*, 1692), vol. 2, 2 *ura*–3 *omote*. Courtesy of the National Diet Library, Tokyo

and forthcoming book titles attached to the end of *Mount Asahi* (figure 4.6). Such publisher's catalogues (*zōhan mokuroku*) began to be produced in the eighteenth century. They advertised titles issued by the publisher of the book to which they were attached.[38] The majority of the books appearing in the catalogue at the end of *Mount Asahi* are intended for women, as is evident from titles such as *Women's Calligraphy: The Fields of Kasuga* (*Nyohitsu kasugano*), *Women's Calligraphy: Bamboo and Pampas Grass* (*Nyohitsu shinosusuki*), and *Notes on Women's Cultivation* (*Fujin yashinaigusa*). Although one can never know who exactly purchased and read any given work, the inclusion of the catalogue suggests that this adaptation of *The Pillow Book* was advertised as reading material for young women. According to the title of the catalogue, the catalogue is of the publisher Uemura Gyokushiken. As Yamamoto Yukari has observed, this is one of the names with which Naitō Dōyū, a Kyoto-based publisher, signed himself. Other names include Uemura Gyokushishi, Banka Sanjin Gyokushi, Banka Sanjin Naitō Gyokushi,

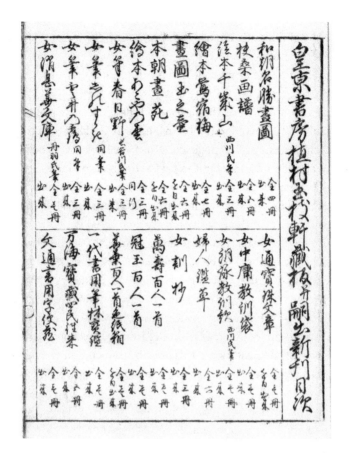

FIGURE 4.6 The catalogue of the publisher Uemura Tōemon (Naitō Dōyū) attached to the end of *Picture Book Mount Asahi* (*Ehon Asahiyama*, 1741), vol. 3, 15 *omote*. Courtesy of Shunsho Bunko, Sōai University Library, Osaka

and Naitō Gyokushi. The majority of writing-practice textbooks produced in Kyoto under the name Uemura Tōemon came out of Dōyū's publishing house.[39] In fact, as Yamamoto has further shown, Dōyū was also involved in the production of such texts as both a writer and editor. Some of his works include *Phoenix Tower of One Hundred Poems by One Hundred Poets* (*Ogura hyakunin isshu hōōdai*), *Women's Educational Songs to Chant* (*Onna rōei kyōkunka*), and *Auspicious Book of Women's Letters* (*Onna shōsoku sakae bunko*).[40] He collaborated with Sukenobu on several projects, one of which was *Mount Asahi*.[41] Thus, considering the context in which *Mount Asahi* was published allows us to situate the eighteenth-century adaptation of *The Pillow Book* within the body of texts related to women.

The preface to the first edition of *Mount Asahi* reads as follows:

> Shōnagon, known from the past, was a daughter of Kiyohara no Motosuke. She served Jōtōmon'in and was a lady-in-waiting of unmatched talent and intelligence. When she lived in Sanuki in her later years, she remembered the past with great fondness, and her thoughts went back to the capital. As a way to pass the time while in the countryside, she selected moving words from the notes she had written, illustrated them with pictures, and titled the book *Mount Asahi*. I had for years desired to see it, and when I recently unexpectedly spotted these three volumes as I was looking at someone's collection of old tales, I was greatly delighted, but keeping them to myself would bring no satisfaction, so, wishing to share them with others, it was by no means senseless to apply to those original pictures a more contemporary brush. Regardless, the happiness of the publisher will be great should this book be transmitted broadly and become a companion to ladies in their bedchambers.[42]

The preface claims that Sei lived in Sanuki[43] in Shikoku after her service at court had ended and erroneously introduces her as a lady-in-waiting to Jōtōmon'in (Fujiwara no Shōshi, 988–1074).[44] Although the title does not refer directly to *The Pillow Book*, the preface claims that Sei wrote *Mount Asahi* as a digest of her work and illustrated it herself. It further explains that the producers have altered the pictures but does not acknowledge the fact that the text, too, has been changed. In short, despite the fact that *Mount Asahi* is a male-authored rewriting of Sei Shōnagon's work, the preface presents it as a supplementary text to *The Pillow Book* and asserts Sei's authorship, thus constructing *Mount Asahi* as a work composed by a female with a female readership in mind. By repackaging a literary text of the past and attributing the product to a Heian woman writer, Sukenobu and Sekkō created a work purporting to be a source of knowledge relayed by an experienced female from the past to younger women. Sei Shōnagon's image reinforces the credibility of *Mount Asahi*, and the Heian writer's affiliation with the imperial court lends the eighteenth-century adaptation an aura of a repository of aristocratic culture that further enhances the work. By extension, *The Pillow Book* within *Mount Asahi* is constructed as a predecessor of the early modern books for women. Within this genre, however, *Mount Asahi* replaces and comes to represent *The Pillow Book* for the remainder of the Edo period, giving rise to new adaptations of Sei Shōnagon's text.

MARRIAGE AND EROTICISM: *EROTIC BOOK SPRING DAWN*

A few months after its reprint in 1772, *Mount Asahi* inspired the production of the parody *Erotic Book Spring Dawn*.[45] Authored by *gesaku* writer Komatsuya Hyakki (1720–1794), it was published in Edo and illustrated by ukiyo-e artist Kitao Shigemasa (1739–1820). Both Komatsuya and Shigemasa were also active *haikai* poets[46] and had produced together several parodies of Sukenobu's works.[47]

Like *Mount Asahi*, this adaptation is in three volumes. Each opens with a love poem drawn from an imperial anthology.[48] While the lists and their associated examples are thematically diverse, the seasonal sequence of the poems signals the themes dominating each volume. For example, book 1 opens with a spring poem on the crying of a young warbler still inside the family nest and continues with multiple examples related to a newly married couple's first night, a woman's deflowering, and lovers considering marriage. Book 2 begins with a summer poem depicting a deer longing for its mate. This second volume includes many examples of frustrated sexual desire, including love triangles, impotent or sexually inept men, and women rejecting marriage proposals because of vows to another man. The autumn poem of the third volume describes a cricket crying in yearning. This volume contains vignettes about waned passion, specifically arguing couples, fleeting affection between a man and a woman, and disloyal customers of courtesans.

Spring Dawn comprises a selection of lists with headings in the same order as those included in *Mount Asahi*. Its preface adapts the preface of the earlier work as follows: "The book titled *Mount Asahi* states that when Sei remembered the capital fondly while she was in Sanuki, she selected moving words from her writings and illustrated them with pictures. Now I have restored the work to its most elegant form, titled it *Spring Dawn*, and circulated it widely. It would bring this publisher no little happiness should this work become a companion to ladies in their bedchambers. Published one glorious spring."[49]

This preface follows the preface of *Mount Asahi* and explicitly states that the intended audience is women. The phrase *rankei no moteasobi*, "a companion for ladies in their bedchambers," or something that brings "consolation to ladies in their bedchambers,"[50] which also appears in the preface of *Mount Asahi*, most likely refers to women's amusement.[51] The publisher's focus on women here, however, does not exclude men but rather emphasizes the inclusion of a female audience.[52] Having transformed the content of *Mount Asahi* into an erotic narrative and replaced Sukenobu's pictures with ones portraying heterosexual intercourse, the publisher claims that this is the best version of Sei's work. The women that populate the pages of *Spring Dawn* are townswomen, servants, and courtesans. Each section contains a picture featuring a couple or couples in the residences of wealthy townsmen or in brothels, an inscribed list, and a dialogue between the figures included in the picture.

The first section of both *Mount Asahi* and *Spring Dawn* is titled "Common Things That Suddenly Sound Special" (Tsune yori mo koto ni kikoyuru mono). The caption in *Mount Asahi* reads as follows:

The sound of carriages on the first day of the first month of the year.
The song of the birds on that day.
The sound of a cough—and also, I need hardly say, of a musical instrument—at dawn.[53]

As figure 4.7 shows, the *Mount Asahi* picture features an oxcart accompanied by several courtiers passing by the gate of a residence. The pine tree decoration in front of the gate indicates a scene in the New Year season. Although this passage appears much later in *The Pillow Book*, it was no doubt perceived as appropriate for the opening of the work because of its focus on the beginning of the year, as well as the beginning of the new day.[54] This opening imitates the first section of *The Pillow Book*, with its passage about spring and dawn, as well as the seasonal structure of imperial poetry anthologies, which open with a selection of spring poems. This rearrangement of the passages to prioritize spring sets a celebratory tone for the work. The producers of *Spring Dawn*, on the

FIGURE 4.7 Section "Common Things That Suddenly Sound Special" (Tsune yori mo koto ni kikoyuru mono). The pine tree decoration (*kadomatsu*) signals the beginning of the New Year; *Picture Book Mount Asahi* (*Ehon Asahiyama*, 1741), vol. 1, 2 *ura*–3 *omote*. Courtesy of Shunsho Bunko, Sōai University Library, Osaka

other hand, retained the focus of the passage on *beginnings* and *sounds* but adapted it as follows:

> The breathing of newlyweds
> The laughter of the madam of a brothel having received a tip from a
>   client
> The wife's greeting after one has spent the night away[55]

The beginning of the year has been replaced with the beginning of a married life, and the sound of a carriage, birdsong, coughing, and the sound of a musical instrument have given way to breathing, laughter, and greetings. All three examples of *Mount Asahi* have been rewritten to feature relations between a man and a woman, specifically married couples, and a female owner of a brothel and a male client. The picture in *Spring Dawn* (figure 4.8) represents the first example—that is,

FIGURE 4.8 . Section "Common Things That Suddenly Sound Special" (Tsune yori mo koto ni kikoyuru mono). A man embraces his wife under the bedding on their wedding night as servants toy with a dildo in the next room; *Erotic Book Spring Dawn* (*Ehon Haru no akebono*, 1772), vol. 1. Courtesy of the International Research Center for Japanese Studies, Kyoto

"newlyweds huffing and puffing on their first night together"—and depicts an intimate moment between a newly married couple. The "island shelf" (*shimadai*) placed in the alcove (*tokonoma*) next to the bride and bridegroom, along with other auspicious symbols such as the pine pattern of the bedding, the crane, and the bamboo that is partly seen on the shelf, suggest a wedding. In the next room, two maids, aroused by the lovers' talk that they overhear, have brought out a dildo, which they scrutinize while taking turns toying with it. The two scenes are placed on separate pages—the one with the maids occupies the right page and the one with the couple the left. The dialogue between the characters included within the pictures is as follows:

SERVANT GIRL ONE: "There's no way I'm going to be able to sleep tonight. Do you think you could help me with my little secret man?"
SERVANT GIRL TWO: "Oh, let me use it, too. You can really hear them doing it. Oh, it's too much."

HUSBAND: "Are you all right? You're not too cold? Here, turn this way! Shall I extinguish the lamp?"
WIFE: "No, I'm fine, really."[56]

The reader's gaze, moving from right to left, first encounters the picture of the girls playing with a dildo and then sneaks into the bedroom of the newlyweds. In other words, readers are first introduced to the dildo and then shown a scene of actual lovemaking. Hayakawa Monta has asserted that each of the pictures accompanying the lists triggers laughter via the juxtaposition of disparate images or misunderstanding between the characters.[57] While the contrast between the titillated maids and the reticent bride provokes amusement, the picture also sends the message that female masturbation is inferior to sexual intercourse with a man.[58] The work thus opens with a section featuring the beginning of a married life and continues with lists that present various aspects of intimate relationships that are evaluated by the headings of the respective lists. Within this collection, many lists focus on conjugal relations. For example, illustrating the list headed "Things Pleasing to Watch" (Mite kokochi yoki mono) is a depiction of a couple in intimate embrace in the inner quarters of a townsman's residence; the accompanying text reads, "[A couple] kissing in a tight embrace—what a pleasure to behold."[59] The list titled "Things That Give a Pleasant Feeling" (Kokoro yuku mono) features "a handsome man with a beautiful wife,"[60] and the picture shows a couple drinking together. The idea of marriage and gratifying sex is further reinforced by the last illustrated section of the book, titled "Splendid Things" (Medetaki mono). The text reads, "A harmonious couple. A man who can keep doing it without ever exhausting himself. Erotic tales stirring laughter, what joy!"[61]

The picture features a man and a woman making love with an erotic book open next to them and suggests a definition of "spouses being on good terms" (naka no yoi fūfu) that centers on sex, which is hailed by the work as "a splendid thing" (figure 4.9).

The dialogues of the couples populating the pages of Spring Dawn are a new element not found in Mount Asahi. All the conversations, which are concise but sensuous, reveal the characters' passion and affection for their partners. The characters depicted in Spring Dawn flirt, praise their partner's sex organs, and express sexual desire. As Nakano Setsuko's

FIGURE 4.9 Section "Splendid Things" (Medetaki mono). A couple make love as an erotic book lies open next to them; *Erotic Book Spring Dawn* (*Ehon Haru no akebono*, 1772), vol. 3. Courtesy of the International Research Center for Japanese Studies, Kyoto

examination of seventeenth-century stories in vernacular prose, anachronistically labeled as *kanazōshi* (kana booklets), has shown, sexual intercourse and intimate talk were considered essential for married couples.[62] Thus, the dialogues included in *Spring Dawn* might be interpreted as attempts to provide its female readers with models for love talk, an important aspect of intimate relations with one's husband.

In addition to the assortment of illustrated lists, the erotic book *Spring Dawn* offers readers two stories about the marriages of merchants' daughters. O-Taka, the protagonist of the first story, is the daughter of a small merchant in the vicinity of Asakusa.[63] Readers are told that "[she] has been taught the shamisen from a tender age, has a beautiful voice from birth and sings well, dresses properly, and has a personality that everyone would appreciate."[64] At the age of seventeen O-Taka marries a man of high station, but after three years she is sent back to her parents because of her inability to bear a child. Becoming mentally unstable and developing an eye disease, O-Taka begins visiting an eye doctor on a daily basis. It is during these visits that a wealthy sixty-year-old pawnbroker named Yojiemon takes a fancy to O-Taka and eventually marries her. When O-Taka recovers her sight, she is terrified upon realizing that she has married a much older man and wonders about the future of their intimacy. Yojiemon becomes sexually obsessed from their first night, but, after two years of lovemaking, he is bedridden because of his excessive sexual activity.[65] When Yojiemon discovers his twenty-two-year-old wife's affair with a cotton merchant from Echizen named Tesuke, he is outraged but eventually comes to terms with it by divorcing O-Taka, giving her half his wealth, and becoming a recluse.

This story echoes the medieval narratives known as *hiren-tonsei-tan*, or "tales of taking Buddhist vows after a heartbreak," in which failure in love leads to the male protagonist's religious awakening. Although the typical plot of such stories centers around the sudden death of a female lover, in the story about O-Taka, it is the wife's infidelity that causes the husband to take holy vows. Haruo Shirane has noted that the medieval structure of *hiren-tonsei* tales reveals that "love, being transitory and illusory, carries within it the seeds of its own destruction and that excessive attachment can only result in frustration and suffering."[66] Similarly, in *Spring Dawn* the oversexed older man, whose lasciviousness has destroyed his body, is spiritually awakened by the unexpected loss of his wife to a much younger man. The early modern story parodies its medieval predecessors by substituting the death of the woman with her infidelity. Yet despite the fact that sterility and adultery were two of the seven grounds for divorce in the Edo period, the heroine is not punished for her transgressions. The story does end with a divorce, but it is a happy ending for O-Taka, who walks away from an onerous marriage with significant wealth.

The second story is about O-Tsuya, the daughter of a famous wealthy merchant in Edo.[67] She marries at fourteen but is returned to her parents after three days for unknown reasons. Within the next four to five years she remarries unsuccessfully seven times. In the end, when her parents decide to make her a nun, O-Tsuya's wet nurse opposes them and attempts to intervene. When the girl tells her wet nurse about the "embarrassing thing about her body" (*ware mi no jō ni hazukashii koto*), the older woman realizes that O-Tsuya's marriages have failed because of her excessive and uncontrollable sexual desire. The wet nurse takes the girl to a famous lecherous man named Shikijirō, who heals her through intense intercourse and makes her "like a normal woman" (*tsune no onna no goto ni*).[68]

O-Tsuya's parents are overjoyed and marry her to the owner of a liquor shop. The story ends as follows: "The couple got along well, and even had a child, and lived happily for many years into old age."[69] This anecdote marks the end of the *Spring Dawn* text.

Unlike the previous story, this narrative ends with a successful marriage. The sexually insatiable female protagonist is converted into a "normal woman" who becomes a wife and mother. The two stories share similarities in plot, however. The sexual urges of the man in the story about O-Taka and of the woman in the story of O-Tsuya are presented as faults, and are resolved by the end of each narrative. The old man becomes sexually inactive because of illness and enters onto the Buddhist path, while the young woman, faced with the prospect of a similar outcome, has her excessive sexuality placated and enters a successful marriage. The moral that the two tales convey is that insatiable sexuality destroys marriages and triggers misfortune, as illustrated by Yojiemon and O-Tsuya. Each of the narratives depicts in detail the girl's first bridal night, explains the reasons for her failed initial marriage (owing to the sterility of one and the sexual obsession of the other), and describes each girl's subsequent marriages. In other words, the stories tell readers what makes a marriage succeed or fail, with sexuality and fecundity being central to both.

The final picture of *Spring Dawn* (figure 4.10) features a woman writer, most likely designed to be understood as Sei Shōnagon, holding a brush and sitting at a writing table in front of an open book. Next to her is a pile of books, and in front of the table is a blooming cherry branch in a vase. The *tsuitate* screen next to the table depicts a Chinese landscape with a plum branch in its center. The image of the woman writer and the cherry and plum branches evoke ancient aristocratic culture. Since Heian women were held as exemplary in early modern manuals for women, as Nakano has argued,[70] the image of the Heian female at the end of the work further reinforces the idea that *Spring Dawn* aimed at fostering courtly comportment. The claim of the preface that Sei Shōnagon had authored this work, and the picture of a woman writer at the end of *Spring Dawn*, also construct this adaptation as a text through which a knowledgeable woman from the distant past shares her wisdom with early modern female readers.

The two stories about marriage and women's sexuality, along with the majority of scenes, which feature male-female sexual encounters, and

FIGURE 4.10 An Edo-period Sei Shōnagon sits at her desk; *Erotic Book Spring Dawn* (*Ehon Haru no akebono*, 1772), vol. 3. Hayashi Yoshikazu, *Enpon kenkyū: Shigemasa* (Tokyo: Yūkō Shobō, 1966), 219

topics such as weddings, matrimony, deflowering, and spousal relations, transform *The Pillow Book* into a narrative about successful marriage, at the core of which are harmonious sexual relations between a husband and wife. The opening scene of the book, which, as mentioned, features the first night of a married couple, might suggest that this work was intended as a trousseau item for young brides. Although erotic, *Spring Dawn* can be viewed as sharing similarities with female educational texts, which construct women as subservient to their husbands and provide practical advice for improving spousal relations. One such example is *A Mirror of Womanhood: The Book of Secret Transmissions* (*Jokyō hidensho*, 1650), which, thanks to its popularity, was published several times in both Kyoto and Edo between 1688 and 1704.[71] Taking examples from this work, Nakano demonstrates the existence of books that provided women with strategies on how to improve their spousal relations, specifically how to win their husband's affections. The strategies included unconditional obedience to a husband's will and taste and cajoling him into a good mood by planting flowers, pouring sake and drinking together, and playing the *biwa* or koto.[72] Nakano also points out that one of the common themes in books for women's education is the focus on interpersonal relations, such as with one's husband, father-in-law, mother-in-law, servants, family, and friends. Among these, the woman's relation to her husband was viewed as central since the securing of one's husband's affection played an essential role in a woman's life.[73]

Andrew Gerstle has further shown that erotic books that closely parodied works for women were also included in young women's trousseaux.[74] He argues that both types of works are didactic. Whereas books for women, imbued with Confucian overtones, create an image of the ideal female as one who is a spiritless servant of her husband, erotic books, by means of laughter and parody, construct their heroines as "proactive and attractive for men."[75] Unlike the Confucian works, which unilaterally delineate the duties and expectations of a woman, the erotic parodies portray successful couples as those able to build a mutually acceptable relationship.[76] For example, to alleviate a husband's anger, *The Treasure Chest of Great Learning for Women* urges its readers to simply obey their husbands and avoid arguing with them. Its erotic parody, *Great Pleasures for Women and Their Treasure Boxes*, on the other hand, provides detailed instructions about how a woman should sexually please her husband during the night following a quarrel. The relevant passage ends, "No doubt that [because] a prudent [*tsutsushimu*] woman never makes domestic quarrels known to others, her husband understands his wife's heart, and the family will be able to continuously thrive."[77] Thus, Gerstle demonstrates that erotic parodies of Confucian texts for women offered a new type of education that viewed a woman's enjoyment of her sexuality as essential to the well-being of her family. Central to such texts, Gerstle notes, was laughter, which functioned as a device to mitigate the embarrassment related to the topic of sex across gender and class.[78]

Likewise, although *Spring Dawn* does not appear in lists of books for women because erotic books and prints were removed from publishers' catalogues after 1722, it can still be viewed as a work for female readers.[79] As a humorous rewriting of the woman-oriented *Mount Asahi*, it educated women who were married or were soon to enter matrimony about the sexual aspect of spousal relations, and it did so through parody and laughter. Anne Walthall's discussion of representations of female masturbation and sexual practices in early modern Japan has shown that although female sexuality was frequently constructed by men and at the service of men, beginning in the eighteenth century some erotic works discussed "not just sex for recreation, but also sex for procreation."[80] In this context, the large number of scenes of harmonious couples engaged in sexual intercourse in *Spring Dawn* can be viewed not as promoting the concept of romantic marriage but rather that of "household harmony" (*kanai wajun*), which, as Yonemoto has pointed out, pervaded instruction manuals for women but was hardly mentioned in educational texts aimed at men.[81]

What settings can be imagined in which women read erotic parodies? Many of the pictures in *Spring Dawn* include a couple looking at another couple engaged in sexual intercourse. In other cases, a couple is depicted making love while looking at erotica (figure 4.9). Such pictures are an imaginative rendering of possibilities and do not necessarily depict reality, but they allow us to discern some of the intended readership, specifically couples who consumed these works together while enjoying their erotic and entertaining content.[82]

WOMEN'S LITERARY ERUDITION AND IDEALS OF FEMININITY: "SEI SHŌNAGON'S UNMATCHED TALENT"

In 1818 *Mount Asahi* became the base text for yet another adaptation of *The Pillow Book*, "Sei Shōnagon's Unmatched Talent." [83] It was published by Suharaya Mohei of Nihonbashi, one of the preeminent publishers in the latter half of the Edo period.[84] Suharaya is also known as the father of Kitao Shigemasa, the artist for *Erotic Book Spring Dawn*.[85] The title of this adaptation projects an image of an exceptionally gifted woman of the past, as emphasized by the words "unmatched talent" (*kisai*) and "prodigious words" (*kigo*). The work features sixteen lists in exactly the same form as they appeared in the 1741 *Mount Asahi*, though reordered. It occupies the upper register of the pages of *A Collection of Model Texts for Women*. The lower register features *Illustrated Selections and Commentaries: Thirty-Six Immortal Poets* (*Sanjūrokkasen eshō*), a collection of the exemplars of Japanese poetic prowess. Its preface does not acknowledge *Mount Asahi* as its base text, but, like the prefaces of the earlier two works, it introduces Sei as Kiyohara no Motosuke's daughter and a lady-in-waiting to Jōtōmon'in, and it states that the work is a digest of *The Pillow Book* that Sei produced while in Sanuki. In other words, the preface of "Sei Shōnagon's Unmatched Talent" closely follows the content of the *Mount Asahi* preface. Unlike the earlier two works, however, the preface of this work includes the episode about the snow of Kōro Peak with the aim of creating a fuller portrait of Sei Shōnagon (which I discuss in detail in the next chapter). "Sei Shōnagon's Unmatched Talent" transforms the episode as follows:

> One snowy day when the emperor asked his courtiers, "What does Kōro Peak look like?" Sei quickly stood up and raised the blind that was in front of the emperor. This is a repartee based on an allusion to a Chinese poem that says, "I raise the blind and gaze at the snow of Kōro Peak." The emperor was greatly impressed. The following illustrated fictions [*soragoto*] are based on a selection from *The Pillow Book* that Sei wrote while she was in Sanuki. Girls with heart, read *The Pillow Book* in its entirety! If you attend to it intently, your daily comportment will no doubt become self-possessed, your feelings will be understood when you mingle with friends, your heart will acquire natural gracefulness, and when you compose poems about the moon and the flowers, they will be imbued with feeling.[86]

In *The Pillow Book* this episode features Empress Teishi surrounded by a group of ladies-in-waiting.[87] The preface of the 1818 adaptation, however, has transformed the original all-female setting of Empress Teishi's salon and placed Sei in the company of men. Sei emerges as more quick-witted and knowledgeable than any of the men present and, by raising the blind, shows that she has recognized the allusion to Bo Juyi's (772–846) poem.[88] In *The Pillow Book*, Empress Teishi laughs, and the other ladies-in-waiting express their astonishment at Sei's quick-wittedness, but in "Sei Shōnagon's Unmatched Talent" the praise comes from the emperor. In other words, Sei's behavior is not commended within a community of women but evaluated by a man in the exclusive company of men. The strong presence of the male gaze through which Sei is constructed is further evident in the accompanying illustration (figure 4.11).[89] It depicts Sei from behind, raising the blind, while surrounded by elite men. Although omitted from the illustration, the emperor in front of whom she is lifting the blind can be imagined as the primary bearer of the gaze, which overlaps with that of the reader.

An even more sexualized representation of Sei raising the blind, which was based on the illustration reproduced in figure 4.11, appeared in the same year. *Seedling Library of Women's Learning* (*Onna yūshoku mibae bunko*, 1818), recapitulates the same episode about the snow of Kōro Peak by situating Sei at a drinking party attended by the emperor and male and female courtiers. The setting is depicted as follows: "One snowy morning when the snow had piled up beautifully, the emperor came out near a corner of the main ceremonial hall of the inner palace. Male courtiers and female attendants were nearby attending the emperor, and they were served sake. As things became more entertaining, the

FIGURE 4.11 Surrounded by elite men, Sei Shōnagon raises the blind; *A Collection of Model Texts for Women* (*Onna yōbunshō yukikaiburi*, 1818), 3 *omote*. Courtesy of Toyota City Library, Toyota

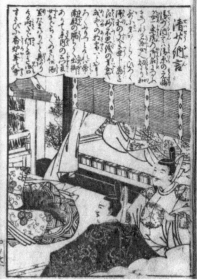

FIGURE 4.12 Surrounded by elite men, Sei Shōnagon raises the blind at a drinking party; *Seedling Library of Women's Learning (Onna yūshoku mibae bunko*, 1818), *ro* 7. Collection of the Ajinomoto Foundation for Dietary Culture, Tokyo; photography National Institute of Japanese Literature, Tokyo

emperor happened to say, for amusement, "What does the snow of Kōro Peak look like?" and no one guessed the allusion."[90]

Although the text mentions that court women also took part in the banquet, the accompanying illustration (figure 4.12) portrays Sei as the only woman in the presence of the emperor and high-ranking men. Sei emerges as the only one who could solve the emperor's riddle, since "the others did not know what [the riddle] meant."[91]

These textual and visual representations of Sei as a knowledgeable and attractive female seen through men's eyes construct her as a woman to be emulated within a male-centered society and, at the same time, evoke the image of a talented courtesan. Unlike the illustrated courtly tales from the Heian period, in which women are hidden from the male gaze and the only way to catch a glimpse of a woman with whom one was not intimate was by "peeking through the hedge" (*kaimami*),[92] this text depicts her as being surrounded and viewed directly by several men, and powerful men at that. Bearing the male gaze, Sei lifts the blind and brings smiles and expressions of delight to the men's faces. Although highly sexualized, she is not depicted as unguarded, unlike in Heian-period illustrated tales. As Mostow has explained, these narratives present women exposed to a voyeuristic gaze as "oblivious" and "absorbed," which implies "a loss of control" and "vulnerability."[93] Although portrayed as a Heian-period woman, in these late-Edo illustrations Sei is completely aware of the masculine gaze upon her, although she has turned her back to the three high-ranking courtiers shown in the picture. She appears as if performing onstage after being challenged by the emperor. The depiction of Sei in the company of men, the emphasis on her femininity, and the focus on her as a poet rather than the author of *The Pillow Book* in the two pictures conjure up an image of a high-ranking courtesan (*keisei*) who excelled in the arts, such as poetry composition, calligraphy, flower arrangement, and tea ceremony.[94] Presenting Sei as exceptionally gifted and appealing in the eyes of men, or, in other words, as the embodiment of ideal femininity, this work instructs readers about the skills necessary to acquire feminine appeal.[95]

This image of the woman writer as an object of desire follows the conventional depiction, found in educational books for female readers, of aristocratic women and courtesans as representatives of a court culture known for *yasashisa* (courtliness, refinement, and allure).

Yasashisa encompassed various aspects of demeanor, but poetry composition and elegant handwriting were hailed as two of its main components. The ability to compose poems extempore (*tōi sokumyō*) was deemed particularly alluring in a woman.[96] In books for women featuring this episode of Sei Shōnagon raising the blind, the author of *The Pillow Book* is frequently praised for her quick-wittedness, which is also expressed by the phrase *tōi sokumyō*. The opening section of "Sei Shōnagon's Unmatched Talent" commends her courtly comportment (*miyabi*) regarding her ability to quickly recognize the allusion to the Chinese poem and demonstrate it in an elegant way. Although this particular text does not use the phrase *tōi sokumyō* to describe her behavior, what it defines as "courtly comportment" can be linked to Sei Shōnagon's competence in Chinese poetry and ability to provide an impromptu response, very much in the manner of composing a poem on the spot.

"Sei Shōnagon's Unmatched Talent" presents a selection of sixteen of the forty lists appearing in *Mount Asahi*.[97] Having further abridged

Mount Asahi and, by extension, *The Pillow Book*, the producers have selected sections with entries focusing on courtship and relations between men and women, topics deemed worthy of inclusion in the 1818 collection of exemplary texts for women. "Sei Shōnagon's Unmatched Talent" uses Sei's writing to introduce women's literary erudition demonstrated in the presence of men ("Pleasing Things," "Things of Elegant Beauty"); a man's upsetting behavior ("Depressing Things"); a lover who fails to visit ("Things That Move the Heart," "Depressing Things," "Startling and Disconcerting Things"); a disappointing lover ("Things That Are Frustrating and Embarrassing to Witness"); a husband's neglect of his wife ("Things That Are Frustrating and Embarrassing to Witness," "Unreliable Things"); jealousy ("People Who Look as Though Things Are Difficult for Them"); and letters from a former lover ("Things That Make One Feel Nostalgic"). Thus the strong focus on relations between men and women in the lists in this condensed version of Sei Shōnagon's text projects an image of *The Pillow Book* as a work in which the motif of love prevails.

The pictures resemble those in *Mount Asahi* but, as with the text of *The Pillow Book*, they have been adapted by altering, zooming in, or cropping. For example, although the list under "Things That Move the Heart" suggests longing for a loved one, the picture portrays the lovers together. The text in *The Pillow Book* under "Things That Move the Heart" reads, "A child who is full of filial piety. The cry of a deer. River bamboo swaying in the evening breeze. A mountain village in the snow. A dilapidated house overgrown with goosegrass; the garden is rank with mugwort and other weeds; the moon shines so brightly over the whole scene that there is not a single dark corner; and the wind blows gently."[98]

The picture in *Mount Asahi* (figure 4.13) depicts each aspect of the text, including a man digging out bamboo shoots, a deer, a dilapidated house, a garden, the moon, and a mountain covered with snow. The figure of the man evokes one of the stories included in the *Twenty-Four Examples of Filial Piety (Nijūshikō)*, specifically the tale of the devoted son Meng Zong, whose tears because of his powerlessness to provide bamboo-shoot soup to his gravely ill mother cause bamboo shoots to grow in the midst of the winter.[99] This scene occupies the right-hand side of the page and is the first element in the picture to catch the reader's attention. In addition to its centrality in the picture, this reference to filial piety is the first entry in the list. In "Sei Shōnagon's Unmatched

FIGURE 4.13 Section "Things That Move the Heart" (Aware naru mono). A man pulls up a bamboo shoot in the foreground as a deer looks into the distance in the background; *Picture Book Mount Asahi* (*Ehon Asahiyama*, 1741), vol. 1, 3 *ura*–4 *omote*. Courtesy of Shunsho Bunko, Sōai University Library, Osaka

Talent," however, the figure of the devoted son is replaced by an image of two deer, a motif suggesting love between a man and a woman rather than love for one's parents (figure 4.14). Placed on the right-hand side of the picture in "Sei Shōnagon's Unmatched Talent," the two deer become central to the picture and to the message it transmits to readers. Contrary to the text, in which "the cry of a stag" suggests longing for one's mate, the picture portrays a scene of the reunion of the two deer, rather than their separation.[100]

Another change to the illustrations suggests an emphasis on women's erudition as sexually alluring. In *Mount Asahi*, the picture for the section "Pleasing Things" features a woman and a man facing each other with a book open in front of the man, as well as three women engaged in grooming in the next room (figure 4.3). Whereas in the *Mount Asahi* text the picture includes other people as well, "Sei Shōnagon's Unmatched Talent" provides a close-up of the man and the woman, with the woman ardently engaged in conversation with the man, who is now holding a book (figure 4.15). As mentioned earlier, the scene recalls the one of Emperor Murakami testing the Sen'yōden Consort's knowledge of the

FIGURE 4.14 Section "Things That Move the Heart" (Aware naru mono). Two deer stand next to each other as a man digs bamboo shoots in the distance; *A Collection of Model Texts for Women* (*Onna yōbunshō yukikaiburi*, 1818), 6 *omote*. Courtesy of Toyota City Library, Toyota

Kokin wakashū poems. Both pictures suggest a private rather than a public context, but the focus on the two figures in "Sei Shōnagon's Unmatched Talent" underscores the intimate overtones of the scene. It also places an emphasis on women brimming with confidence and erudition, which the producers of the work cast as alluring.[101]

Another example of a scene featuring a woman's learnedness is the illustration to "Graceful Things" (Namamekashiki mono). The picture is reminiscent of episode 23 in *The Ise Stories*. In that episode a man is spying on his wife, who has made up her face and is reciting a poem revealing her affection for her husband (figure 4.16). The woman's fidelity and lack of jealousy rekindle the husband's affection and help her win him back. The two adaptations of *The Pillow Book* portray the women as educated. In the *Mount Asahi* picture the woman is reading (figure 4.17), and in "Sei Shōnagon's Unmatched Talent" she is writing (figure 4.18). Moreover, in the latter work, the man is not behind a fence but in front of the woman, and although she is fully aware of his presence she continues writing, smiling at him. In other words, by appropriating the illustration of the *Ise* episode, the two adaptations of *The Pillow Book* hail

FIGURE 4.15 . Section "Pleasing Things" (Ureshiki mono). A man and woman face each other as the woman points to the open book the man holds; *A Collection of Model Texts for Women (Onna yōbunshō yukikaiburi*, 1818), 4 *ura.* Courtesy of Toyota City Library, Toyota

women's education, particularly reading and writing skills, as powerful enough to attract a man.

As the representation of Sei in its preface and the illustrations suggest, this last adaptation of *The Pillow Book* abounds with images of women who display their erudition in front of men. As a section of a book of exemplary texts for women, "Sei Shōnagon's Unmatched Talent" demonstrates that in the early nineteenth century the image of Sei Shōnagon was employed to foster the link between women's sexuality and literacy. In addition, the preface's approbation of *The Pillow Book* as a text essential for women's education suggests that literary erudition as well as sexual allure were important aspects of the construction of early modern femininity.

Although the three works discussed here have different foci, they can all be situated in the same category of edifying texts for women. The 1741 *Mount Asahi* can be viewed as a digest of *The Pillow Book*, which instead of presenting Heian court life centers on women's work and pastimes. The 1772 *Spring Dawn* features topics such as marriage and erotic

FIGURE 4.16 A man hiding in the bush clover spies on his wife
as she gazes sadly before her; episode 23 ("Kawachi-goe"), *Sagabon Ise stories* (*Sagabon Ise monogatari*, 1608), vol. 1. Courtesy
of the National Diet Library, Tokyo

behavior and provides insight into the intimate aspects of male-female
relations. The 1818 "Sei Shōnagon's Unmatched Talent" focuses on
women's literary erudition as an essential aspect of the ideal of womanhood in male-centered society.

These works frame themselves as supplementary to the real *Pillow
Book* by adding educational overtones to what was originally a narrative
about the cultural salon of an empress defeated by a rival. They present

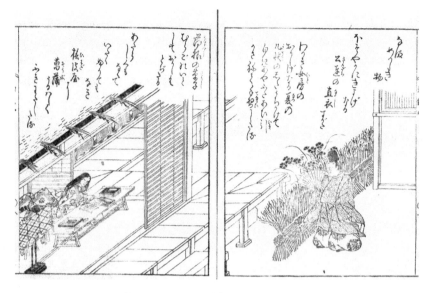

FIGURE 4.17 Section "Graceful Things" (Namamekashiki mono). A man spies on his wife through a fence as she reads a book; *Picture Book Mount Asahi* (*Ehon Asahiyama*, 1741), vol. 2, 7 *ura*–8 *omote*. Courtesy of Shunsho Bunko, Sōai University Library, Osaka

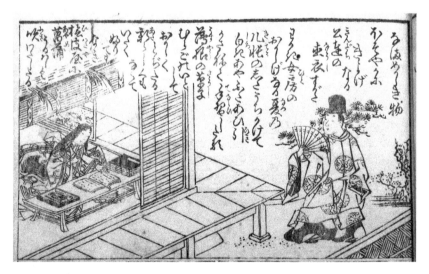

FIGURE 4.18 Section "Graceful Things" (Namamekashiki mono). A man gazes over his fan at his wife as she writes; *A Collection of Model Texts for Women* (*Onna yōbunshō yukikaiburi*, 1818), 7 *ura*–8 *omote*. Courtesy of Toyota City Library, Toyota

their fictitious author Sei Shōnagon as exceptionally gifted and intelligent and transform her from a lady-in-waiting serving a Heian-era empress into a talented courtesan. This courtesan-like image is reminiscent of the Sei one encounters in the pages of the *sharebon* works discussed in the previous chapter but produces a different effect. Specifically, Sei is no longer well versed in the culture of pleasure seeking associated with brothel districts but offers wisdom that could strengthen a woman's position in marriage.

The rewritings of *The Pillow Book* intended for a female audience further show the correlation between the two trends of women's education in early modern Japan, specifically Confucian virtues and courtly comportment.[102] *Mount Asahi* emphasizes the role of literary works centering on aristocratic culture in increasing a young woman's desirability as a bride. *Spring Dawn* constructs Sei Shōnagon as an experienced courtesan who offers advice on maintaining harmony in the household, whereas "Sei Shōnagon's Unmatched Talent" shows that the image of the Heian writer, even outside the realm of erotica, was still imbued with a sexual allure and was consistently held up as a model for female comportment. Although the latter narratives focus on women's sexuality and display of erudition, they do not convey anxiety over unruly feminine sexuality and do not present this Heian writer as a transgressor of social norms. Instead, women's sexuality in these works is trained by the dominant male, and female erudition is constructed within a woman's relation to a man. By hailing *The Pillow Book* as a source of important knowledge for women's conduct, thereby endorsing the "feminine" nature of Heian literature, the male producers of these early modern rewritings of Sei's work transformed the eleventh-century text into a tool for training women. The ability of *The Pillow Book* to perform such functions, which were perceived as desirable in the eighteenth and nineteenth centuries, contributed to the endurance of the text as reading material to which women were advised to devote time.[103]

CHAPTER FIVE

Shaping the Woman Writer

Today, Sei Shōnagon is typically described as a boastful aristocratic woman writer from Japan's distant past. Although there is not sufficient evidence to substantiate such a portrayal, it is important, both for what it reveals about attitudes toward women's creativity and because it has achieved wide currency within and outside Japan. However, this representation does not offer a full picture of readers' views of Sei over the centuries. The image of *The Pillow Book*'s author has undergone dramatic metamorphoses, ranging from an impoverished crone in medieval anecdotes, to a sexually attractive exemplary woman in early modern educational texts, to a female libertine in modern literary scholarship, to a cute and adorable girl in present-day comic books. Despite the fact that little is known about Sei's life except for scant mentions in poems and comments recorded in her contemporaries' and later literary works,[1] scholars and writers have repeatedly tried to re-create her, thus giving rise to multiple anecdotes about her personality and destiny.[2] Sei's career as a lady-in-waiting to an empress, her authorship of *The Pillow Book*, and insufficient information about her life have transformed her into a useful allegory for addressing a wide range of issues, including gender roles, tradition and change, and Japan's place in the world. Similar to the many rewritings of *The Pillow Book* over the centuries, Sei has taken on multiple identities, performing various functions in diverse contexts.

Although *The Pillow Book* has offered rich material to generations of readers to reinvent its author, it does not relate Sei's fate following the death of her patron, Empress Teishi. In fact, a scholarly consensus has been reached that the latest event depicted in *The Pillow Book* is the one recounted in the section "When Her Majesty Was in the Sanjō Palace" (Sanjō no miya ni owashimasu koro).[3] It describes the move of Empress Teishi and her retinue to Taira no Narimasa's residence in the fifth month of the year 1000 to give birth to her third child.[4] Teishi died in the twelfth month of the same year. Narratives about Sei from the thirteenth to the early twentieth century drew from *The Pillow Book* and various anecdotes and resulted in contrasting images of the Heian writer often based on identical sources. For example, drawing on the episode of the snow of Kōro Peak, educational literature for women in the Edo and Meiji periods portrayed Sei as exceptionally talented and knowledgeable, whereas Meiji literary scholars viewed her as the antithesis of femininity. Furthermore, Meiji and Taishō literary histories and scholarship continue to shape our understanding of the attitudes toward her in the nineteenth and early twentieth centuries because researchers have paid much heed to these works of literary criticism, ignoring other genres, especially educational literature for women.[5] In other words, although from the latter half of the Edo period to the early twentieth century Sei's image was shaped in diverse ways for different readerships, modern scholarship has disregarded Sei's reception in genres targeted toward women readers and has privileged the image of Sei constructed by elite male scholars as representative of the mainstream perception of the Heian writer.

This chapter examines how Sei was re-created in discourses of gender norms, women's education, and nationalism in the Edo and Meiji periods to demonstrate that even in the same historical period, writers asserted contrasting ideas by means of the symbolic representation of a woman from the distant past. Situating these diverse images in particular settings and delving into the motives of such portrayals reveal their constructed nature and implications about changing views of femininity and women's creativity in Japan. My analysis begins with a consideration of how Buddhist and poetic discourses shaped Sei in medieval Japan. This is followed by a discussion of the inclusion of the Heian writer in lists of exemplary women in early modern instruction manuals for female readers. Then I turn to the discourse known as the Sei and Murasaki debate and analyze how scholarly works and texts for mass consumption in the Edo and Meiji periods engaged with it. I expand the pool of sources by drawing attention to works targeted at audiences of women readers, specifically early modern popular texts with wide dissemination, modern state-sanctioned official textbooks, and a Meiji-period popular journal, to show that although the constructed rivalry between Sei Shōnagon and Murasaki Shikibu was used in debates over women's education, it was not actually incorporated into texts used to cultivate girls and women. Before turning to Edo and Meiji depictions of Sei, I describe how Heian women writers first came to be viewed as allegorical devices in premodern Japan.

THE TROPE OF THE HEIAN LITERARY WOMAN

As aristocrats' economic and political power waned in the twelfth century, following the establishment of the first military government, a yearning for an idealized past instigated the production of an extensive body of narratives related to the imperial court. These texts included many anecdotes regarding accomplished literate women who had been active in the Heian period in the households of preeminent aristocrats and the imperial court. Concocting historical "facts" and creatively manipulated stories, the producers of such works employed women writers, including Ono no Komachi, Sei Shōnagon, Murasaki Shikibu, Izumi Shikibu, and Akazome Emon, in accounts intended for a larger audience beyond aristocratic readers. The deficiency of records of these women's later years encouraged the production of narratives that offered glimpses into the fictitious future of professionally active women, specifically how they struggled through old age and declining fortunes. Viewed as "symbols of the elegance, sophistication, and decadence of the Heian court,"[6] images of women writers from the ninth to the eleventh century began to populate various forms of literature, including anecdotes (*setsuwa*), late-medieval fiction (*otogizōshi*), Noh and puppet plays, and conduct books. Many of these literary women were regarded as having a similar destiny in their later years because of their common background as daughters of provincial governors, their association with the Heian imperial court, and their literary prowess.

The dominant representations of Heian women during the Kamakura and Muromachi periods were greatly influenced by Buddhist attitudes toward women in general and, specifically, the view of women as inherently evil.[7] In medieval narratives known as stories of fall and wandering (*reiraku rurōtan*), women are incessantly punished for their beauty, creativity, erudition, and gender. As R. Keller Kimbrough has noted, "Heian and medieval Japanese literature displays a fetishistic fascination with the plight of aristocratic women in distress."[8] For instance, the Noh plays *Komachi and the Hundred Nights* (*Kayoi Komachi*) and *The Stupa Komachi* (*Sotoba Komachi*) portray Ono no Komachi as an old woman living "in moors of Ichiwara where the wild pampas grass grows,"[9] who asks a priest to pray for her repose because her relentless attitude toward her suitor, Fukakusa no Shōshō, has impeded her salvation.[10] One variant of *The Tale of Jōruri* (*Jōruri monogatari*) depicts Izumi Shikibu as a woman who makes a vow to sleep with one thousand men to save her parents, who have fallen into hell because of their daughter's unparalleled beauty and poetic talent.[11] Murasaki Shikibu, on the other hand, in *A Sutra for Genji* (*Genji kuyō*, 1168) appears in people's dreams pleading with them to destroy their copies of *The Tale of Genji* and to write out the chapters of *The Lotus Sutra*, thus emancipating her from hell, where she has been sent and suffers for having produced an immoral literary work.[12]

Medieval accounts of Sei Shōnagon's later years frequently depict her as an old and impoverished nun or a wanderer in Sanuki and Awa.[13] These stories appear in *A Nameless Tale* (*Mumyōzōshi*, 1198–1202), *Tales of the Past* (*Kojidan*, 1212–1215), *Matsushima Diary* (*Matsushima nikki*, mid-Kamakura period), and the postscript to the *Nōinbon* manuscript of *The Pillow Book* (late fifteenth to early sixteenth century). *A Nameless Tale* lists Sei among the few "women famous for their natural refinement"[14] and depicts her as living in the remote countryside, dressed in shabby clothes and longing for her glorious past.[15] A few years later, Sei appeared as even more unattractive and decrepit in two stories in *Tales of the Past*. The first narrative centers on Sei's witty remark "Won't you buy the bones of a fast horse? Someone else did."[16] It shows how, by means of an allusion to a Chinese story, Sei teases the courtiers who have commented on her destitution as they pass by her run-down dwelling. The second story presents Sei as a nun who shows her sexual organs to a group of warriors to dispel their doubts about her female identity and thus escape death.[17]

Matsushima Diary, traditionally read as Sei's lost diary, also depicts her as an aged and impoverished nun, this time traveling from the capital to Matsushima in search of a relative.[18] Finally, the *Nōinbon* postscript reports that Sei lived in Shikoku, specifically in Awa, and concludes, "Thus it seems that the things one would think about a person at the end of her life are not the things one would expect from the glory of her youth."[19] Kimbrough has observed that this postscript, which offers readers a glimpse into Sei's life after her service at court, shows "the unfortunate future of [the] elegant, arrogant author" and transforms *The Pillow Book* into a "medieval morality play."[20] He further argues that "by informing readers of Sei Shōnagon's supposedly sad fate, the postscript also contributed to the medieval reshaping of Sei Shōnagon's persona, recreating her [in the context of *The Pillow Book*] as a haughty woman author who blithely passes judgment on others while unaware of her own approaching destiny."[21] Read in its current form, the *Nōinbon* manuscript can indeed be viewed as didactic. It is unclear, however, when exactly this textual lineage took shape and specifically in what century the postscript was attached to the main text. The earliest extant manuscripts date from the Muromachi period (1338–1573) and succeed the compilation of the thirteenth-century texts discussed earlier.

Despite the conventional modern representation of Sei as arrogant and derisive, there is insufficient evidence that she was commonly viewed as a "haughty woman author" in premodern Japan. Although medieval and early modern texts portray her unfavorably, they do not explicitly criticize her. Rather, Sei's reception is shaped by the perception of her as a Heian woman associated with the court, and the construction of her gloomy old age results from the tendency to treat all women writers of the past equally. Except for Murasaki Shikibu's well-known comment on Sei, which describes the author of *The Pillow Book* as "dreadfully conceited"[22] because of her profuse use of Chinese characters in her writing and the two *Tales of the Past* anecdotes, medieval and early modern texts do not present her as a woman who flaunted her erudition. On the contrary, many narratives from the thirteenth through nineteenth centuries hail her as an exceptionally accomplished woman by virtue of her erudition and elegant way of displaying it.

In her study of the prominent *waka* poet Ono no Komachi's representations in Japan from the tenth to the fourteenth century, Terry Kawashima argues that images of Ono no Komachi as "a prosperous woman who becomes a destitute hag"[23] result from the desire to domesticate her power to attract men—namely, by negating her sexuality and undermining her literary prowess.[24] In a similar way, we can read representations of Sei as attempts to negate her subjectivity as presented in *The Pillow Book*. Specifically, the stories in *Tales of the Past* that present a highly sexualized image of the Heian writer ridicule her by focusing on her femininity. The one that features Sei comparing herself to a "fast horse" draws from her knowledge of the Chinese literary canon and re-creates her as strong and capable of outwitting men. Her portrayal as an impoverished old woman, however, removes her from the social center and prevents her from attracting men. The second episode ridicules Sei by depicting her as having lost her feminine looks. Exposing her genitalia to the male gaze is her only way of proving that she is a woman.

Outside Buddhist discourses concerned with how the lives of Heian women writers unfolded as they aged, medieval narratives depict these women as accomplished poets and feature them at the peak of their youth and talent. The earliest work to present Heian court women as distinct from their male peers and "valued predecessors as well as scions of important poetic lineages" is Fujiwara no Kiyosuke's (1104–1177) poetic treatise *A Bag of Notes* (*Fukuro zōshi*), as Roselee Bundy has argued.[25] Bundy's examination of anecdotes about female poets reveals that this compilation of poetic knowledge casts literary women who were active two centuries earlier as "the possessor[s] of a verbal facility capable of reducing the male poet to silence."[26] She situates this view of Heian women poets in the context of the rise of patrilineal poetic houses and the establishing of poetic authority in the twelfth century. Although Sei Shōnagon was not included in *A Bag of Notes*, her portrayal in the later medieval collection of anecdotes *Stories Selected to Illustrate Ten Maxims* (*Jikkinshō*, 1252) and poetry treatise *Pleasing Selections and Commentaries* (*Etsumokushō*, mid-Kamakura period) as an exceptionally talented woman is not surprising considering the importance of literary knowledge that both works uphold.

Ono no Komachi, Sei Shōnagon, Murasaki Shikibu, Akazome Emon, Izumi Shikibu, Koshikibu no Naishi, Shunzei's Daughter, and many other literary women of the Heian period appear among legendary figures of the past in a large number of texts. This cataloguing of Heian women and their poetic talents originated in medieval Japan but continued throughout the Edo period and thrived in the genre of texts for women's education. Re-created using brief episodes from their lives and illustrations, such images of aristocratic women were put to use by writers and scholars concerned with girls' education. Evocation of legendary women of the past served as an effective tool in constructing a concept of traditional femininity, which, although constantly revised at various historical junctures, was promoted to female readers as universal and abiding.

The tendency to edify women through accounts about idealized legendary female figures originated in China more than two thousand years ago. The earliest extant text aimed at women's moral education is Liu Xiang's (79–8 B.C.E.) *Categorized Biographies of Women* (Ch. *Lienü zhuan*, J. *Retsujoden*). By means of 125 accounts of women whose actions had either bolstered or sapped the prosperity of a family or dynasty, the text instills such Confucian virtues as maternal rectitude, sage intelligence, benevolent wisdom, purity and obedience, chastity and righteousness, and skill in argument, as summarized by Lisa Raphals.[27] Raphals has noted that despite the misleading reference to biographies in the title, these narratives should be viewed as "(exemplary) life stories" in contrast to the full biographies recorded in Sima Qian's *Records of the Historian* (Ch. *Shiji*, J. *Shiki*, 91 B.C.E.) and the dynastic histories composed in the subsequent centuries.[28] Anne Behnke Kinney has further added that each narrative about an exemplary woman attempted "to preserve for memory or emulation the signal acts that made her life worthy of consideration and exemplified the crucial moral messages of her age."[29] *Categorized Biographies of Women* was first translated into Japanese by Kitamura Kigin as *Biographies of Women in Japanese* (*Kana retsujoden*, 1655) and inspired many didactic works that were targeted at women, including Kigin's own *Tales of the Maidenflower*. Its publication marked the beginning of a series of images of Sei that emphasized new ideas of femininity to women for the remainder of the Edo period.

SEI SHŌNAGON AS A PARAGON OF FEMININITY

Early modern texts for female readers frequently linked ideal woman-hood to literary women of the past. Some examples of section headings in such works include "A Section of Talented Women Writers" (Bungaku saijo no bu), "Biographies of Women Poets of Our Country" (Honchō kajin den), "Biographies of Famous Exceptional Ladies of the Past" (*Kokon meifuden*), and "A Collection of Famous Exceptional Women of Our Country" (Honchō meijoshū).[30] Although the women featured in these lists vary, from Heian writers to fictional characters, they are usually portrayed by reference to a particular episode, one that had, however, undergone continuous modifications. For example, since the thirteenth century Sei Shōnagon has consistently been presented via the episode concerning the snow of Kōro Peak. This episode is recorded in one of the final sections of *The Pillow Book* in the *Sankanbon* and *Nōinbon* lineages, and although it consists of only a few lines, it has become representative of *The Pillow Book* and has been repeatedly reproduced in introducing Sei Shōnagon and her work to generations of readers across a broad range of texts. Texts highlighting this episode include medieval collections of anecdotes, Edo-period educational books for women, multicolored woodblock-printed "brocade pictures" (*nishiki-e*) such as Kunisada's *Biographies of Famous Exceptional Ladies from the Past* (*Kokin meifu den*, 1860–1864), Meiji-period Japanese-language readers (*kokugo tokuhon*), and modern-day junior high school textbooks.[31]

The earliest adaptation of this episode, as recorded in *Stories Selected to Illustrate Ten Maxims*,[32] introduces Sei at the beginning of the work in a section titled "Be of Consistent Temperament in Your Actions" (Hito ni megumi o hodokosu beki koto).[33] It reads,

> The same ex-emperor [Ichijō] one morning when the snow was falling elegantly went out to the veranda to watch it and said, "I wonder what Kōro Peak looks like?" Sei Shōnagon was in the royal presence, and without saying a word she raised the bamboo lat-tice. This story has been handed down to the present day as an outstanding example of sensibility.
>
> This Kōro Peak appears in a poem composed by Bo Juyi when he was old and in retreat in a grass hut at its foot:

Leaning my head on my pillow I listen to the bell of Iai Temple;
Raising the blind, I look upon the snow of Kōro Peak.

This Sei Shōnagon was the daughter of Kiyohara no Motosuke, one of the Five Poets of the Pear Chamber of Tenryaku times. In addition to carrying on the family traditions of learning and the arts, she was of elegant and straightforward character, frequently displaying an uncanny ability to fit her actions to the occasion. In addition, at that time there were many sensitive ladies such as Murasaki Shikibu, the author of *The Tale of Genji*, Akazome Emon, Izumi Shikibu, Koshikibu no Naishi, Ise no Ōsuke, Dewa no Ben, Koben, Kura no Naishi, Taka no Naishi, Gō no Jijū, Otsu no Jijū, Shin Saishō, Konoe no Naishi, and Chūjō.[34]

The narrator's assessment following the recapitulation of the episode introduces Sei as well versed in poetry composition and of a sensitive nature. In her study of the reception of this episode in medieval and early modern *setsuwa* collections, Nakajima Wakako argues that the phrase "superior example" (*yū naru rei*)[35] included in this episode to describe Sei refers to the way she displayed her knowledge—namely, by raising the blind without saying a word (*mōsu koto wa naku*).[36] Nakajima notes that unlike *The Pillow Book*, this adaptation excludes the word "snow" from the riddle, effectively making the test more difficult.[37] Sei's preeminence is further underscored by the fact that she heads the list of exemplary women included in the last paragraph of this episode. This image of Sei emerges in a work that was intended "to serve as an aid in forming the moral character of youth as yet untutored in the ways of the world,"[38] as the preface of *Stories Selected to Illustrate Ten Maxims* states, which suggests that it was not targeted at a specifically gendered audience. In its ten chapters, the text recounts episodes from the lives of male and female figures of the past and presents them as models to be emulated or shunned. Among these exemplary figures Sei appears as superior on her own, neither pitted against other talented writers nor placed in an antagonistic dyad with Murasaki Shikibu, which, centuries later, would become the dominant representation of the two Heian literary women.

A similar image of Sei appeared less than a century later in *Pleasing Selections and Commentaries.* The text introduces Sei as Kiyohara no

Motosuke's daughter and notes that during her time there were other famous women, including "Murasaki Shikibu, who wrote *The Tale of Genji*, and Akazome Emon, Ise no Tayū, Izumi Shikibu, and Uma no Naishi."[39] The author further states that although these women were all different, they were all sensible and refined.

Following the Chinese tradition of presenting the life stories of legendary women, the majority of these texts introduce Sei as a descendant of a family of famous poets—that is, as Kiyohara no Motosuke's daughter and Fukayabu's great-granddaughter—and then recount the episode in which Sei raises the blind in front of the emperor. Interestingly and of importance, from the thirteenth century throughout the Edo period, Emperor Ichijō, rather than Empress Teishi, appears as the interlocutor in this episode. He commends Sei's quick-wittedness and knowledge of Chinese literary sources as she emerges as the only one to solve the riddle. Although some texts comment briefly on *The Pillow Book* as well, it is the writer's character that is pointed to and hailed as laudable. The texts stress the fact that Sei stood out as the most accomplished among court men and women and that her erudition was acknowledged by the highest authority. Some narratives comment that "the emperor was extremely impressed" (*mikado wa hanahada eikan arikeru to ya*),[40] and others that "the emperor was boundlessly impressed" (*mikado eikan kagiri nakarishi to nari*)[41] or "the emperor was greatly moved" (*imijiku kanzesasetamaishi to ka ya*).[42] *The Pillow Book*'s author is thus portrayed as a gentlewoman who not only outshone men but also excelled in the imperial court for her talent and learnedness.

In fact, throughout the Edo period Sei's predominant image even beyond the genre of conduct books for women was that of a talented and intelligent woman (*saijo*). Erotic parodies and texts related to the pleasure quarters also refer to her as *saijo* and praise her exceptional learnedness. This perception of Sei spread even beyond the realm of literature and led to the naming of a tangram, "Sei Shōnagon's Wisdom Plates" (Sei Shōnagon chie no ita), in the early eighteenth century.[43] Consisting of seven plates (three triangles, two trapezoids, one square, and one parallelogram) rearrangeable in multiple ways, the tangram was introduced in a 1742 book with the same title. Its preface states,

When looking at the old text that Sei Shōnagon wrote, one realizes that it brims with wisdom and contains many episodes that amuse people. In it there is a chapter titled "Wisdom Plates" [Chie no ita] that features patterns [zu]. When looking at them, small children, depending on how shrewd they are, can easily produce various forms. This puzzle functions in a truly amazing way, but since the patterns are based on items that existed in the past and were used in the imperial court, children nowadays find them hard to understand.[44]

The preface further explains that the book introduces patterns based on contemporary objects to facilitate the enjoyment of the puzzle by young people. The fifty-two patterns recorded in the book vary greatly, from paper (shikishi) and a knife (chōhō) to a lotus flower (renge) and a paper lantern (ando). According to the Chronology of Edo, Musashi Province (Bukō nenpyō, 1847), this tangram was listed as a game for children in a collection of trendy things in the spring of 1745.[45] In addition, a work by Kitagawa Utamaro I (1753–1806) titled Tagasode of the Kado-Tamaya, Kamuro Kikuno and Shimeno featuring two courtesans enjoying the game reveals that the puzzle attracted not only children but women as well (figure 5.1).

One of the earliest books for women in the Edo period highlighting Sei Shōnagon's extraordinary talent is Kitamura Kigin's Tales of the Maidenflower. By way of a collection of fifty-five illustrated narratives of Chinese and Japanese literary women of the past, the text presents itself as a preliminary handwriting manual for girls and at the same time promotes virtues such as sexual chastity (teijo no michi), forbearance (kannin no kokoro), filial piety (oya ni kō aru kokoro), obedience (otoko no yakko nari), and avoidance of jealousy (monoitami o sezu). As Paul Gordon Schalow has noted, this work made "women's discursive practice visible for the first time as distinct from men's."[46] The majority of women discussed in the text are Heian-period poets.[47]

Compared with books for women produced in the subsequent decades of the Edo period, Kigin's text draws considerable attention to Sei Shōnagon as a writer.[48] Her literary talent is revealed by two episodes that appear in The Pillow Book. In both men of high station put Sei's

FIGURE 5.1 Two courtesans with a tangram and guide with patterns in front of them; Kitagawa Utamaro I, *Tagasode of the Kado-Tamaya, Kamuro Kikuno and Shimeno*. Courtesy of Museum of Fine Arts, Boston

erudition to the test and applaud her response, which attests to her accomplishments—namely, poetic mastery and competence in the Chinese classics. In each account Sei solves a riddle by guessing an allusion to a poem by Bo Juyi. The first episode centers on the poetic exchange between Sei and Fujiwara no Kintō (966–1041), one of the leading poets and critics in mid-Heian Japan. As recounted in *Tales of the Maidenflower*, this anecdote states that on a windy winter day Fujiwara no Kintō sent the final lines ("lower verse" made up of fourteen syllables) of a poem, urging Sei to provide the opening lines ("upper verse" consisting of seventeen syllables) impromptu. Sei capped Kintō's verse[49] and was later praised by Minamoto no Toshikata (960–1027), who, along with Kintō, belonged to the cultural and political elite of the day, specifically the celebrated quartet of so-called Four Counselors (Shinagon) during the reign of Emperor Ichijō.[50] Toshikata suggested that Sei be appointed to the Handmaid's Office.[51] In other words, Sei's ability to cap verses extemporaneously—that is, her *waka* and Chinese literary prowess—offers her an opportunity for advancement to a high-ranking official position available to women at court. However, *Tales of the Maidenflower* does not reveal to readers that Sei, as described in *The Pillow Book*, was perplexed and under time pressure when asked to complete the poem. Neither does it say that she wished she could receive advice from her patron, Empress Teishi, who at that time happened to be secluded with Emperor Ichijō. The recapitulation of this episode is followed by the narrator's comment, "It seems that women, too, understand linked verses [*renga*] and the like. This is probably appropriate. It is unbecoming if [a woman] deliberately speaks flauntingly, but, depending on the occasion, it is natural to invite someone's participation. Having knowledge of everything that may be valuable is surely not a bad thing."[52]

Literary knowledge and poetic talent are presented as important attributes that increase a woman's desirability and consequently her chances for advancement and a rise in status. Similarly, the second story recounts the episode of the snow of Kōro Peak and, along with the first episode, highlights Sei's erudition and the praise she received from powerful men. The inclusion of episodes with a similar structure underscores Sei's mastery of the Chinese classics and poetry composition and presents this as appealing in men's eyes, because both the challenges and praises come from men of a high social rank. Sei is depicted as a woman poet who excels in the composition of linked verse. In the case of the Kōro Peak episode she is able to symbolically complete the poem to which the emperor has alluded by silently lifting the blind, and in the episode concerning Kintō's challenge she verbally caps the poem. The presence of a male interlocutor who initiates the test and evaluates the woman's performance seems of great importance here, because Sei's representation as a paragon of femininity is endorsed by a man. Although in his commentary on *The Pillow Book, Spring Dawn Commentary*, Kigin points to the fact that in the Kōro Peak episode the challenge comes from Teishi, here he follows the *setsuwa* adaptation.[53] In doing so, he continues the tradition of transforming the original all-female setting of Empress Teishi's court as described in *The Pillow Book* into a male-centered setting with the emperor posing the riddle and then praising Sei, as described in chapter 4. The latter half of the section comments on *The Pillow Book's* didactic nature and states that it is equal in quality to the *Genji*, Japan's utmost treasure (*shihō*), and by no means inferior to texts written in the male hand (*otoko moji*), implying *kanbun* literature.[54] Thus, Sei entered the world of educational books for female readers as an exemplary woman and writer, whose image had been sanctioned by powerful men.

A similar representation of Sei appeared in *A Mirror for Women of Our Country* (*Honchō jokan*), published in the same year as *Tales of the Maidenflower*. Drawing attention to her knowledge of Chinese poetry via the same two episodes in which Kintō and the emperor test Sei, the text introduces her as the talented author of *The Pillow Book*. It reads, "She wrote *The Pillow Book* and expressed herself within it. The language is elegant and boundlessly refined."[55]

Both *Tales of the Maidenflower* and *A Mirror for Women of Our Country* view Sei's writing as intimate and extemporaneous and show as much interest in *The Pillow Book* as in the writer's learnedness. Edo-period conduct books for women frequently present *The Pillow Book* as being as worthy of praise as *The Tale of Genji*. For example, *Japanese Stories of Women's Patience* (*Onna kanninki yamatobumi*, 1713) extols the elegance of language and the depth of *The Pillow Book* and hails it as equal to the *Genji* in a way that is strongly reminiscent of Kigin's evaluation in his *Spring Dawn Commentary*.[56] *A Mirror for Women's Epistolary Education* (*Jokyō bunshō kagami*, 1742), a collection of fifty-six model letters, even presents *The Pillow Book* as superior to the *Genji* and an

FIGURE 5.2 . Sei Shōnagon leans against a writing table and a girl sits by her side; *A Mirror for Women's Epistolary Education* (*Jokyō bunshō kagami*, 1742). Courtesy of The British Museum, London

essential text for mastering the art of letter writing.[57] The accompanying illustration features a woman facing a writing table and includes no reference to the Kōro Peak episode, which in the majority of early modern conduct books emphasizes Sei's superior qualities as a woman rather than writer (figure 5.2). A shorter version of the description of Sei in *The Mirror for Women's Epistolary Education* appeared in *A Young Crane's Elegant Selection of One Hundred Poets, One Poem Each* (*Hinazuru hyakunin isshu hana monzen*, 1757), and the accompanying illustration likewise features a woman facing a writing table.[58] As these examples show, the image of Sei Shōnagon in some early modern conduct books was intended to encourage women's literary education, and her *Pillow Book* was hailed as a work that could cultivate women's creativity.

In the following centuries, particularly from the mid-eighteenth through the nineteenth century, books for women focused more on Sei's character than her writing style. Eliding the anecdote about Kintō's poetic challenge and abandoning Kigin's neo-Confucian reading of her work, many of the later conduct books showed little concern with her writing. As discussed in the previous chapter, presenting Sei as an exemplary woman skilled in poetry composition, knowledgeable in Chinese classics, and good at repartee, later books for female readers used *The Pillow Book* to justify their view of Sei as a woman worthy of emulation.[59] In other words, while earlier educational texts characterized Sei as an exemplary woman writer by demonstrating the value of her writing, later texts domesticated her, focusing on her superior qualities as a woman and approaching *The Pillow Book* mainly as a means to paint a more vivid portrait of its author.

VILIFYING SEI SHŌNAGON: GENDER AND NATIONAL LITERATURE

Books for women frequently presented *The Pillow Book* and *The Tale of Genji* as works of equal literary excellence. At the beginning of the eighteenth century, however, one scholar disagreed. In his text *Seven Essays on Murasaki Shikibu* (*Shijo shichiron*, known also as *Shika shichiron*, 1703), Andō Tameakira (1659–1716) contrasted the *Genji* author with Sei Shōnagon. By that time in scholarly circles *The Tale of Genji* had been characterized as immoral and "senseless and deceiving fiction" that ran counter to both Buddhist and Confucian tenets, thus causing "moral depravity."[60] Using *Murasaki Shikibu's Diary* (*Murasaki Shikibu nikki*, eleventh century) as an unbiased and reliable source that revealed Murasaki's virtuous nature and unsurpassed literary talent, Tameakira hailed *The Tale of Genji* as a work of moral value.[61] He argued that an awareness of Murasaki's character was central to fully understand *The Tale of Genji* and, citing extensively from her diary, presented her as "an ultimate woman: discreet and humble, she is a mother but simultaneously a celibate widow; in other words, she is a nurturer devoid of her (threatening) sexuality," in Satoko Naito's words.[62] To underscore the virtuous character of the *Genji* author, Tameakira contrasted her with Sei, stating, "Shikibu, whose brush is brilliant and extraordinary, should be regarded as having a talent unparalleled in all ages. Since the days of old it has been customary to speak of them as 'Sei and Murasaki' [*Seishi*], but, as is evident in her writing, which is most disagreeable, Sei Shōnagon was not very talented, and she thought herself clever. They cannot be discussed on an equal footing."[63]

Without justifying his claim, Tameakira reiterated Murasaki Shikibu's criticism of Sei Shōnagon as recorded in Murasaki's diary:

> Sei Shōnagon, for instance, was dreadfully conceited. She thought herself so clever, and littered her writings with Chinese characters, but if you examined them closely, they left a great deal to be desired. Those who think of themselves as being superior to everyone else in this way will inevitably suffer and come to a bad end, and people who have become so precious that they go out of their way to be sensitive in the most unpromising situations, trying to capture every moment of interest, however slight, are bound to look ridiculous and superficial. How can the future turn out well for them?[64]

In her diary Murasaki Shikibu comments on her own ability to read and understand Chinese, criticizes various women in Empress Shōshi's service, and documents in detail multiple events during her court service. In other words, she disparages Sei for having behaved in a similar way a few years earlier. Tameakira's Confucian-informed approach to *The Tale of Genji* was not embraced by his contemporaries, especially national learning scholars, who, in the view of literature, favored traditional Japanese poetics rather than foreign ideologies.[65] Most likely, his condemnation of Sei Shōnagon was not espoused for the same reason. It was only three centuries later that scholars revived the vilified image of Sei that Tameakira had created.

Over the course of the Meiji Restoration (1868), various reforms took place as part of an effort to situate Japan on an equal footing with the advanced nations of the West.[66] This concern for the state of Japan and its position in the world manifested itself in gendered terms. The perception that Japan was a "'feminine' nation vis-à-vis the more 'masculine' and more civilized Anglo-European world" resulted in new attitudes toward women.[67] As Rebecca Copeland has shown, "woman," as a designation, became "a metaphor for all that was backward and shameful in Japan," and reformers of the new nation-state regarded women's education as central to their efforts to raise Japan's status in Westerners' eyes.[68]

Women's status was further addressed in debates surrounding the formation of a national literature (*kokubungaku*) and national language (*kokugo*) in the 1880s, where Heian literature with its predominantly female contribution was mobilized to project advanced cultural achievements and the high position of women. A number of histories and anthologies of Japanese literature were produced during the next decade in order to systematize this newly configured national literature.[69] Summarizing their objectives, Tomi Suzuki has noted: "All of them considered literature as 'reflections of national life' (*ikkoku seikatsu no shaei*) and tried to present, through concrete literary examples, the development of the mentality of the nation' in order that 'the nation's people will deepen their love for the nation,' that 'the national spirit' (*kokumin no seishin*) will be elevated, and that the 'social progress and development of the nation will be furthered.'"[70]

Suzuki has additionally argued that these works focused on native literary works and aimed for "a comprehensive representation of the historical development of national literature, stressing both the continuity and the progress of the national spirit—'continuity' and 'progress' being signs of a civilized and advanced nation."[71] Heian literature played a central role in the construction of a Japanese literary tradition. Women's writing offered the basis for genre categorization and the authors acted as models of "traditional" Japanese womanhood. However, even within the field of literary criticism, a strong focus was placed on the women writers rather than their works. Contesting views of literature prevailed from the 1890s until the beginning of the twentieth century, and despite the ambivalent position and shifting assessments of Heian literary works, Meiji scholars concurred in their views of Sei and Murasaki, shaping the former as the bad girl and the latter as the good girl.[72] Because of their gender and literary talent, Heian women writers offered rich material for debates on nonconformance to what was viewed as the traditionally feminine Meiji schoolgirl (*jogakusei*), the new woman (*atarashii onna*), and the modern girl (*moga*), thus becoming vehicles for conveying views on feminine virtues and women's literary expression.[73]

In this new context Japanese literary scholars again faced the challenge of reconciling the gap between the erotic content of *The Tale of Genji* and the moral agenda of the state. National literature scholars revisited Tameakira's focus on the virtuous character of the *Genji* author and, viewing it as a legitimate approach, once again juxtaposed Murasaki and Sei. Placed in an antagonistic dyad, Sei Shōnagon was criticized for her arrogance, haughtiness, and impertinence for displaying superiority over men, while Murasaki Shikibu's image was shaped in accordance with the newly constructed parameters of "traditional" femininity predicated on the "good wife, wise mother" (ryōsai kenbo) ideology.[74]

Male scholars repeatedly recognized *The Pillow Book* and *The Tale of Genji* as masterpieces of Japanese literature but pitted their authors against each other and drew conclusions about their personalities. For example, in "the first full-length modern survey of Japanese literary history,"[75] titled *History of Japanese Literature* (*Nihon bungakushi*, 1890), Mikami Sanji (1865–1939) and Takatsu Kuwasaburō (1864–1921) referred to *The Tale of Genji* and *The Pillow Book* (in the order they are introduced in their literary history) as the two finest works ("treasures," *sōheki*) of Japanese literature. The two young critics asserted that Sei and Murasaki were unsurpassed writers of their time, neither inferior to the other, both highly educated and equally accomplished, and the differences in their writing styles were naturally the result of their contrasting personalities. Mikami and Takatsu explained that a calm, gentle, and virtuous woman writer like Murasaki was bound to produce a continuous narrative (*tsuzuki monogatari*) such as *The Tale of Genji*, whereas someone too modern (*imayō*) and boastful of her learnedness like Sei would naturally write a "fitful" (*danzoku*) and "fickle" (*tsune naki*) zuihitsu such as *The Pillow Book*. Therefore, they described Murasaki's style as pure and Sei's writing as slightly flawed. Mikami and Takatsu defined *zuihitsu* as "a collection of things that have impressed [the writer]—things that have been seen, heard, or come to one's mind in succession."[76] According to them, what made Sei modern was the fact that she "did not think men were men. She argued vigorously drawing from past events and old texts, leaving men dumbfounded by her unparalleled vehemence."[77] In other words, Sei's ability to outshine men diminished her femininity. Mikami and Takatsu further noted that the contrasting personalities of the two female writers had led to differences in the styles of *The Pillow Book* and *Murasaki Shikibu's Diary*; specifically, that the former brimmed with "emotionally saturated, rampant, and eccentric" accounts, while the latter abounded in "calm and peaceful events."[78]

A few years later, literary scholar Haga Yaichi (1867–1927) expressed his view on *The Pillow Book* and *The Tale of Genji* by positioning them on an equal footing and labeling them as "the two unsurpassed works in the national literature of our country" (*waga kuni no kokubun ni sōzetsu*).[79] However, his criticism did not spare Sei Shōnagon. In his *Ten Lectures on the History of National Literature* (*Kokubungakushi jikkō*, 1899), Haga acknowledges the fact that a lack of records prevents us from learning about Murasaki Shikibu's personality. Citing Andō Tameakira's *Seven Essays on Murasaki Shikibu*, Haga introduces the *Genji* author by simply highlighting her extraordinary learnedness. After his ten-page introduction to *The Tale of Genji* and brief remarks on *Murasaki Shikibu's Diary*, he turns to Sei Shōnagon. His logic takes an abrupt turn, and although he previously stated that it would be difficult to know what Murasaki Shikibu's character was like because of insufficient evidence, he expounds on Sei Shōnagon's personality drawing entirely from her writing. Haga introduces Sei as follows: "It was in her nature to not lose to men. Relying on her own scholarly ability, she was frequently hard on men. As becomes evident from an episode like that about the snow of Kōro Peak, she seems to have been apt and quick-witted. She was not mild-mannered like Murasaki Shikibu but extremely sharp-witted, and therefore her writing abounds in criticism."[80]

Haga presents *The Pillow Book* as a reflection of the author's character and describes it as full of critical remarks.[81] He contrasts a "mild-mannered" nature (*onkō na tokoro*) with sharp-wittedness, displays of learnedness, and attitudes that challenge men and uses Sei and Murasaki to offer two models of feminine behavior, both of which are determined by women's attitudes to men. Haga views *The Pillow Book* as a collection of Sei's judgment on various people and comments on numerous aspects of life. Although he does not see her literary work as problematic, he uses *The Pillow Book*'s content to justify his view of its author. Unlike Mikami and Takatsu, who explained the different styles of *The Tale of Genji* and *The Pillow Book* as reflecting the writers' characters, Haga used *The Pillow Book* as a primary source for re-creating Sei Shōnagon.[82]

This juxtaposition of Sei and Murasaki in the discourse of the new nation-state appealed to literary scholars and educators as a persuasive tool for addressing contemporary social issues triggered by the newly developed relationship with the West. In 1902, the Japanese literary scholar and art critic Umezawa Waken (1871–1931) completed a monograph titled *Sei Shōnagon and Murasaki Shikibu* (*Sei Shōnagon to Murasaki Shikibu*), which launched a sequence of book-length monographs and scholarly articles with the same title that continue to be published to this day.[83] Shaping Sei as the forerunner of the "new woman," he underscored Japan's superiority over Western countries, arguing that women who challenged traditional gender norms in Japan had preexisted those in Europe and the United States by hundreds of years. Specifically, in the opening chapter, "The Age of the New Woman," he describes the emergence of talented women writers and politically active women in Europe and the United States as a result of the flourishing of women's education. Such women included Anne Steele (1717–1778), George Sand (1804–1876), the Brontës (nineteenth century), George Eliot (1819–1880), Elizabeth Cady Stanton (1815–1902), and Millicent Fawcett (1847–1929), and their prominence resulted from the efforts of advocates of women's rights, such as Olympe de Gouges (1748–1793), Mary Wollstonecraft (1759–1797), Lucy Stone (1818–1893), and Henry Browne Blackwell (1825–1909). In Japan, however, as Umezawa contended, women's education had emerged in the Heian period and given rise to women writers, such as Sei Shōnagon, Murasaki Shikibu, Izumi Shikibu, Ono no Komachi, and Akazome Emon. Among them, Sei and Murasaki were the two unsurpassed literary women and sources of pride for Japan. Umezawa went further to position *The Pillow Book*, which he described as a miscellany (*zuihitsu*), a diary (*nikki*), and random notes (*manroku*), as the predecessor of impressionist literature that developed in the latter half of the nineteenth century in Europe and the United States. He hailed *The Tale of Genji* as the masterpiece among all realist novels in the world.[84]

Umezawa's interest in the two women writers, however, seems to have pertained to their personalities and not so much to their literary works, which he called Japan's unrivaled prose masterpieces. As he notes, his examination of Sei's and Murasaki's characters aimed at aiding in finding "a solution to the woman problem" (*fujin mondai no kaiketsu*).[85] The so-called woman problem referred to widespread debates in the late nineteenth and early twentieth centuries about the status of women in modern society. Within this discourse, improvement of the purported "backwardness" of Japanese women was viewed as essential to projecting an image of the nation as strong and civilized. The state's good wife, wise mother vision of the ideal modern female was predicated on chastity before marriage and a gentle temperament.[86]

In this context, Umezawa portrayed Sei Shōnagon as a "new woman," mainly because she was "single [dokushin], vagrant [hōrō], arrogant [kyōkan], unrestrained [gōtō], almost like the new rebels of the present" and viewed Murasaki Shikibu as "a literary widow, good wife and wise mother, chaste and mild-mannered, representing the women of the past as portrayed in the seventeenth-century educational work for women titled *Greater Learning for Women* [*Onna daigaku*]."[87] It was not Sei's display of knowledge that Umezawa regarded as her greatest vice but the fact that she was unmarried. He explains that, unlike Murasaki, Sei was "a proponent of free love, a romanticist, and a lover,"[88] did not aspire to become a good wife and wise mother, and viewed "marriage as a woman's grave" (*kon'in wa onna no funbo*).[89] According to Umezawa, Sei's lack of experience as a married woman prevented her from seeing men through a wife's or a mother's eyes, and, like the new woman, she repeatedly disparaged men. Umezawa concluded that in every aspect Sei was evil (*hinekurete iru*) precisely like the new woman.[90] He specified that Sei's loyalty and devotion to the empress she had served was the only aspect that could evoke sympathy in modern readers and asserted that had she lived in the present, she would have become a self-centered new woman comparable to those featured in European dramas and novels. In sum, using Sei's image, Umezawa claims that modernity, as marked by women's literary prowess, and the new woman, as marked by education and independence, had their origins not in the West but in Heian Japan. Yet on the other hand, he denigrates the same image of Sei he has used to underscore Japan's superiority over the West.

Disparagement of Sei's failure to fulfill modern gendered norms of femininity appears even more pointedly in Fujioka Sakutarō's (1870–1910) *Complete History of Japanese Literature: The Heian Court* (*Nihon bungaku zenshi: Heianchō-hen*, 1905), published six years later. In the only chapter dedicated to *The Pillow Book*, Fujioka repeatedly presents Sei Shōnagon as lacking in femininity (*ikani onnarashikarazaru onna*), using carefully selected episodes to support his claim. The reason why Fujioka viewed Sei as masculine was the abundance of episodes of seeming self-praise. He interpreted them as highlighting her erudition and not her appealing looks. The majority of the eleven examples he offers center on elite men's praise of Sei's ability to guess an allusion to a Chinese literary source. In this new context, the Kōro Peak episode, which had been used to underscore Sei's femininity in early modern Japan, came to symbolize her lack of modesty.

Sei's boastfulness was brought even further to light by her lack of compassion, according to Fujioka. He describes Sei's callousness by way of examples in which she passes judgment on parents who fail to scold mischievous children, laughs at the news that a man's house was burning, and looks down on lowly people. He also notes, "If Sei Shōnagon had had a feminine nature, she would have treated with compassion those who were naively honest and belittled by others; however, she was too boastful and willful and [therefore] does not deserve any sympathy."[91]

Here again ideal womanhood is defined by compassion and self-denial. Viewing *The Pillow Book* as Sei's personal memoir, Fujioka selects episodes in which politically powerful people praise Sei's learnedness and thus characterizes the work as a collection of her boastful stories. Removing them from their actual historical background and political context and disregarding the possibilities that *The Pillow Book* was commissioned by a politically influential figure or was a work of fiction, Fujioka takes Sei's statements about herself at face value and argues that Sei's writing reflected her personality.[92]

This tendency to discuss the two Heian writers' personal qualities rather than analyze their works continued throughout the Meiji period. Sei's perceived "arrogant" display of knowledge was justified by references to her own accounts recorded in *The Pillow Book* and Murasaki Shikibu's criticism of Sei as documented in *Murasaki Shikibu's Diary*. As Fujimoto Munetoshi has observed, self-praise was not unique to Sei Shōnagon but was seen also in other Heian works written by women, including *The Kagerō Diary* (*Kagerō nikki*, tenth century) and *The Sarashina Diary* (*Sarashina nikki*, eleventh century).[93] However, Sei was selected to represent the boastful literary woman, whose negative image was used in debates about ideal femininity. Despite Sei's inclusion of episodes that portray her as being embarrassed by her insufficient knowledge or unsatisfactory poetic skills, Meiji scholars disregarded these sections of the text and focused on what was later labeled self-praise episodes (*jisandan*)—those portraying the Heian author as accomplished and confident.

PROMOTING CULTURAL NATIONALISM: MEIJI SCHOOL TEXTBOOKS

How did the views of literary scholars on Sei and Murasaki and the new state ideology affect the images of the two literary women in educational literature for female readers in Meiji Japan? In 1899, one of what was referred to as Japanese-language readers (*kokugo tokuhon*)—a type of textbook approved by the Ministry of Education and a predecessor to state-compiled textbooks (*kokutei kyōkasho*)—paired Sei and Murasaki. Titled *High-School Japanese-Language Reader: Girls' Edition* (*Kōtō kokugo tokuhon: Joshiyō-hen*, 1899), it states that "the reign of Emperor Ichijō was a time when literary women noted for their talent emerged. Among them, those who became well known were Murasaki Shikibu and Sei Shōnagon."[94] Sei is introduced by way of the Kōro Peak episode and the empress's praise of her quick-wittedness (*binsai*). The text continues, "This woman [Sei Shōnagon] took pride in her learnedness, relied on her sharp, clever nature, and outwitted aged scholars. She wrote of this amusingly in her own book, yet Murasaki Shikibu does not speak of this in her diary and censures Sei for her unladylike [*fujin ni nigenaki*] behavior."[95]

The section next turns to Murasaki Shikibu and tells of her outstanding knowledge of Chinese and her discretion, since she never flaunted her erudition. It concludes, "The novel titled *The Tale of Genji*, which she wrote at that time, is not only interesting in content but also has never been surpassed and has served as a model for Japanese [vernacular] writing for a long time. Shikibu's daughters, too, must have inherited their mother's virtues, [since] the elder, Daini no Sanmi, was a prominent poet and was appointed a wet nurse to Emperor Go-Ichijō. The younger, Ben no Tsubone, was appointed a wet nurse to Emperor Go-Reizei."[96]

Clearly, the authors of this textbook lavish praise on Murasaki, introducing her as exceptionally knowledgeable, discreet, talented, and fecund. On the other hand, they criticize her for belittling Sei and her work. Sei Shōnagon's literary erudition—deemed sexually alluring in the Edo period, as discussed in the previous chapter—did not fit the agenda of the Meiji reformers. The focus on asceticism and restrained natural impulses in support of their notion of nationalism precluded attention to women's appeal as sexual partners.[97] Although this passage emphasizes the difference between the women writers, it does not place Sei in an inferior position to Murasaki, nor does it criticize her.

Even in state-compiled textbooks that emerged in 1903, Sei Shōnagon was not portrayed antagonistically, in opposition to an idealized Murasaki Shikibu. Among the three editions of the *Upper Elementary Reader* (*Kōtō shōgaku tokuhon*), Sei Shōnagon appears only once, in the second edition. She is again paired with Murasaki and is introduced after the *Genji* author. Following a summary of the Kōro Peak episode, the author notes Sei's competence in all things (*yorozu ni kokoro kikitaru*), though this commendation is tempered by the emphasis placed on Murasaki's humbleness and discretion. The positive images of the two women writers of the past, who continued to be labeled as *saijo*, emphasizing their exceptional talent and learnedness, were used to promote cultural nationalism and spark pride among the children of the new nation-state rather than provide moral admonition regarding gender roles.

A PRECEDENT FOR FEMALE STRENGTH AND TALENT: *WOMAN'S EDUCATION MAGAZINE*

Further examples revealing that the negative image of Sei constructed by elite male scholars in literary histories does not represent the mainstream view of the Heian writer in the Meiji period come from "the first mass-circulated journal to address women and women's concerns."[98] Titled *Woman's Education Magazine* (*Jogaku zasshi*, 1885–1904), this periodical did not employ the images of Sei and Murasaki as vehicles for defining the bounds of ideal womanhood but rather used them as precedents for female strength and talent. Their appearance in the inaugural issue of the magazine in 1885 in an article titled "Women's Status" (Fujin no chii) reveals this attitude. Mentioned along with Ise no Tayū and Izumi Shikibu, the Heian writers are hailed as "exceptional women writers who surpassed men." The article states that in the Heian period women were able to devote time to cultivating various talents, and men did not see that as problematic. It further states that later "with the advent of feudalism, as in any other country, women's roles were limited to giving birth and passing on the blood lineage," thus presenting women's literary expression as impeded by women's domesticity.[99]

The same magazine continues to emphasize the idea of the Heian women writers' superiority over men as shown in writings about Sei and Murasaki. Another article, "Sei's Talent in Mastering Japanese and Chinese Writing" (Seijo no shūsai wakan o tsuranuku), depicts Sei as exceptionally knowledgeable, recounting the Kōro Peak episode as it appears in the Edo-period educational texts. In other words, it keeps the male interlocutor (the emperor) and presents Sei as the only one who can guess the allusion to the Chinese poem while the male courtiers are completely clueless. The emperor is greatly moved and pleased, and Sei is praised for her quick-wittedness and ability to understand allusions and to display this in an elegant way—without saying a word. The text further underscores her superiority over men by recounting an episode involving a courtier who spelled out his demand to have a sliding door installed rather than just alluding to it through a poem, concluding that there was an immeasurable difference (ten'en no chigai nari) between the two with regard to elegant demeanor. This section is accompanied by an illustration featuring a woman lifting a blind, reminiscent of early modern texts for women.[100]

The positive view of Sei's superiority over men is underscored again in an 1886 article titled "Literature" (Bungaku) in the same journal that again pairs Sei and Murasaki.[101] In a section on Priest Kenkō's (1284–1350) *Essays in Idleness* (*Tsurezuregusa*, 1329–1333) *The Pillow Book* and *The Tale of Genji* are introduced as the sources that shaped the foundation of Kenkō's literary work (*taitei Seishi no nijo yori koto okorite*). The text states that Kenkō imitated Sei's writing style and borrowed phrases from Murasaki's work, thus emphasizing female ability by juxtaposing literary works by women writers with the work of a man.

The long tradition of drawing links between Sei Shōnagon's personality and her work, and viewing the latter as a natural consequence of the former, yielded multiple images of the Heian writer, ranging from destitute hag to female exemplar. Shaped by dominant ideologies rather than references to historical documents and in-depth studies of *The Pillow Book*, these representations reflect shifting gender and cultural norms over time. Although the motives and outcomes vary according to the context, each attempt to re-create the author of *The Pillow Book* reveals the importance she has held for generations of readers over the course of a millennium.

Medieval Buddhist narratives imagined her old age amid desolation to emphasize the impermanent nature of life. This representation was influenced by predominant Buddhist views of women as the ultimate source of suffering and resulted from the tendency to depict aristocratic women associated with the imperial court as marginalized from the center of power. Educational texts from the thirteenth to the early twentieth century presented Sei as an accomplished poet and exemplary woman to promote aristocratic ideals of femininity and encourage female literary erudition and empowerment. They frequently constructed her as the gifted author of a literary work whose excellence paralleled that of *The Tale of Genji* and commended her learnedness. As new subjectivities for women began to challenge traditional gender norms in the late nineteenth and early twentieth centuries, literary scholars transformed the image of Sei Shōnagon into an antithesis of ideal femininity, drawing inspiration from Andō Tameakira's work in the eighteenth century. No longer portrayed on her own but paired with her contemporary Murasaki Shikibu, the author of *The Pillow Book* came to represent negative qualities, ones strongly discouraged in Meiji-period women. Although this image of Sei developed in debates about women's education, it had no impact on actual educational literature for women.

Originating and initially holding sway in scholarly circles, the constructed rivalry between Sei Shōnagon and Murasaki Shikibu is still prominent. Despite the outdated nature of the view in academic discourse of the two women as antagonistic figures, Sei's image as the boastful literary woman from Japan's past perseveres in present-day popular culture, where Sei and Murasaki stand as representatives of Heian women writers. For example, a comic book titled *Japanese Literature a Japanese Should Know* (*Nihonjin nara shitte okitai Nihon bungaku*, 2011)[102] introduces her as a writer who speaks without reserve (*iitai hōdai*), another comic book, titled *How Splendid Even Today: "The Pillow Book"* (*Honjitsu mo ito okashi Makura no sōshi*, 2014),[103] portrays her as indomitable (*kachiki*), and the educational television program *NHK for School: Bewildering History* (*Rekishi ni dokiri*, 2014)[104] features her as the jealous rival of Murasaki Shikibu who cannot tolerate the success of

The Tale of Genji. No longer intended to directly enhance a woman's marriageability and instill moral values, these current representations in works aimed as study guides for university entrance exams present *The Pillow Book* as a literary masterpiece that transcends time and use Sei as a tool to address issues concerning feminine subjectivity. Thus the image of the Heian writer continues to be readapted and reinvented not so much in search for the real Sei Shōnagon but rather to impart ideological messages in new historical settings.

CHAPTER SIX

New Markets for Japanese Classics

Having examined some of the ways in which readers from the seventeenth to the early twentieth century accessed and interpreted *The Pillow Book*, let us consider the question, "What is *The Pillow Book*?" It is a text, which we believe Sei Shōnagon produced in the early eleventh century and despite the absence of an accessible version written in Sei's hand, has continued to draw readers through its multiple manifestations for more than a thousand years. As I have shown, *The Pillow Book* instigated diverse readings not only over time but also even within the same historical setting. In the early Edo period, for example, scholars regarded the work as a collection of logically ordered sections, while others viewed it as a "play of the brush" that resulted in randomly organized musings. In the eighteenth century, Sei's writing was further categorized as a miscellany (*zuihitsu*) and hailed as the progenitor of the genre, while in the late nineteenth and early twentieth centuries it was described as an anomaly whose literary value was based on its relation to the Heian imperial court and its presumed similarity to Western literature. In popular culture, including *haikai* collections, texts for women's education, and erotic literature from the seventeenth to the nineteenth century, Sei's work repeatedly emerged as a compilation of lists that catalogued knowledge rather than representing an assemblage of random jottings. In the same Edo period, readers of literature related to the pleasure quarters encountered Sei as a courtesan of the past who was well versed in the ways of love, while for many young women she was an embodiment of quick-wittedness and literary erudition, as presented in instruction manuals for female audiences. Despite being hailed as a paragon of femininity in early modern Japan, Sei Shōnagon came to represent negative qualities that were discouraged in Meiji-period women.

In each context of reception, Sei was presented in a way that readers could comprehend: as a female attendant in the Heian imperial court she was described as a courtesan to Edo-period audiences, a new woman in the early twentieth century, and a career-driven female in modern-day Japan. These examples shed light on how people imagined this woman writer from the distant past and reveal the resources they had to make sense of their world. Although contradictory at times, these multiple versions of the literary past influenced and informed one another, giving rise to further interpretations of the text and representations of its author that resonated with new audiences. Likewise, it was not the work that Sei composed in the eleventh century but later versions of it that were deemed the most authoritative, accessible, or convenient for specific purposes. These later versions served as source texts for consequent rewritings.

Brought into the present in the form of multiple versions, Sei and her work have offered diverse views to readers depending on their age, gender, and cultural identity. As demonstrated in previous chapters, the versions of *The Pillow Book* available to readers from the seventeenth to the early twentieth century differ from the editions of the work commonly read today. Considering this plurality of the text, describing *The Pillow Book* becomes an unfeasible task, unless we specify exactly which *Pillow Book* we have in mind.

In this study, I have shown that much more can be learned by considering multiple versions of *The Pillow Book* as elements of a wider discourse than by focusing on one specific textual manifestation. *The Pillow Book* transcends material textuality and presents itself as an idea, reminiscent of a foundation myth that has been utilized for various purposes, whether legitimizing Japan's superiority, affirming views on femininity, or claiming ownership of knowledge. As such, it challenges the ways we think about textual identities, transmission, and canonization. Moreover, *The Pillow Book*'s various transformations suggest that set notions of identity, authenticity, and (thematic and stylistic) coherence are not productive when discussing works that encompass multiple textual variants, narratorial voices, and readings. Therefore, instead of continuing to center on one aspect or one version and thus symbolically loosening the pages, or "unbinding" *The Pillow Book*, we need to acknowledge that there is no stable and unified text. Engaging the work's plurality provides a better understanding of what *The Pillow Book* is, how its versions have interacted, and why we continue to read it.

The Pillow Book's presence in the book market and on television is indicative of the significance that Sei Shōnagon and her writing continue to hold in present-day Japan. Museum and gallery displays of centuries-old manuscripts of the text and woodblock prints featuring its author, multimedia adaptations broadcast on national television and streamed on the internet, as well as scholarly annotated editions, children's books, and graphic novel (*manga*) adaptations of the Heian text, all shelved side-by-side in bookstores, are only some of the endeavors that have been made to cultivate greater appreciation of *The Pillow Book*. Amulets (*omamori*) carried in wallets or attached to handbags promise to help one become (even more) gifted in both intelligence and beauty (*saishoku kenbi*) like Sei Shōnagon.[1] Cell-phone cases and handkerchiefs portraying Sei along with her poem recorded in *One Hundred Poets, One Poem Each* similarly transpose the eleventh-century writer into current everyday life. This ongoing dialogue between the irretrievable past and the dynamic present continues to sustain modern-day literary production within and outside Japan, as the corpus of works inspired by Sei's text expands every year. What fuels the appeal of *The Pillow Book* today?

THE PILLOW BOOK IN NATIONAL LITERATURE

Following the late nineteenth century, when literary scholars selected Sei Shōnagon's writing as one of the texts to represent Japan's "national literature" (*kokubungaku*), the import of European views on literature, literary genres, modernism, and individualism, as well as the growing visibility of women in the public sphere, triggered new interpretations of the Heian text. Scholars debated over what constituted the "most authentic" textual variant, the meaning and style of the work, the character of its author, and its literary value. *The Pillow Book* continued to be viewed as a miscellany, while being further classified within categories such as "women's literature" (*joryū bungaku*), "women's diary literature" (*joryū nikki bungaku*), and "self-reflexive literature" (*jishō bungaku*) established in the 1920s. In the following decades, the work's merit was assessed through the aesthetic of *okashi* (amusement), and in the 1960s it was dismissed as a mere record of Empress Teishi's milieu devoid of any literary value.

In contrast to this dynamic shift in the interpretation of *The Pillow Book* in scholarly circles, a relative stability has reigned in the way the eleventh-century text has been taught in the Japanese educational system. As early as the late nineteenth century, *The Pillow Book* became part of the national language (*kokugo*) curriculum. Initially, textbooks focused on the author and her self-cultivation—under the heading "Sei Shōnagon" rather than "*The Pillow Book*"—and featured only the episode concerning the snow of Kōro Peak (as discussed in chapter 5). Since the 1920s, the opening passage "In spring, the dawn" and a few other sections have been taught to middle- and high-school students. With the establishment of a category on "Traditional Linguistic Culture and Characteristics of the National Language" in the curriculum guidelines announced in 2008 by Japan's Ministry of Education, Culture, Sports, Science and Technology, this passage entered the elementary school curriculum as well. Since 2011, it has been the only passage from classical literature taught at every stage of the educational system in Japan.[2]

The increased focus on tradition and culture in the revised teaching guidelines sheds light on the redefined roles of literary works of the past in Japan today. The guidelines hail the country's "traditional linguistic culture" (*dentōteki na gengo bunka*) as crucial for Japan and state that early exposure to literary sources from the past will nurture and deepen the interest of the young in the country's heritage and inspire them to become future innovators.[3]

This perceived importance of classical literature in Japanese education, however, stands in contrast to the general lack of interest in ancient texts, as the common phrase *koten girai* (contempt for the classics) suggests. As Komori Kiyoshi has noted, the section "In spring, the dawn" has been taught in the same way for decades following government teaching guidelines, which impose "a correct reading" and specific learning activities, thus allowing little freedom to teachers and students to engage with the text in new ways.[4] Seeing no relevance to their lives, many young learners consider these texts out-of-date (*dasai*) and useless. To many Japanese, classical literature conjures up memories of studying for high school and university entrance exams centering on a rigid analysis of classical grammar, vocabulary, memorization of the opening passage and the name of the author.

Attempts to redeem *The Pillow Book* despite the inflexibility of the educational system can be discerned in the large number of educational graphic novel (*gakushū manga*) adaptations and translations into colloquial Japanese published since the 1990s, as well as the recent inclusion of Sei's work in television shows about Japanese literature and history. Emphasizing Sei's similarities with young women of today and shaping *The Pillow Book* as an autobiographical essay, these adaptations consistently present the eleventh-century text as one belonging to the present.

Hashimoto Osamu's translation, titled *"The Pillow Book": Translated into Peach Hip Girls' Language* (*Momojiri goyaku Makura no sōshi*, 1998), which became a best seller, is a case in point. It makes explicit reference to the stilted and alienating way in which Sei's work is taught in schools by announcing its dedication to "those who felt furious about university entrance exam preparation" and those who are "currently goaded by anger."[5] This translation of *The Pillow Book* includes a rendition of the complete *Sankanbon* text of *The Pillow Book* into current girls' slang, followed by a research-informed explanation of various aspects of Heian political life and culture presented in an engaging way. Alluding to the *Collection of Ancient and Modern Poems* (*Kokin wakashū*, ca. 905), it opens with two prefaces: a male and a female version. The narrator of the male version explains the choice of this particular linguistic register, insisting that girls' slang is best suited for a literal translation of the eleventh-century text. Considering the "freshness" of *The Pillow Book*, the lack of punctuation in premodern handwritten manuscripts, and the colloquial nature of vernacular writing in the past, the narrator claims that rewriting *The Pillow Book* in the language of teenage girls would shorten the distance between Sei and the reader and thus would convey her work in a more intimate manner.[6]

The female version of the preface, too, endorses the value of *The Pillow Book*. Written in Sei's voice, this preface challenges views of her as an old-fashioned (*naukunai*) and unattractive middle-aged woman with "frizzled hair."[7] The female narrator notes with confidence that she had a professional career one thousand years ago, when America was yet to be discovered and Europe was still undeveloped.[8] The fictional Sei further explains that her mastery of Chinese was an important asset, as important as English proficiency in Japan is today. Addressing Murasaki Shikibu's critical remarks about her, Hashimoto's Sei Shōnagon repeatedly stresses that she is modern (*naui*) and not part of the "moldy national literature" (*kabi no haeta kokubungaku*) like Murasaki's *The Tale of Genji*.[9] Comparing her work with *The Tale of Genji*, Sei argues that the antiquity of Murasaki's tale has necessitated the large number of translations into modern Japanese, whereas *The Pillow Book*'s modern nature makes it readable without any intervention. Expressing disdain for canonical literary works that are put on a pedestal and worshipped, and thus echoing the sentiments of many of her readers, Sei distinguishes her work from "national literature," which conjures an image of literary texts that are included in school and university curricula as relics from the past. According to the narrator Sei, *The Pillow Book*, unlike *The Tale of Genji* with its aristocratic aura, transcends time.[10] Hashimoto gives the Heian writer a new voice to redeem herself from the inferior position she has occupied in the constructed rivalry with Murasaki for more than a century. Sei is also able to speak directly to readers and promote her work. Walking them through the pages of *The Pillow Book* and constantly drawing parallels between the Heian period and modern-day Japan, Sei is no longer a distant and imposing cultural icon. Her "girl next door" image brings accessibility and appeal to the aura of the Heian writer and transforms the ancient text into one that belongs to the present. Hailed by scholars of *The Pillow Book* and often preferred over other annotated editions and translations into modern Japanese, *The Pillow Book: Translated into Peach Hip Girls' Language* combines the merits of both scholarly and popular editions and offers a new approach to understanding and appreciating writings from the past.

In a similar way, educational manga adaptations of *The Pillow Book* emphasize the work's freshness despite the fact that it was completed a thousand years ago. By means of a careful textual selection and focus on themes that resonate with modern readers, these rewritings present the eleventh-century text as a "super essay" about Sei's observations during "her longed-for employment in the imperial court,"[11] "a story about the life of a working woman,"[12] or a collection of essays about female bonding.[13] Shaped as first-person narratives, these adaptations offer readers direct access to the Heian woman's inner world. Sei is no longer the exceptional writer from the past, in the way Edo- and Meiji-period textbooks describe her through a third-person narrative perspective. Readers of the present encounter her as a diligent employee who blushes when praised by her superiors, feels tense in the workplace, and is exhausted at the end of the workday.[14] At other times, Sei is a single mother who questions ingrained gender expectations for women pertaining to marriage and childbirth,[15] and at still other times she stands out because of her "unique sensibility" and acute observation skill,[16] or outspokenness[17] (figure 6.1). The psychological access to the protagonist of these adaptations inspires readers' identification with her. Sei is relatable, and although of a distant age she acts as if she belonged to the same generation as young readers. Emanating cuteness, images of the Heian writer as a kimono-dressed girl with long hair and big eyes further shorten the distance between the past and the present and invite a degree of emotional affinity.

On television, Sei is described using concepts that readily resonate with modern viewers. One example comes from the NHK show *A Masterpiece in 100 Minutes* (*Hyappun de meicho*), aired in 2014. It begins with

FIGURE 6.1 Sei Shōnagon argues with a male courtier about women's life paths; Hebizō and Umino Nagiko, *Nihonjin nara shitte okitai Nihon bungaku: Yamato Takeru kara Kenkō made jinbutsu de yomu koten* (Tokyo: Gentōsha, 2011), 10. Courtesy of Gentōsha Inc., Tokyo

an introduction of Sei as "a talented staff member" who was the best fit for the imperial court, describing Teishi as a "superwoman" who was beautiful, well versed in Japanese and Chinese, and skillfully managed a cultural salon and referring to Sei's father as a "superstar" in the poetry circles of the day. The four episodes devoted to *The Pillow Book*, twenty-five minutes each, present passages that reveal Sei's "exceptional mastery of subtle observation and expression," her views on manners and compelling qualities in men and women, and some of the factors that made her a successful essayist. Sei appears on the screen as a young woman who connects with viewers through shared experiences and worldviews. According to this program, *The Pillow Book* regards women who are educated, pursue professional careers, and emanate an aura of mystery as attractive. Sei's depiction of her rewarding experience in Teishi's cultural salon is communicated as an urging of female viewers to quit their traditional role of homemaker and find employment. The show even emphasizes that *The Pillow Book* would not have come into existence if there had been no working women. Moreover, Sei's success as a writer is regarded as ensuing from her free spirit, original thinking, and creativity, qualities coveted in Japan today.

The episodes of *A Masterpiece in 100 Minutes* focus on passages that resonate with viewers and omit those that center on specific historical events, rituals, and aesthetics related to the Heian period. Emphasizing the relevance of *The Pillow Book* to modern-day Japanese and the commonality of values between the eleventh century and the present,[18] this television program aims at reviving interest in Japan's literary heritage for a reason. The perception conveyed on national television, as well as in manga adaptations and colloquial translations, of *The Pillow Book* as a timeless work with a universal value signals a desire to fill the growing gap between traditional approaches to literary works in Japanese school curricula and students' shifting interests and learning habits. Replacing the "be like her" and "do not be like her" attitudes from previous centuries with a "she is like you" perspective, these recent reimaginings of *The Pillow Book* invite audiences to discover how much they have in common with those who preceded them. Thus, they construct a long cultural continuity between ancient and modern Japan and perpetuate the notion of a unified Japanese ethnic identity. These nationalistic overtones resonate with recent trends in society to cultivate self-esteem and national pride in Japan's youth, who were born or have come of age during the prolonged economic stagnation since the 1990s. At a time when the country is moving toward increased female participation in the labor force while grappling with the strong influence of traditional gender roles, images of Sei as a young working woman who passionately expounds on issues related to female subjectivity not only advocate the work's relevance to present-day life but also offer a source of inspiration to many on their journey of self-discovery.

THE PILLOW BOOK IN WORLD LITERATURE

Outside Japan, *The Pillow Book* has offered a popular theme for writers and filmmakers since the 1980s, as the large number of works inspired by Sei's text, including collections of poems, observations, essays, and films, attests. Most of these works produced before the mid-1990s imitate the style of Sei's writing, have Western protagonists, are set outside Japan, and scarcely allude to the eleventh-century text.[19] Since the late 1990s *The Pillow Book* has offered authors a productive means of using Japan's ancient court culture to construct an imaginary world of erotic fantasies. Through these works of popular culture, a "pillow book" has come to be associated with a woman's diary imbued with erotic overtones. Many of the works produced in the past two decades that have drawn inspiration from Sei's writing focus on female-male relationships, are set in Japan's past, have protagonists who keep erotic diaries, or pillow books, and portray Japanese women as licentious.[20]

Undoubtedly, the geisha fixation since the late 1990s has fostered an image of Japan as an exotic country filled with sexually alluring women. Fueled by Arthur Golden's best seller *Memoirs of a Geisha* (1997) and its film adaptation in 2005, as well as the *maiko* (apprentice geisha) boom in Kyoto, the mass popularity of geisha in the United States has blurred the lines between history and fantasy and perpetuated the stereotype of the sensual exotic Asian woman.[21] In this context, the production of a number of works that construct an erotic image of the Heian woman writer can be viewed as a consequence of the misrepresentation of the geisha world. Another important factor fostering the eroticization of *The Pillow Book* outside Japan is the film *The Pillow Book* (1996) by globally renowned film director Peter Greenaway that attracted much attention around the world in the late 1990s.[22] By means of its beautiful imagery, focus on the art of calligraphy and fetishism, and many love scenes, Greenaway creates an erotic image of the Heian period, *The Pillow Book*, and Sei Shōnagon that reverberates in several historical fiction novels published after the release of the film.

Greenaway initially encountered Sei's writing through Arthur Waley's translation, titled *The Pillow-Book of Sei Shōnagon* (1928).[23] By virtue of this translation *The Pillow Book* made its debut as an independent work in English. It appeared in England in the early twentieth century, when Japan was frequently presented as an aesthetic realm and Japanese art was often viewed as a mirror of Japanese reality. The translation introduces the eleventh-century text using a small portion of passages, "about a quarter" of *The Pillow Book*, in Waley's words.[24] Waley's selection includes a large number of sections that focus on Sei's relationship with male courtiers and remarks about the desirable behavior of a good lover and the time most suited for trysts. In the unabridged version of *The Pillow Book*, there are no passages that explicitly describe Sei's intimate relationship with men, except for a hint of her former relationship with Norimitsu, to whom Sei Shōnagon is said to have been married prior to her service at court. Moreover, in Sei's work these passages are interspersed among narratives on diverse subjects, including depictions of the beauty of nature, lists of various topics, and observations of festivals, religious rituals, and human behavior. Waley's selection of passages thus distorts Sei's text into one permeated with accounts of her relationships, presenting it, and Sei, as focused on her sexuality. He justifies his selection of passages by stating that "omissions have been made only where the original was dull, unintelligible, repetitive, or so packed with allusion that it required an impracticable amount of commentary."[25] In other words, Waley transformed the eleventh-century text into a version he believed would best capture the attention of readers outside Japan.

To demonstrate how different Waley's translation is from Sei Shōnagon's writing, Tsushima Tomoaki translated it back into Japanese. The frequent omission of the subject in Japanese leads to considerable ambiguity. Waley's introduction of a first-person narrator in his translation, however, generates an account based on Sei Shōnagon's own experiences rather than her observations, as Tsushima observes.[26] By viewing *The Pillow Book* as a collection of personal accounts, Waley distills the experiences of various people whom Sei Shōnagon observed into her own personal story. He introduces *The Pillow Book* as a work that "consists partly of reminiscences, partly of entries in diary-form,"[27] while viewing it as "a plain record of facts" and "the most important document of the period."[28] He hails *The Pillow Book* along with *The Tale of Genji* as the two sources of information about Heian Japan but claims that *The Tale of Genji* has "the disadvantage of being fiction."[29] Waley selects and reorders passages chronologically, thereby producing a work reminiscent of a diary but interspersed with his own commentary. Despite his perception of Sei's work as a historical record, he disregards the purposeful omissions of accounts of the actual historical events that occurred at the end of the tenth century, specifically Fujiwara no Michitaka's death, the exile of Empress Teishi's brothers, Empress Teishi's loss of political backing, and the humiliation she endured in the last months of her life. Thus effacing the literary value of Sei Shōnagon's *Pillow Book* and removing it from the context of its creation, Waley transforms it into a diary focused on a woman's relations with men and a "reliable" source documenting life in the Heian period.

Although Waley's translation is incomplete, selective, and remote from its Japanese source, in the past decade it has been republished more frequently than the other two translations of Sei's work, Ivan Morris's and Meredith McKinney's.[30] To readers who are unaware of the outdated nature of Waley's translation, *The Pillow-Book of Sei Shōnagon* functions as the authoritative "version" and shapes their understanding of Japan, its literary heritage, and its people. Because it is the shortest and most accessible translation of the work as a result of its oversimplification of the source text, it is frequently preferred by readers over the other two translations and assigned in courses on world literature and Asian literature.

The image of Sei Shōnagon that Waley creates in his translation resonates with Greenaway's reworking of her into a licentious court lady who recorded her countless trysts in her diary. Greenaway's female protagonist, Nagiko, who lives in the late twentieth century, becomes a modern Sei Shōnagon through the striking similarities between the two.[31] Sei Shōnagon's *Pillow Book* serves as an ultimate source of inspiration for Nagiko, and scenes of her life are often juxtaposed with passages from

Sei Shōnagon's work. *The Pillow Book* appears in the film as a text from Japan's distant past that is a record of Sei's sexual experiences. Among the passages from the eleventh-century text quoted in the film, even the few that she actually penned do not appear in full but are chiseled down to create statements about the relationships between men and women.[32] The remainder of passages through which Sei Shōnagon's *Pillow Book* is introduced to the viewer are centered on discussions of the link between writing and sex.[33] Greenaway mixes citations from Waley's translation with statements he himself has crafted and draws on the image of Heian women as passive and immobile, as presented in Waley's work. Disregarding the political significance of the act of writing in eleventh-century Japan, Greenaway views it as a form of diversion. Nagiko's claim—"Perhaps like Sei Shōnagon I would fill my diary with accounts of all my lovers"—reinforces the image of the Heian text as one featuring Sei's numerous lovers and erotic ruminations (figure 6.2). Thus the film portrays *The Pillow Book* as a text that despite its antiquity continues to inspire modern

FIGURE 6.2 Greenaway's Sei Shōnagon is juxtaposed with the modern-day female protagonist. Peter Greenaway, *The Pillow Book*, 1996

Japanese women. It also imparts to them that sexuality and love of litera-ture are indispensable aspects of womanhood.[34] Greenaway's Sei Shōnagon appears on the screen to add an aura of authenticity to the exotic image of Japan and to justify the perception of Japanese women's hypersexuality as inherent and long established. Her identification with the modern-day protagonist, who is half Japanese, half Chinese, projects an ahistorical and monolithic image of the Asian woman as irresistibly attractive and sensual throughout the film.

The perception of *The Pillow Book* as an erotic diary is perpetuated by way of various adaptations, including *The Pillow Book of Lady Kasa* (2000), a narrative of longing and passion set in the eighth-century imperial court; *The Pillow Book of Lady Wisteria* (2002), in which a seventeenth-century former courtesan from the Yoshiwara pleasure quarter records her trysts with lovers; and *The Pillow Book of the Flower Samurai* (2009), which tells the Cinderella story of a prostitute in the twelfth century. These works of historical fiction claim they are related to Sei's *Pillow Book*, thus creating a lineage of texts related to Japan's past. With their claims to authenticity, they present themselves as rare texts that offer a valuable insight into Japan's history.

In a way reminiscent of later readers' purposeful selection of ele-ments deemed as representative of the writer and her work, I selected only a limited number of texts—among the myriad manifestations of Sei and reworkings of her writing since the eleventh century—to consider what *The Pillow Book* has signified to various audiences over time. My focus on sources from the seventeenth to the early twentieth century was determined by the fact that much of how *The Pillow Book* is taught today arises from constructions originating in the Edo and Meiji periods. Both the scholarly works and texts for mass consumption that I examine here confirm that subsequent rewritings, rather than the "original" text, have kept Sei alive for a millennium, bringing her work to readers far outnum-bering its initial audience.

Notes

1. WHAT IS *THE PILLOW BOOK*?

1. NHK is Japan's national broadcasting organization. *Haru wa akebono* appears as the title of the first section of *The Pillow Book* in many modern editions. Historically, however, the phrase marked the beginning of the work as part of the larger narrative.

2. I use the terms "pleasure quarters" and "pleasure districts" throughout as translations of the Japanese euphemisms *yūkaku* and *yūri*.

3. In addition to the *History's Secret Stories* episode mentioned earlier, another source that describes *The Pillow Book* as a blog is Machiko Midorikawa, "Reading a Heian Blog: A New Translation of *Makura no Sōshi*," review of *The Pillow Book*, by Sei Shōnagon, trans. Meredith McKinney, *Monumenta Nipponica* 63, no. 1 (spring 2008): 143–60.

4. Motosuke belonged to the group of the Five Men of the Pear Chamber (Nashitsubo no Gonin). The other four members were Ōnakatomi no Yoshinobu (921–991), Minamoto no Shitagō (911–983), Sakanoue no Mochiki (d. 957?), and Ki no Tokibumi (dates unknown). Commissioned by Emperor Murakami (926–967, r. 946–967), the five poets and scholars compiled the second imperial anthology of Japanese poetry and added glosses to *The Collection of Ten Thousand Leaves* (*Man'yōshū*, late eighth century) to make it readable in Japanese. The Thirty-Six Poetry Immortals refers to a list of the most accomplished Japanese poets from the eighth century to the mid-Heian period identified by Fujiwara no Kintō in the eleventh century.

5. Miyakawa Yōko, "Fujiwara no Teishi," in *Makura no sōshi daijiten*, ed. Makura no Sōshi Kenkyūkai (Tokyo: Bensei Shuppan, 2001), 538.

6. Paper was a precious commodity in the Heian period.

7. Mitamura Masako, *Makura no sōshi: Hyōgen no ronri* (Tokyo: Yūseidō Shuppan, 1995); Naomi Fukumori, "Sei Shōnagon's *Makura no sōshi*: A Re-visionary History," *Journal of the Association of Teachers of Japanese* 31, no. 1 (April 1997): 1–44.

8. Haruo Shirane, ed., *Traditional Japanese Literature: An Anthology, Beginnings to 1600* (New York: Columbia University Press, 2007), 248.

9. Kigoshi Takashi, "Shutten, gensen, senshō," in *Makura no sōshi: Shosetsu ichiran*, ed. Shioda Ryōhei, 133–64 (Tokyo: Meiji Shoin, 1970); Yahagi Takeshi, "*Makura no sōshi* to kanseki," in Makura no Sōshi Kenkyūkai, *Makura no sōshi daijiten*, 599–615.

10. Joshua S. Mostow, "Mother Tongue and Father Script: Sei Shōnagon and Murasaki Shikibu," in *The Father-Daughter Plot: Japanese Literary Women and the Law of the Father*, ed. Rebecca L. Copeland and Esperanza Ramirez-Christensen (Honolulu: University of Hawai`i Press, 2001), 121–27.

11. Jonathan Chaves, "Chinese Poems in *Wakan rōei shū*," in *Japanese and Chinese Poems to Sing: The "Wakan rōei shū*," trans. and annot. J. Thomas Rimer and Jonathan Chaves (New York: Columbia University Press, 1997), 20–25.

12. Minamoto no Tsunefusa was a middle general of the left from 998 until 1015. See Matsuo Satoshi and Nagai Kazuko, eds., *Makura no sōshi: Nōinbon*, Genbun ando gendaigoyaku shirīzu (Tokyo: Kasama Shoin, 2008), 365.

13. Ikeda Kikan, "*Makura no sōshi* no genkei to sono seiritsu nendai," in *Kenkyū Makura no sōshi* (Tokyo: Shibundō, 1963), 30–31.

14. Matsuo and Nagai, *Makura no sōshi*, 369.

15. Tanaka Jūtarō, "Shohon no denryū," in *Makura no sōshi hikkei*, ed. Kishigami Shinji (Tokyo: Gakutōsha, 1967), 32.

16. Ikeda Kikan, "*Sei Shōnagon Makura no sōshi* genson shohon no kaisetsu," in "*Sei Shōnagon Makura no sōshi* no ihon ni kansuru kenkyū," special issue, *Kokugo to kokubungaku* 5, no. 1 (1928): 83–184

17. Gergana Ivanova, "Textual Variations of Sei Shōnagon's *Makura no sōshi*: Perception of the Text and the Narratorial Voice" (master's thesis, University of Toronto, 2006).

18. Examples include Nagai Kazuko, "Dōtai toshite no *Makura no sōshi*: Honmon to sakusha to," *Kokubun* 91 (August 1999): 10–19; Tsushima Tomoaki, *Dōtai toshite no Makura no sōshi* (Tokyo: Ōfūsha, 2005).

19. Hazama Tetsurō, "*Makura no sōshi* kenkyūshi," in *Gengo, gensen, eikyō, kenkyū*, vol. 4 of *Makura no sōshi kōza*, ed. Yūseidō Henshūbu (Tokyo: Yūseidō, 1976), 304–7.

20. Ikeda Kikan was the first modern scholar to draw attention to the *Sankanbon* textual line by introducing extensively varying manuscripts within it; see Ikeda, "*Sei Shōnagon Makura no sōshi*," 115–61. Two years earlier, a transliteration of two of the *Sankanbon* manuscripts was published for the first time. See Yamagishi Tokuhei, ed., *Sei Shōnagon Makura no sōshi*, in *Nihon bungaku taikei: Kōchū*, vol. 3 (Tokyo: Kokumin Tosho, 1926). In postwar Japan the annotated editions of the *Sankanbon* textual line that were commonly used for research include Tanaka Jūtarō, ed., *Makura no sōshi*, Nihon koten zensho (Tokyo: Asahi Shinbunsha, 1947); Ikeda Kikan and Kishigami Shinji, *Makura no sōshi*, Nihon koten bungaku taikei (Tokyo: Iwanami Shoten, 1958); Ishida Jōji, ed., *Makura no sōshi: Fu gendai goyaku*, 2 vols. (Tokyo: Kadokawa Shoten, 1979–1980); Hagitani Boku, ed., *Makura no sōshi*, 2 vols., Shinchō Nihon koten taisei (Tokyo: Shinchōsha, 1977); Hagitani Boku, *Makura no sōshi kaikan*, 4 vols. (Tokyo: Dōhōsha Shuppan, 1981–1983). Currently Tsushima Tomoaki and Nakajima Wakako, eds., *Shinpen Makura no sōshi* (Tokyo: Ōfūsha, 2010), is the most highly regarded scholarly edition. Not all scholars have regarded *Sankanbon* as the most authoritative textual line.

21. Mitamura Masako, "*Makura no sōshi* no kenkyū no ashibumi," *Nihon bungaku* 31, no. 2 (February 1982): 58–59. In the early 1980s, when this article was published, there were 132 scholarly works on the *Genji* and only 19 on *The Pillow Book*; see Fujimoto Munetoshi, "Kenkyū, hyōronshi," in Makura no Sōshi Kenkyūkai, *Makura no sōshi daijiten*, 823.

22. Stanley Fish, "Interpreting the *Variorum*," in *Is There a Text in This Class? The Authority of Interpretative Communities* (Cambridge, Mass.: Harvard University Press, 1982), 171–72.

23. Mitamura, *Makura no sōshi: Hyōgen no ronri*, 402.

24. Some of these studies include Mark Morris, "Sei Shōnagon's Poetic Catalogues," *Harvard Journal of Asiatic Studies* 40, no. 1 (June 1980): 5–54; Tzvetana Kristeva, "the pillow hook (*the pillow book* as an 'open work')," *Japan Review* 5 (1994): 15–54; Fukumori, "Sei Shōnagon's *Makura no sōshi*"; Edith Sarra, "The Poetics of Voyeurism in *The Pillow Book*," in *Fictions of Femininity: Literary Inventions of Gender in Japanese Court Women's Memoirs*, 222–64 (Stanford, Calif.: Stanford University Press, 1999); and Mostow, "Mother Tongue."

25. Jennifer Guest, "Primers, Commentaries, and Kanbun Literacy in Japanese Literary Culture, 950–1250 CE" (PhD diss., Columbia University, 2013).

26. Murasaki Shikibu served as a lady-in-waiting in the court of Fujiwara no Shōshi, Fujiwara no Michinaga's daughter. Shōshi was a principal consort to Emperor Ichijō. She oversaw the rule of her sons Go-Ichijō (r. 1016–1036) and Emperor Go-Suzaku (r. 1036–1045) and her grandsons Emperor Go-Reizei (r. 1045–1068) and Emperor Go-Sanjō (r. 1068–1072). In 1072, a year

before her death, the throne passed to her great-grandson Emperor Shirakawa (r. 1072–1086).

27. Kigoshi Takashi, "Kōsei e no eikyō: Omo toshite chūsei e no eikyō," in *Makura no sōshi: Shosetsu ichiran*, ed. Shioda Ryōhei, 165–82 (Tokyo: Meiji Shoin, 1970).

28. Neither Fujiwara no Teika nor Fujiwara no Suetsune (1131–1221) commented on *waka* in Sei's *Pillow Book* in their own copies of the work. It seems that their primary interest lay in personal names and years. In Imagawa Ryōshun's (1326–1420?) *Ryōshun isshiden*, attention is drawn to the importance of *waka* in *Tales of Ise*, *The Pillow Book*, and *The Tale of Genji*, as well as the poems included in the first three imperial anthologies of Japanese poetry, the *Kokin wakashū*, the *Gosenshū* (951), and the *Shūishū* (1005–1007), and the private poetry collections of the Thirty-Six Poetry Immortals. See Asada Tōru, "Kagakusho, karonsho," in Makura no Sōshi Kenkyūkai, *Makura no sōshi daijiten*, 717.

29. Rebecca Copeland, discussant comments for panel "Heian Writers and Female Readers," Association for Asian Studies Annual Conference, Chicago, March 2015.

30. Robert H. Brower and Steven D. Carter, trans., *Conversations with Shōtetsu (Shōtetsu monogatari)*, Michigan Monograph Series in Japanese Studies 7 (Ann Arbor: Center for Japanese Studies, University of Michigan, 1992), 96.

31. Linda H. Chance, *Formless in Form: Kenkō, "Tsurezuregusa," and the Rhetoric of Japanese Fragmentary Prose* (Stanford, Calif.: Stanford University Press, 1997), 280.

32. See, for example, Watanabe Minoru, ed., *Makura no sōshi*, Shin Nihon koten bungaku taikei 25 (Tokyo: Iwanami Shoten, 1991), 2.

33. Linda H. Chance, "*Zuihitsu* and Gender: *Tsurezuregusa* and *The Pillow Book*," in *Inventing the Classics: Modernity, National Identity, and Japanese Literature*, ed. Haruo Shirane and Tomi Suzuki, 120–47 (Stanford, Calif.: Stanford University Press: 2000).

34. Hans Robert Jauss, *Toward an Aesthetic of Reception*, trans. Timothy Bahti (Minneapolis: University of Minnesota Press, 1982), 21.

35. Nakajima Wakako, "*Makura no sōshi* 'Kōrohō no yuki' no dan no juyō o megutte: Chūsei, kinsei no setsuwashū o chūshin ni," *Kokubun ronsō* 18 (March 1991): 1–15; Numajiri Toshimichi, *Heian bungaku no hassō to seisei*, Kokugaku Daigaku Daigakuin kenkyū sōsho, Bungaku Kenkyūka 17 (Tokyo: Kokugakuin Daigaku Daigakuin, 2007); Tsushima, *Dōtai*.

36. R. Keller Kimbrough, "Apocryphal Texts and Literary Identity: Sei Shōnagon and *The Matsushima Diary*," *Monumenta Nipponica* 57, no. 2 (summer 2002): 133–71; Valerie Henitiuk, *Worlding Sei Shōnagon: "The Pillow Book" in Translation* (Ottawa: University of Ottawa Press, 2012); Evelyne Lesigne-Audoly, "Du

texte à l'œuvre: L'édition commentée du Livre-oreiller de Sei Shōnagon par Kitamura Kigin (1674)" (PhD diss., INALCO, 2013).

37. Chance, *Formless in Form*; Chance, *"Zuihitsu* and Gender."

38. Michael Emmerich, *The Tale of Genji: Translation, Canonization, and World Literature* (New York: Columbia University Press, 2013), 11.

39. Joshua S. Mostow, *Courtly Visions: "The Ise Stories" and the Politics of Cultural Appropriation*, Japanese Visual Culture 12 (Honolulu: University of Hawai'i Press, 2014), 5.

40. "Pillow" comes from "pillow books" (*makura sōshi* or *makura zōshi*), which served as notebooks for recording casual reflections and observations.

41. Tsushima and Nakajima, *Shinpen Makura no sōshi*, 304. Unless otherwise indicated, all translations are my own.

2. (RE)CONSTRUCTING THE TEXT AND EARLY MODERN SCHOLARSHIP

1. Some recent examples include Kurosawa Hiromitsu and Takeuchi Kaoru, *Kokoro ni gutto kuru Nihon no koten* (Tokyo: NTT Shuppan, 2012); Shimizu Yoshinori, *Gakkō de wa oshiete kurenai Nihon bungakushi* (Tokyo: PHP Kenkyūjo, 2013); and Steven Carter, ed. and trans., *The Columbia Anthology of Japanese Essays: Zuihitsu from the Tenth to the Twenty-First Century* (New York: Columbia University Press, 2014).

2. I borrow Berry's term "common knowledge," which she uses to refer to the ways through which seventeenth-century informational texts presented Japanese society; see Mary Elizabeth Berry, *Japan in Print: Information and Nation in the Early Modern Period* (Berkeley: University of California Press, 2007), 17.

3. The colophon is found in the manuscripts attributed to the *Sankanbon* manuscript lineage.

4. The last sentence seems to have been added by the person who produced this copy of a preexisting manuscript, as suggested by the phrase "the book says" (*to zo hon ni*).

5. Tsushima Tomoaki and Nakajima Wakako, eds., *Shinpen Makura no sōshi* (Tokyo: Ōfūsha, 2010), 304.

6. Episode 136 in both Morris's and McKinney's translations depicts Sei as being viewed as disloyal to Teishi after Tsunefusa's visit to her following Michitaka's death. See Ivan Morris, trans., *The Pillow Book of Sei Shōnagon* (London: Oxford University Press, 1967), 1:149–52; Sei Shōnagon, *The Pillow Book*, trans. Meredith McKinney (New York: Penguin Books, 2006), 143–46; Tsushima and Nakajima, *Shinpen Makura no sōshi*, 171–76 (episode 138). Tsunefusa's proximity to

Michinaga is described in later sources as well, including *Murasaki Shikibu's Diary, A Tale of Flowering Fortunes*, and Michinaga's diary *Records of the Midō Chancellor* (*Midō kanpakki*).

7. Saitō Kiyoe et al., eds., *Makura no sōshi Tsurezuregusa*, Kokugo kokubungaku kenkyūshi taisei 6 (Tokyo: Sanseidō, 1960), 37–38.

8. Matsuo Satoshi and Nagai Kazuko, eds., *Makura no sōshi: Nōinbon*, Genbun ando gendaigoyaku shirīzu (Tokyo: Kasama Shoin, 2008), 369.

9. Watanabe Minoru has conjectured that the book of the princess of the first order may have been the source text for the *Sankanbon* and thus has tried to justify the proximity of the *Sankanbon* to the original text produced by Sei Shōnagon; see Watanabe Minoru, ed., *Makura no sōshi*, Shin Nihon koten bungaku taikei 25 (Tokyo: Iwanami Shoten, 1991), 380–81.

10. Scholars have referred to her as Tachibana no Motoyasu's daughter. Tachibana no Motoyasu is known as Nōin's father. See Nakanishi Kenji, "Den-Nōin-shoji-hon," in *Makura no sōshi daijiten*, ed. Makura no Sōshi Kenkyūkai (Tokyo: Bensei Shuppan, 2001), 85n9. Norinaga is a son to Sei and Tachibana no Norimitsu (b. 965).

11. Kakitani Yūzō, "Sankanbon," in *Makura no sōshi daijiten*, ed. Makura no Sōshi Kenkyūkai (Tokyo: Bensei Shuppan, 2001), 66.

12. Hayami Hiroshi, "Maedakebon," in *Makura no sōshi daijiten*, ed. Makura no Sōshi Kenkyūkai (Tokyo: Bensei Shuppan, 2001), 86.

13. Kusunoki Michitaka, *Makura no sōshi ihon kenkyū* (Tokyo: Kasama Shoin, 1970).

14. Hayami Hiroshi, "Sakaibon," in *Makura no sōshi daijiten*, ed. Makura no Sōshi Kenkyūkai (Tokyo: Bensei Shuppan, 2001), 88–89, 100–101.

15. Sasaki Takahiro, "Teika-bon toshite no *Makura no sōshi*," in *Nihon koten shoshigakuron* (Tokyo: Kasama Shoin, 2016), 412–28.

16. According to the dated postscripts, the text was copied in 1228 (Antei 2), between 1228 and 1447, and in 1447, 1473, and 1583. See Hashimoto Fumio, *Genten o mezashite: Koten bungaku no tame no shoshi* (Tokyo: Kasama Shoin, 1977), 184–94.

17. Tsushima and Nakajima, *Shinpen Makura no sōshi*, 306–7.

18. For an English translation of the work, see Robert H. Brower and Steven D. Carter, trans., *Conversations with Shōtetsu (Shōtetsu monogatari)*, Michigan Monograph Series in Japanese Studies 7 (Ann Arbor: Center for Japanese Studies, University of Michigan, 1992). The mention of a three-volume manuscript of *Makura no sōshi* is included on p. 126.

19. Sasaki, *Nihon koten shoshigakuron*, 404–5. Sasaki has further noted that it would be more accurate to call the *Sankanbon* lineage of manuscripts "Teika's book."

20. I borrow the translation of the title from Lewis Edwin Cook, "Genre Trouble: Medieval Commentaries and Canonization of *The Tale of Genji*," in *Envisioning "The Tale of Genji": Media, Gender, and Cultural Production*, ed. Haruo Shirane (New York: Columbia University Press, 2008), 135.

21. Numajiri Toshimichi, *Heian bungaku no hassō to seisei*, Kokugaku Daigaku Daigakuin kenkyū sōsho, Bungaku Kenkyūka 17 (Tokyo: Kokugakuin Daigaku Daigakuin, 2007), 172.

22. It is arguable whether other commentaries on *The Pillow Book* were produced before 1674. Several titles are mentioned in secondary sources, but none of them have survived. See Hamaguchi Toshihiro, "*Makura no sōshi* chūshakusho kaidai," in *Makura no sōshi daijiten*, ed. Makura no Sōshi Kenkyūkai (Tokyo: Bensei Shuppan, 2001), 790–91.

23. The Kawachi school refers to the family of poets and scholars headed by the governor of Kawachi province, Minamoto no Mitsuyuki (1163–1244).

24. I borrow the translation of the title from Cook, "Genre Trouble," 135.

25. Jamie L. Newhard, *Knowing the Amorous Man: A History of Scholarship on "Tales of Ise,"* Harvard East Asian Monographs 355 (Cambridge, Mass.: Harvard University Press, 2013), 59.

26. What came to be known as the authoritative texts were Fujiwara no Teika's copies in the case of *Ise monogatari* and Teika's and Minamoto no Michiyuki's copies in the case of *Genji monogatari*. See Joshua S. Mostow and Royall Tyler, trans., *The Ise Stories: Ise Monogatari* (Honolulu: University of Hawai`i Press, 2010), 5. See also Royall Tyler, trans., *The Tale of Genji* (New York: Penguin Books, 2003), xix.

27. *Kokatsujiban* refers to books printed using movable type, each font cut from wood or cast from metal. Movable-type printing was used extensively from the late sixteenth to the mid-seventeenth century.

28. The woodblock technique was dominant from around the mid-seventeenth century until the end of the early modern period.

29. Kakitani, "Sankanbon," 63. Scholars refer to this edition as the book of 1649 (*Keian ninenbon*).

30. Lewis Edwin Cook, "The Discipline of Poetry: Authority and Invention in the *Kokindenju*" (PhD diss., Cornell University, 2000), 18.

31. The citation comes from Cook, "The Discipline of Poetry," 22.

32. Haruo Shirane, ed., *Early Modern Japanese Literature: An Anthology, 1600–1900* (New York: Columbia University Press, 2002), 172.

33. Ii Haruki, "Kochūshaku kenkyū no igi," in *Heian bungaku no kochūshaku to juyō*, ed. Jinno Hidenori, Niimi Akihito, and Yokomizo Hiroshi, 1:2–6 (Tokyo: Musashino Shoin, 2008).

34. Shioda Ryōhei, ed., *Shosetsu ichiran Makura no sōshi* (Tokyo: Meiji Shoin, 1970), 188.

35. Watanabe Kenji, *Kinsei daimyō bungeiken kenkyū* (Tokyo: Yagi Shoten, 1997), 177–80.

36. Alternative titles of this annotated edition include *Commentary on "The Pillow Book"* (*Makura no sōshishō*), *Bansai's Commentary* (*Bansaishō*), and *Bansai's Commentary on "The Pillow Book"* (*Makura no sōshi Bansaishō*).

37. The last commentary that used *Shunshoshō* as a base text was *Makura no sōshi shūchū* (1931) by Sekine Masato. See Hamaguchi, *"Makura no sōshi,"* 789–806.

38. Thomas Harper, *"The Moonlit Lake Commentary,"* in *Reading "The Tale of Genji": Sources from the First Millennium*, ed. Thomas Harper and Haruo Shirane (New York: Columbia University Press, 2015), 368–76.

39. The commentary is also known as *Sei Shōnagon's Marginal Notes* (*Sei Shōnagon bōchū*) and *Notes on Gathered Grains of "The Pillow Book"* (*Makura no sōshi shūsuishō*).

40. Shirane, *Early Modern Japanese Literature*, 174–75.

41. For a brief description of each commentary, see Hamaguchi, *"Makura no sōshi,"* 791–97.

42. For the importance of *The Pillow Book* to nineteenth-century national learning scholars, specifically Nagasawa Omotoo (1808–1857) and Nakanishi Tazuki (1810–1864), see Kamei Shin, "Kinsei kōki *Makura no sōshi* kenkyū ippan," *Gazoku* 11 (June 2012): 30–44.

43. Cook, "The Discipline of Poetry," 21, translates the term alternatively as "authorized texts"—i.e., manuscripts with colophons certifying their authority and assessing their authority as the standard text for a given family or lineage.

44. Suzuki Tomotarō, *"Makura no sōshi* shohanpon no honmon no seiritsu: Toku ni Keian hanpon, Bansaishō, Shunshoshō, Bōchūbon ni tsuite," in *Heian jidai bungaku ronsō* (Tokyo: Kasama Shoin, 1968), 494.

45. As I mention in chapter 1, the extant manuscripts of *The Pillow Book* were divided into four textual lines in the 1920s.

46. Suzuki Tomotarō, *"Makura no sōshi,"* 493.

47. Katō Bansai, *Makura no sōshishō*, ed. Kokubun Meicho Kankōkai, Nihon bungaku kochū taisei (Tokyo: Kokubun Meicho Kankōkai, 1934), 1–2.

48. Officially known as the *Kajūji okugakibon*. See Suzuki Tomotarō, *"Makura no sōshi,"* 494.

49. On Yūsai, see Donald Keene, *Seeds in the Heart: Japanese Literature from Earliest Times to the Late Sixteenth Century*, A History of Japanese Literature 1 (New York: Holt, 1993), 1136. After taking the tonsure, Yūsai was known as Priest Gensō (Gensō Hōin).

50. Kitamura Kigin, *Makura no sōshi: Shunshoshō*, ed. Ikeda Kikan (Tokyo: Iwanami Shoten, 1951), 1:36.

51. Bishū is an alternative name for Owari province, situated in the western part of present-day Aichi prefecture.

52. Kitamura, *Makura no sōshi*, 1:36.

53. Kitamura, *Makura no sōshi*, 1:36–37.

54. Kitamura, *Makura no sōshi*, 1:36.

55. Kitamura, *Makura no sōshi*, 1:36–37. According to Kigin, such literary works include poetry collections such as *A Later Collection of Gleanings* (*Goshūishū*, 1086), *A Collection of a Thousand Years* (*Senzai wakashū*, 1188), *A New Collection of Ancient and Modern Poems* (*Shinkokin wakashū*, 1205), *A Collection of Ancient and Modern Poems Continued* (*Shokukokin wakashū*, 1266), and *A Collection of Jeweled Leaves* (*Gyokuyō wakashū*, 1312); poetry treatises such as *The Sovereign's Eightfold Cloud Treatise* (*Yakumo mishō*, thirteenth century) and *Pleasing Selections and Commentaries* (*Etsumokushō*, mid-Kamakura period); as well as the guide to imperial ceremonies and customs *Summary of Court Practices* (*Kinpishō*, 1213–1221) and Kenkō's *Essays in Idleness*.

56. Okanishi Ichū and Katō Bansai, *Makura no sōshi bōchū, Makura no sōshishō*, ed. Muromatsu Iwao et al., Kokubun chūshaku zensho 4 (Tokyo: Sumiya Shobō, 1967), 1.

57. This manuscript is known as the Yūsai transcription in the Hosokawa family collection. See Suzuki Tomotarō, "*Makura no sōshi*," 494. See also Kishigami Shinji et al., eds., *Makura no sōshi, Tsurezuregusa*, Kokugo kokubungaku kenkyūshi taisei 6 (Tokyo: Sanseidō, 1977), 232.

58. Modern scholars have divided the texts from the *Nōinbon* lineage into 323 sections; see Tanaka Jūtarō, *Kōhon Makura no sōshi* (Tokyo: Koten Bunko, 1953–1957); Numajiri Toshimichi, "'*Sei Shōnagon Makura no sōshishō*' no shōdan kubun hōhō," *Nihon Bungaku* 59, no. 5 (May 2010): 42.

59. The content and order of the passages were heavily influenced by the *Sankanbon* text. See Suzuki Tomotarō, "*Makura no sōshi*," 464–65.

60. Katō, *Makura no sōshishō*, 23.

61. Matsuo and Nagai, *Makura no sōshi*, 28–38.

62. In my study of *The Pillow Book* in early modern Japan I follow Ivan Morris's translation because, being based primarily on the *Nōinbon*, it contains all the passages included in the adaptations of the work published during the Edo period. Moreover, the choices he has made when there are multiple possible meanings are closer to what the early modern producers of these adaptations most likely had in mind, as reflected in the illustrations of the adaptations discussed in chapter 4. See Ivan Morris, *The Pillow Book*, 1:5–6, 6–9, 9–13.

63. Bansai divided the episode about Narimasa into seven subsections while combining episodes "On the First Day of the First Month" and "I Enjoy Watching the Officials" into one.

64. Katō, *Makura no sōshishō*, 23.

65. Tsushima Tomoaki, *Dōtai toshite no Makura no sōshi* (Tokyo: Ōfūsha, 2005), 104.

66. Linda H. Chance, *Formless in Form: Kenkō, "Tsurezuregusa," and the Rhetoric of Japanese Fragmentary Prose* (Stanford, Calif.: Stanford University Press, 1997), 70.

67. Katō, *Makura no sōshishō*, 24.

68. Katō, *Makura no sōshishō*, 23.

69. Ivan Morris, *The Pillow Book*, 5; Katō, *Makura no sōshishō*, 23.

70. Katō, *Makura no sōshishō*, 24.

71. Katō, *Makura no sōshishō*, 24.

72. Katō, *Makura no sōshishō*, 27.

73. Katō, *Makura no sōshishō*, 51.

74. Katō, *Makura no sōshishō*, 85.

75. "Seigan chawa" is the title of the second book of *Shōtetsu monogatari*.

76. Brower and Carter, *Conversations with Shōtetsu*, 126.

77. Katō, *Makura no sōshishō*, 2.

78. The translation here is adapted from Linda H. Chance, "*Zuihitsu* and Gender: *Tsurezuregusa* and *The Pillow Book*," in *Inventing the Classics: Modernity, National Identity, and Japanese Literature*, ed. Haruo Shirane and Tomi Suzuki (Stanford, Calif.: Stanford University Press, 2000), 141. See the original in Katō, *Makura no sōshishō*, 2–3.

79. Chance, "*Zuihitsu* and Gender," 141.

80. Regarding Sei, Bansai quotes from *Zoku yotsugi monogatari* and *Jikkinshō*. He retells the episode of Kōro Peak, which highlights Sei's exceptional literary erudition, as recorded in *Jikkinshō*, and presents her as a descendant of a family of poets. This episode is discussed in chapter 4.

81. Kitamura, *Makura no sōshi*, 1:63, 70, 131.

82. Joshua S. Mostow, *Pictures of the Heart: The "Hyakunin Isshu" in Word and Image* (Honolulu: University of Hawai'i Press, 1996), 15.

83. These lists are the focus of the next chapter. I follow the pronunciation *monohazuke* as included in Ijichi Tetsuo, et al., eds., *Haikai daijiten*, rev. 7th ed. (Tokyo: Meiji Shoin, 1961), 752–53.

84. Kitamura, *Makura no sōshi*, 1:35.

85. Kitamura, *Makura no sōshi*, 1:35.

86. Kitamura, *Makura no sōshi*, 1:38.

87. Shirane, *Early Modern Japanese Literature*, 173.

88. Okanishi and Katō, *Makura no sōshi bōchū*, 28.

89. Modern commentaries interpret this passage as containing praise for Sei.

90. This passage is usually read as banter between Narinobu and Sei regarding the bishop.

91. Tanaka Jūtarō used the Yōmei Bunkobon (type 2 text of the *Sankanbon* line) for his commentary on *Makura no sōshi*. He supplemented the missing sections at the opening of that text with "the text formerly in Yatomi Hamao's collection" (type 1 text of the *Sankanbon* line), which is currently held at Sōai University. See Tanaka Jūtarō, ed., *Makura no sōshi*, Nihon koten zensho (Tokyo: Asahi Shinbunsha, 1947). See also Hamaguchi, "*Makura no sōshi*," 806.

92. Mostow, *Pictures of the Heart*, 14.

93. Katō, *Makura no sōshishō*, 3.

94. Okanishi and Katō, *Makura no sōshi bōchū*, 1.

95. Kitamura, *Makura no sōshi*, 1:35.

96. It is unclear how broadly the term *monohazuke* was known in the latter half of the seventeenth century. As a subgenre of *zappai* it gained independence in the eighteenth century, but as a technique in *zappai* composition it had developed much earlier.

97. See Inoue Masami, ed., *Shorin shuppan shoseki mokuroku shūsei*, 3 vols. (Tokyo: Inoue Shobō, 1962). From the late seventeenth century into the early eighteenth, the commentaries appeared as part of "vernacular works" (*kanasho*).

98. Tomiko Yoda, *Gender and National Literature: Heian Texts in the Construction of Japanese Modernity* (Durham, N.C.: Duke University Press, 2004), 37.

99. Yoda, *Gender and National Literature*, 37.

100. Yoda, *Gender and National Literature*, 29, 35.

101. Thomas Harper, trans., "*The Tale of Genji: A Little Jeweled Comb*," in *Reading "The Tale of Genji": Sources from the First Millennium*, ed. Thomas Harper and Haruo Shirane (New York: Columbia University Press, 2015), 455.

102. Harper, "*The Tale of Genji*," 453.

103. Susan Burns, *Before the Nation: Kokugaku and the Imagining of Community in Early Modern Japan* (Durham, N.C.: Duke University Press, 2003), 1.

104. Hazama Tetsurō, "*Makura no sōshi* kenkyūshi," in *Gengo, gensen, eikyō, kenkyū*, vol. 4 of *Makura no sōshi kōza*, ed. Yūseidō Henshūbu, 301–24 (Tokyo: Yūseidō Shuppan, 1976); cited in Hara Masako, "Kamo no Mabuchi no *Makura no sōshi* kō: Mabuchi jihitsu kakiire *Makura no sōshi shunshoshō*," in *Kamo no Mabuchi to sono monryū*, ed. Mabuchi Tanjō Sanbyakunen Kinen Ronbunshū Kankōkai (Tokyo: Heibunsha, 1999), 87.

105. Newhard, *Knowing the Amorous Man*, 4; Harper and Shirane, *Reading "The Tale of Genji*," 383.

106. The translation of the title is taken from Chance, *Formless in Form*, 71. The text appears in Nishio Mitsuo, "Honkoku: Kunitsufumi yoyo no ato," in *Nihon*

bungaku sōkō: Nishio Mitsuo Sensei kanreki kinen ronshū, ed. Nishio Mitsuo Sensei Kanreki Kinenkai, 289–346 (Tokyo: Tōyō Hōki Shuppan, 1968).

107. Nakamura Yukihiko, "Kinsei zuihitsu ni tsuite," in *Kinsei yogo*, vol. 13 of *Nakamura Yukihiko chojutsushū* (Tokyo: Chūō Kōronsha, 1984), 287.

108. Nakamura, "Kinsei zuihitsu ni tsuite," 292.

109. Chance, *Formless in Form*, 73.

110. Ban Kōkei, "Kanden jihitsu," in *Hyakka setsurin zokuhen ge no ichi*, ed. Yoshikawa Hanshichi (Tokyo: Yoshikawa Kōbunkan, 1906), 126.

111. Ban, "Kanden jihitsu."

112. Translation adapted from Chance, *Formless in Form*, 72. See Ishihara Masaaki, "Nennen zuihitsu 1," in *Hyakka setsurin*, 109.

113. Ishihara, "Nennen zuihitsu 1," 210. Chance, *Formless in Form*, 72, explains that, according to Ishihara, "*zuihitsu* is occasional writing that does not call for cross-checking references or exhausting a subject."

114. Chance, *Formless in Form*, 73.

115. Umezawa Waken, *Sei Shōnagon to Murasaki Shikibu* (Tokyo: Kokkōsha, 1902), 151.

116. Rachel DiNitto, "Return of the *Zuihitsu*: Print Culture, Modern Life, and Heterogeneous Narrative in Prewar Japan," *Harvard Journal of Asiatic Studies* 64, no. 2 (December 2004): 253. Some examples of multivolume series on *zuihitsu* include Jinbunkai's *Meiji Taishō zuihitsu senshū* (Selected Meiji and Taishō *zuihitsu*), *Kikō zuihitsu shū* (Collected travel literature and *zuihitsu* essays), *Zuihitsu kansō sōsho* (Library of *zuihitsu* and impressionistic writing).

117. Linda H. Chance, "Japanese Essay," in *Encyclopedia of the Essay*, ed. Tracy Chevalier (London: Fitzroy Dearborn, 1997), 431.

118. Igarashi Chikara, *Shinkokubungakushi* (Tokyo: Waseda Daigaku Shuppanbu, 1912), 155–56. Also cited in Tsushima, *Dōtai*, 73.

119. Tsushima, *Dōtai*, 73.

120. Ikeda Kikan, *Zuihitsu bungaku* (Tokyo: Shibundō, 1968), 231.

3. FROM A GUIDE TO COURT LIFE TO A GUIDE TO THE PLEASURE QUARTERS

1. I borrow the title translation from Robert N. Huey, *Kyōgoku Tamekane: Poetry and Politics in Late Kamakura Japan* (Stanford, Calif.: Stanford University Press, 1989), 192.

2. I borrow the title translation from Esperanza Ramirez-Christensen, *Emptiness and Temporality: Buddhism and Medieval Japanese Poetics* (Stanford, Calif.: Stanford University Press, 2008), 52.

3. Imai Gen'e, *Kazan'in to Sei Shōnagon*, ed. Koga Noriko, vol. 9 of *Imai Gen'e chosakushū*, ed. Imanishi Shūichirō et al. (Tokyo: Kasama Shoin, 2007), 341–42.

4. Ivan Morris, trans., *The Pillow Book of Sei Shōnagon* (London: Oxford University Press, 1967), 1:80 (episode 81); Sei Shōnagon, *The Pillow Book*, trans. Meredith McKinney (New York: Penguin Books, 2006), 75 (episode 80) (McKinney's translation hereafter in these notes cited as McKinney, *The Pillow Book*); Tsushima Tomoaki and Nakajima Wakako, eds., *Shinpen Makura no sōshi* (Tokyo: Ōfūsha, 2010), 99 (episode 82).

5. Ivan Morris, *The Pillow Book*, 1:189 (episode 194); McKinney, *The Pillow Book*, 185 (episode 201); Tsushima and Nakajima, *Shinpen Makura no sōshi*, 221 (episode 203).

6. Mary Elizabeth Berry, *Japan in Print: Information and Nation in the Early Modern Period* (Berkeley: University of California Press, 2007), 52.

7. Ijichi Tetsuo et al., eds., *Haikai daijiten*, rev. 7th ed. (Tokyo: Meiji Shoin, 1961), 252–54.

8. Ijichi, *Haikai daijiten*, 752; Mutō Sadao, "'Monohazuke' zakkō: Medetaki mono wa," *Senryū shinano* 610 (January 1994): 1.

9. Linda Hutcheon, *A Theory of Parody: The Teachings of Twentieth-Century Art Forms* (New York: Methuen, 1985), 27.

10. Joshua S. Mostow, *Courtly Visions: "The Ise Stories" and the Politics of Cultural Appropriation*, Japanese Visual Culture 12 (Honolulu: University of Hawai'i Press, 2014), 203.

11. Examples include *Genji kokagami* (fifteenth century; published several times between 1651 and 1680), *Jūjō Genji* (1650s), and *Osana Genji*. See P. F. Kornicki, "Unsuitable Books for Women? *Genji monogatari* and *Ise monogatari* in Late Seventeenth-Century Japan," *Monumenta Nipponica* 60, no. 2 (summer 2005): 149. See also Satoko Naito, "The Making of Murasaki Shikibu: Constructing Authorship, Gendering Readership, and Legitimizing *The Tale of Genji*" (PhD diss., Columbia University, 2010), 137.

12. For an examination of the functions of these lists in *The Pillow Book* and the influences of the Heian-period literary landscape on their composition, see Mark Morris, "Sei Shōnagon's Poetic Catalogues," *Harvard Journal of Asiatic Studies* 40, no. 1 (June 1980): 5–54.

13. Until the late twentieth century, studies of Edo-period literature were confined largely to the works of Ihara Saikaku (1642–1693), Matsuo Bashō (1644–1694), and Chikamatsu Monzaemon (1653–1725) and were overshadowed by studies and English translations of Heian and medieval literary sources.

14. Linda Hutcheon, A Theory of Adaptation (London: Routledge, 2006), 169.

15. For a translation and a brief introduction to the work, see Edward Putzar, "Inu Makura: The Dog Pillow," *Harvard Journal of Asiatic Studies* 28 (1968): 98–113.

16. Komachiya Teruhiko, "*Inu makura, Mottomo no sōshi, Sei Shōnagon chie no ita*: *Makura no sōshi* no kyōju to rufu," *Kōkō tsūshin tōsho kokugo* 322 (May 1994): 2, defines *inu* as "sham" (*nisete hinaru*).
17. Putzar, "Inu Makura," 100.
18. Mutō, "'Monohazuke' zakkō," 1–6. *Otogishu* served feudal lords as conversational partners and advisers from the fifteenth to the mid-seventeenth century. Nobutada, known for his exceptional calligraphic skills, was the son of the regent Konoe Sakihisa (1536–1612). He served as a regent for about a year following the transfer of the post of shogun from Ieyasu to his son Hidetada (1579–1632), after which he continued to exert political influence on the throne through his nephew Emperor Go-Mizunoo (1611–1629).
19. For more on Sōha's commentary on *Essays in Idleness*, see Linda H. Chance, "Constructing the Classic: *Tsurezuregusa* in Tokugawa Readings," *Journal of the American Oriental Society* 117, no. 1 (January–March 1997): 42.
20. Noma Kōshin, *Kinsei sakka denkō* (Tokyo: Chūō Kōronsha, 1985), 40–45. His reluctance to attribute sole authorship of the work to Sōha sprang from the fact that although not identical to each other, the two manuscripts had been housed in the Konoe family's collection Yōmei Bunko and their production coincided with the period when Nobutada headed the Konoe family.
21. Mutō, "'Monohazuke' zakkō," 1–6.
22. Chance, "Constructing the Classic," 42.
23. See Putzar, "Inu Makura," 101–3. See also Maeda Kingorō and Morita Takeshi, "Inu makura," in *Kanazōshishū*, ed. Maeda Kingorō and Morita Takeshi, Nihon koten bungaku taikei 90 (Tokyo: Iwanami Shoten, 1965), 35–37.
24. Joshua S. Mostow, "The Gender of *Wakashu* and the Grammar of Desire," in *Gender and Power in the Japanese Visual Field*, ed. Joshua S. Mostow, Norman Bryson, and Maribeth Graybill (Honolulu: University of Hawai`i Press, 2003), 2.
25. Margaret H. Childs, "*Chigo Monogatari*: Love Stories or Buddhist Sermons?" *Monumenta Nipponica* 35, no. 2 (summer 1980): 127.
26. I have borrowed the translation of the term *shudō* from Mostow, "Gender of *Wakashu*," 53.
27. For a discussion of male-male relations in terms of difference or sameness between the partners (pederastic or homosexual), see Eve Kosofsky Sedgwick, "Tales of the Avunculate: Queer Tutelage in *The Importance of Being Earnest*," in *Tendencies* (Durham, N.C.: Duke University Press, 1993), 57; cited in Mostow, "Gender of *Wakashu*," 49.
28. Gregory M. Pflugfelder, *Cartographies of Desire: Male-Male Sexuality in Japanese Discourse, 1600–1950* (Berkeley: University of California Press, 1999), 36.

29. Passivity characterized a *wakashu* only in his relations with a *nenja*. When he was involved in a heterosexual relationship, however, he often assumed an active role. See Mostow, "Gender of *Wakashu*," 67–68.

30. Paul Gordon Schalow, "Spiritual Dimensions of Male Beauty in Japanese Buddhism," in *Religion, Homosexuality, and Literature*, ed. Michael L. Stemmeler and José Ignacio Cabezón (Las Colinas, Texas: Monument Press, 1992), 89.

31. Putzar, "Inu Makura," 107. See also Maeda and Morita, "Inu makura," 35.

32. Paul Gordon Schalow, "Theorizing Sex/Gender in Early Modern Japan: Kitamura Kigin's *Maidenflowers* and *Wild Azaleas*," *Japanese Studies* 18, no. 3 (1989): 254.

33. Haruo Shirane, *Traces of Dreams: Landscape, Cultural Memory, and the Poetry of Bashō* (Stanford, Calif.: Stanford University Press, 1998), 8.

34. I have based my translation of the title on a claim in the preface of the work. Specifically, it acknowledges the influence of *The Pillow Book* and *Dog/Fake Pillow* and states that the writer has retained only the right component of the variant character for "pillow" and has therefore named it *Mottomo no sōshi*. My translation of the title emphasizes this "incompleteness" of the character for "pillow."

35. Watanabe Morikuni and Watanabe Kenji, "Mottomo no sōshi," in *Kanazōshishū*, ed. Watanabe Morikuni and Watanabe Kenji, Shin Nihon koten bungaku taikei 74 (Tokyo: Iwanami Shoten, 1991), 54.

36. Noma, *Kinsei sakka denkō*, 45–52.

37. This claim is based on a mention of a prince without an imperial rank (*muhon*) in the colophon.

38. Watanabe and Watanabe, "Mottomo no sōshi," 85–86.

39. J. Thomas Rimer and Jonathan Chaves, trans. and annots., *Japanese and Chinese Poems to Sing: The "Wakan rōei shū"* (New York: Columbia University Press, 1997), 239, poem 803.

40. This opening verse is a variation of a *hokku* by Saitō Tokugen.

41. Some examples of seventeenth-century erotic rewritings of *The Ise Stories* include the courtesan critique *The Funny Man* (*Okashi otoko*, 1662), later renamed *Yoshiwara Ise Stories* (*Yoshiwara Ise monogatari*); the sex manual *Narihira Flirtatious Grasses* (*Narihira taware-gusa*, 1663), and Moronobu's pornographic works. See Mostow, *Courtly Visions*, 243–45. Examples of woodblock prints inspired by *The Tale of Genji* include Sugimura Jihei's (active 1680s–early eighteenth century) *Kashiwagi and the Third Princess* (*Kashiwagi to Onna san no Miya*) and *Tale of Genji Floating World Fukusa Pictures* (*Genji ukiyo fukusa-e*), as well as *Genji Pillows* (*Genji makura*, 1680s). See Keiko Nakamachi, "*Genji* Pictures from Momoyama Painting to Edo Ukiyo-e: Cultural Authority and New Horizons," in *Envisioning "The Tale of Genji": Media, Gender, and Cultural*

Production, ed. Haruo Shirane (New York: Columbia University Press, 2008), 178–203.

42. Kitamura Kigin, *Makura no sōshi: Shunshoshō*, ed. Ikeda Kikan (Tokyo: Iwanami Shoten, 1951), 1:3.

43. Tanaka Jūtarō, *Sei Shōnagon Makura no sōshi kenkyū*, Kasama sōsho 10 (Tokyo: Kasama Shoin, 1942), 521.

44. Hanasaki Kazuo, *Senryū shungashi* (Tokyo: Taihei Shooku, 1989), 40.

45. The character for "pure" (*kiyoraka*) also functions as the family name Sei and thus puns on both contexts here; Hanasaki, *Senryū shungashi*, 40.

46. Tanaka, *Makura no sōshi kenkyū*, 511.

47. Hanasaki, *Senryū shungashi*, 42.

48. Hanasaki, *Senryū shungashi*, 43.

49. Marcia Yonemoto, *Mapping Early Modern Japan: Space, Place, and Culture in the Tokugawa Period (1603–1868)* (Berkeley: University of California Press, 2003), 134.

50. Edo Yoshiwara Sōkan Kankōkai, ed., *Edo Yoshiwara sōkan: Yūjo hyōbanki* (Tokyo: Yagi Shoten, 2010), 1:287.

51. Yonemoto, *Mapping Early Modern Japan*, 134–35, notes that originally *saiken* were appended to courtesan critiques (*yūjo hyōbanki*) but began to be published independently after 1728.

52. Yonemoto, *Mapping Early Modern Japan*, 133.

53. Yonemoto, *Mapping Early Modern Japan*, 137.

54. Shima-no-uchi refers to the entertainment district in Osaka known as Dōtonbori and, more specifically, to an establishment of private courtesans. *Gleanings* consists of twenty-five *mono*-type lists and one *wa*-type list; see Mappira Gomenshi, "*Shūi Makura no sōshi kagaishō* tsūshaku 1," *Kinsei shomin bunka* 11 (1952): 24.

55. Mappira, "*Shūi Makura no sōshi* 1," 25.

56. Mappira Gomenshi, "*Shūi Makura no sōshi kagaishō* tsūshaku 2," *Kinsei shomin bunka* 12 (1952): 28; "Kagaishō," in *Sharebon taisei*, ed. Sharebon Taisei Henshū Iinkai (Tokyo: Chūō Kōronsha, 1979), 3:296.

57. In Ivan Morris's translation, some of the references to writing appear in sections such as "Hateful Things" (section 27) ("I hate people whose letters show disrespect to worldly civilities"), "Unsuitable Things" (section 47) ("Ugly handwriting on red paper"), and "A Young Bachelor" (section 317) (". . . he starts to write his next-morning letter. He does not let his brush run down the paper in a careless scrawl, but puts his heart and soul into the calligraphy").

58. "Maroyama," as it appears in the text, is most likely a typographical error for "Maruyama"; see "Ahō makura kotoba," in *Sharebon taisei*, ed. Sharebon Taisei Henshū Iinkai (Tokyo: Chūō Kōronsha, 1978), 1:239.

59. Ivan Morris, *The Pillow Book*, 1:14. Morris has placed the narrator's thoughts in parentheses in order to keep them separate from the names of the mountains.

60. Yonemoto, *Mapping Early Modern Japan*, 133.

61. "Ahō makura kotoba," 240.

62. J. Scott Miller, "The Hybrid Narrative of Kyōden's *Sharebon*," *Monumenta Nipponica* 43, no. 2 (summer 1988): 134.

63. Gustav Heldt, "Saigyō's Traveling Tale: A Translation of *Saigyō Monogatari*," *Monumenta Nipponica* 52, no. 4 (winter 1997): 514.

64. For other interpretations of the passage, see the following studies: Bernard Faure, *The Power of Denial: Buddhism, Purity, and Gender* (Princeton, N.J.: Princeton University Press, 2003), 265; Janet R. Goodwin, *Selling Songs and Smiles: The Sex Trade in Heian and Kamakura Japan* (Honolulu: University of Hawai`i Press, 2007), 117; Michele Marra, *Representations of Power: The Literary Politics of Medieval Japan* (Honolulu: University of Hawai`i Press, 1993), 94.

65. The earliest version of this episode appears in *Tales of the Past* (*Kojidan*, 1212–1215).

66. Fujimoto Kizan's *The Great Mirror of the Way of Love* (*Shikidō ōkagami*, 1678), an eighteen-volume encyclopedia of the brothel districts throughout Japan, describes Murotsu Port in Harima (present-day Hyōgo prefecture) as a place associated with the origin of prostitution. See Fujimoto Kizan, *Shinpan Shikidō ōkagami*, ed. Shinpan Shikidō Ōkagami Kankōkai (Tokyo: Yagi Shoten, 2006), 407.

67. Terry Kawashima, *Writing Margins: The Textual Construction of Gender in Heian and Kamakura Japan*, Harvard East Asian Monographs 201 (Cambridge, Mass.: Harvard University Asia Center, 2001), 52.

68. "Ahō makura kotoba," 241.

69. "Ahō makura kotoba," 241.

70. The poem appears in *Kokin wakashū* (poem 990) and the *Gunsho ruijū* version of the *Ise shū*. The translation of the poem is from Laurel Rasplica Rodd and Mary Catherine Henkenius, trans., *Kokinshū: A Collection of Poems Ancient and Modern* (Boston: Cheng and Tsui, 2004), 334. The list translation is mine.

71. *Jikkinshō*, vol. 10, story 50.

72. Rodd and Henkenius, *Kokinshū*, 334.

73. According to a version of Japan's creation myth, the heavenly floating bridge (*ama no ukihashi*) is the place where the male deity Izanagi and the female deity Izanami had sexual intercourse for the first time after watching the lovemaking of two wagtails.

74. Kukuri no Mikoto appears in *Nihon shoki*. In the Land of Yomi when Izanami refuses to accompany Izanagi and prefers to stay in the land of the dead, the

deity Kukuri convinces Izanagi to leave. Since she reconciled Izanami and Izanagi, she is considered the deity of matchmaking.

75. "Kagaishō," 302.
76. Matsuo Satoshi and Nagai Kazuko, eds., *Makura no sōshi: Nōinbon*, Genbun ando gendaigoyaku shirīzu (Tokyo: Kasama Shoin, 2008), 366.
77. "Kagaishō," 289.
78. This is an allusion to poem 67 by the Suō Handmaid in *Hyakunin isshu*. See Joshua S. Mostow, *Pictures of the Heart: The "Hyakunin Isshu" in Word and Image* (Honolulu: University of Hawai`i Press, 1996), 340–41. The poem reads as follows:

> With your arm as my pillow
> for no more than a brief
> spring night's dream,
> how I would regret my name
> coming, pointlessly, to 'arm!

79. "Ahō makura kotoba," 238.
80. "Ahō makura kotoba," 240.
81. The title translation is from Goodwin, *Selling Songs*, 13.
82. "Kagaishō," 292
83. Burton Watson, trans., *The Tales of the Heike* (New York: Columbia University Press, 2003), 16.
84. Homi K. Bhabha, *The Location of Culture* (New York: Routledge, 1994), 89.
85. For a detailed discussion, see R. Keller Kimbrough, *Preachers, Poets, Women, and the Way: Izumi Shikibu and the Buddhist Literature of Medieval Japan*, Michigan Monograph Series in Japanese Studies 62 (Ann Arbor: Center for Japanese Studies, University of Michigan, 2008), 62–70, and Kawashima, *Writing Margins*, 130–46. The two scholars discuss Izumi Shikibu's image as a *yūjo* in *Koshikibu* and *Jōruri monogatari*, and Ono no Komachi's representation in *Tamatsukuri Komachi shi sōsuisho* (The prosperity and decline of Tamatsukuri Komachi). See also Saeki Junko, *Yūjo no bunkashi: Hare no onnatachi*, Chūō shinsho 853 (Tokyo: Chūō Kōronsha, 1987), 62–63.
86. Kimbrough, *Preachers, Poets*, 63.
87. Kornicki, "Unsuitable Books," 156–59.
88. Kornicki, "Unsuitable Books," 157–58.
89. Tomiko Yoda, *Gender and National Literature: Heian Texts in the Constructions of Japanese Modernity* (Durham, N.C.: Duke University Press, 2004), 27.
90. Nakamachi, "*Genji* Pictures," 176–78.
91. Yoda, *Gender and National Literature*, 25–30.

92. Amy Stanley, *Selling Women: Prostitution, Markets, and the Household in Early Modern Japan* (Berkeley: University of California Press, 2012), 52.

93. Watanabe Kenji, *Edo sanbyaku nen Yoshiwara no shikitari: Prē bukkusu interijensu* (Tokyo: Seishun Shuppansha, 2004), 127.

94. Yoshiwara stood apart from the other brothels in Edo for the aesthetic pleasures it offered its patrons, and courtly manners were important for all categories of courtesans except the lowest ranking, known as either *kirimise* (partitioned shop) or *zenimise* (cent shop); Watanabe Kenji, *Edo sanbyaku nen*, 50–51.

95. Watanabe Kenji, *Edo sanbyaku nen*, 128–32.

96. Niwa Kenji, "Yūri," in *Genji monogatari no hensōkyoku: Edo no shirabe*, ed. Suzuki Ken'ichi (Tokyo: Miyai Shoten, 2003), 235–38.

97. The title translation is from Mostow, *Courtly Visions*, 253.

98. Called Kōshokushi Naishinnō (Amorous Princess Shokushi).

99. Taihei Shujin, "Fūfu narabi no oka," in *Nishikawa Sukenobu makurabon issō*, Sumizuri ehonsen 2 (Tokyo: Taihei Shooku, 2008), 100.

100. Mostow, *Pictures of the Heart*, 325.

101. Taihei Shujin, "Fūfu narabi no oka," 100.

102. Taihei Shujin, "Fūfu narabi no oka," 106.

103. For examples, see Mostow, *Pictures of the Heart*, 326–27.

4. *THE PILLOW BOOK* FOR EARLY MODERN FEMALE READERS

A substantial portion of this chapter appeared in Gergana Ivanova, "Re-Gendering a Classic: *The Pillow Book* for Early Modern Female Readers," *Japanese Language and Literature* 50 (2016): 105–53.

1. Mitamura Masako, "Tennōsei kara *Makura no sōshi* o yomu," in "*Makura no sōshi*-teki jinsei sekkei," special issue, *Kokubungaku: Kaishaku to kyōzai no kenkyū* 52, no. 6 (2006): 44.

2. The scroll includes the following sections: "When the Lady of the Shigei Sha Entered the Crown Prince's Palace" (section 100) (*Shigeisha tōgū ni*, section 101); "On a Dark, Moonless Night in the Fifth Month" (*Satsuki bakari tsuki mo nō ito kuraki ni*, section 132); "On the Tenth Day of Each Month" (section 128) (*Kotono no otame ni*, section 130); "One Day When the Emperor Visited Her Majesty's Rooms" (section 87) (*Mumyō to iu biwa no okoto*, section 90); two scenes from "Once When Her Majesty Was Residing" (section 83) (*Shiki no mizōshi ni owashimasu koro*, section 84); "When the Emperor Returned from His Visit to Yawata" (section 121) (*Hashitanaki mono*, section 124).

3. For more on the rivalry between the two imperial lines in the thirteenth century, see Michele Marra, *Representations of Power: The Literary Politics of Medieval Japan* (Honolulu: University of Hawai'i Press, 1993), 6–12.

4. Mitamura, "Tennōsei," 46–47. On another monochrome scroll produced in the circle of Retired Emperor Fushimi and its political function, see Joshua S. Mostow, *Courtly Visions: "The Ise Stories" and the Politics of Cultural Appropriation*, Japanese Visual Culture 12 (Honolulu: University of Hawai'i Press, 2014), 129–43.

5. Okanishi Ichū and Katō Bansai, *Makura no sōshi bōchū, Makura no sōshishō*, ed. Muromatsu Iwao et al., Kokubun chūshaku zensho 4 (Tokyo: Sumiya Shobō, 1967).

6. Ivan Morris, trans., *The Pillow Book of Sei Shōnagon* (London: Oxford University Press, 1967), 1:6 (episode 8). See also Tsushima Tomoaki and Nakajima Wakako, eds., *Shinpen Makura no sōshi* (Tokyo: Ōfūsha, 2010), 23 (section 6); Sei Shōnagon, *The Pillow Book*, trans. Meredith McKinney (New York: Penguin Books, 2006), 8 (section 5).

7. Ivan Morris, *The Pillow Book*, 1:15–19 (episode 22). See also Tsushima and Nakajima, *Shinpen Makura no sōshi*, 33–38 (section 21); McKinney, *The Pillow Book*, 17–22 (section 20).

8. Koizumi Yoshinaga, "Learning to Read and Write: A Study of *Tenaraibon*," in *Listen, Copy, Read: Popular Learning in Early Modern Japan*, ed. Matthias Hayek and Annick Horiuchi, Brill's Japanese Studies Library 46 (Leiden: Brill, 2014), 101, defines the genre of *yōbunshō* as "a collection of model official letters and documents on practical matters, more or less ready to use—one just had to insert the proper names, terms, and dates."

9. For a discussion of the role of education in elevating a family's status and increasing a young woman's chance for marriage, see Anne Walthall, "The Life Cycle of Farm Women in Tokugawa Japan," in *Recreating Japanese Women, 1600–1945*, ed. Gail Lee Bernstein (Oakland: University of California Press, 1991), 47–52. See also Eiko Ikegami, *Bonds of Civility: Aesthetic Networks and the Political Origins of Japanese Culture* (Cambridge: Cambridge University Press, 2005), 155–56.

10. Other reasons why these works have been understudied include the marginalization of *The Pillow Book* vis-à-vis the *Genji* and the predominant view of parody as an inferior genre.

11. According to the Union Catalogue of Early Japanese Books (Nihon kotenseki sōgō mokuroku dēta bēsu), http://www.nijl.ac.jp/pages/database/.

12. Marcia Yonemoto, "The Perils of the 'Unpolished Jewel': Defining Women's Roles in Household Management in Early Modern Japan," *U.S.-Japan Women's Journal* 39 (2010): 53.

13. P. F. Kornicki, "Unsuitable Books for Women? *Genji monogatari* and *Ise monogatari* in Late Seventeenth-Century Japan," *Monumenta Nipponica* 60, no. 2 (summer 2005): 160. Kornicki refers to the catalogue of books included in *Shorin shuppan* 1, 160.

14. Matsubara Hidee, *Usuyuki monogatari to otogizōshi kanazōshi*, Kenkyū sōsho 202 (Osaka: Izumi Shoin, 1997), 79–80.

15. A woman's obligations to her father, husband, and son.

16. The seven reasons for which a man could divorce his wife were sterility, adultery, disobedience to her father- or mother-in-law, talkativeness, theft, jealousy, and disease.

17. Very often, however, books fall into more than one category because of the diverse subject matter they include.

18. Kornicki, "Unsuitable Books," 160.

19. Kornicki, "Unsuitable Books," 160.

20. Kornicki, "Unsuitable Books," 152–59.

21. For instance, in the *Moonlit Lake Commentary* (*Kogetsushō*, 1673) Kigin cites Kujō Tanemichi's (1507–1594) commentary *Mōshinshō* (1575) warning *Genji* readers of its moral dangers. See Kornicki, "Unsuitable Books," 165. On the moral implications of *Ise monogatari* and Asai Ryōi's assessment in *Ise monogatari jokai* (after 1655), see Jamie L. Newhard, *Knowing the Amorous Man: A History of Scholarship on "Tales of Ise,"* Harvard East Asian Monographs 355 (Cambridge, Mass.: Harvard University Press, 2013), 139–42.

22. Kitamura Kigin, *Ominaeshi monogatari*, ed. Satō Ritsu, Koten bunko 282 (Tokyo: Koten Bunko, 1975), 222.

23. Kitamura, *Ominaeshi monogatari*, 223–24. The text reads, "If you are diffident with men, strive to improve your comportment! You should not harbor ignoble thoughts, be jealous, and behave selfishly in any way! It is a woman's drawback owing to her shallow-mindedness to be bashful at the beginning of her relationship with a man, but later she opens her heart, and her unseemly behavior becomes visible more and more, and since such conduct can estrange [a man], you should be prudent about such shameful behavior."

24. Joshua S. Mostow, "Illustrated Classical Texts for Women in the Edo Period," in *The Female as Subject: Reading and Writing in Early Modern Japan*, ed. P. F. Kornicki, Mara Patessio, and G. G. Rowley, Michigan Monograph Series in Japanese Studies 70 (Ann Arbor: Center for Japanese Studies, University of Michigan, 2010), 72.

25. Mostow, "Illustrated Classical Texts," 81, 83.

26. Nakano Setsuko, *Kangaeru onnatachi: Kanazōshi kara "Onna daigaku"* (Tokyo: Ōzorasha, 1997), 83–87. For a discussion of the trend of emulating aristocratic culture as revealed in nineteenth-century household encyclopedias, see Toshio

Yokoyama, "In Quest of Civility: Conspicuous Uses of Household Encyclopedias in Nineteenth-Century Japan," *Zinbun* 34, no. 1 (1999): 197–222.

27. Yokota Fuyuhiko, "Imagining Working Women in Early Modern Japan," trans. Mariko Asano Tamanoi, in *Women and Class in Japanese History*, ed. Hitomi Tonomura, Anne Walthall, and Wakita Haruko, Michigan Monograph Series in Japanese Studies 25 (Ann Arbor: Center for Japanese Studies, University of Michigan, 1999), 157.

28. This adaptation does not follow closely any of the extant textual variants in terms of the spelling, the content, order of passages, or the order of the entries within a passage. Tanaka Jūtarō's textual analysis has revealed that the text of *Mount Asahi* bears the strongest resemblance to the *Nōinbon* variant, specifically the 1649 text, and Kigin's *Shunshoshō*, which is based largely on "the book of 1649." See Tanaka Jūtarō, *Sei Shōnagon Makura no sōshi kenkyū*, Kasama sōsho 10 (Tokyo: Kasama Shoin, 1942), 446–48.

29. A full transcription of the work can be found in Tanaka Jūtarō, ed., *Sei Shōnagon inu makurashū*, Koten bunko 49 (Tokyo: Koten Bunko, 1982), 343–57.

30. *Mount Asahi* is the first of two picture books produced through collaboration between Minamoto Sekkō and Nishikawa Sukenobu. The second is titled *Picture Book: Remarks on Warriors* (*Ehon musha bikō*, 1749). Although in *Mount Asahi* Sekkō's name appears at the end of the 1741 preface and is mentioned in the colophon of the 1772 edition of the work, in *Ehon musha bikō* he is listed as the author of the 1749 work.

31. The sections that appear as in *The Pillow Book* are the following: "Common Things That Suddenly Sound Special," "Things That Should Be Small," "Things That People Despise," "Things That Imitate," "Things That Are Hard to Say," "Things That Just Keep Passing By."

32. *Ehon Asahiyama*, vol. 1, 6 *ura*–7 *omote*. See also Tsushima and Nakajima, *Shinpen Makura no sōshi*, 168 (section 135). The translation is from Ivan Morris, *The Pillow Book*, 1:145 (section 133). See also McKinney, *The Pillow Book*, 140 (section 133).

33. *Ehon Asahiyama*, vol. 2, 15 *ura*–16 *omote*. See also Tsushima and Nakajima, *Shinpen Makura no sōshi*, 252–53 (section 260). The translation is from Ivan Morris, *The Pillow Book*, 1:216–17 (section 254). See also McKinney, *The Pillow Book*, 211 (section 257).

34. Some examples include the episodes of the exchange between Fujiwara no Tadanobu (967–1035) and Sei Shōnagon (Tsushima and Nakajima, *Shinpen Makura no sōshi*, 88–89 [section 79]; Ivan Morris, *The Pillow Book*, 1:71–75 [section 78]; McKinney, *The Pillow Book*, 65–67 [section 77]) and between Sei and Fujiwara no Kintō (966–1041) (Tsushima and Nakajima, *Shinpen Makura no*

sōshi, 138–39 [section 103]; Ivan Morris, *The Pillow Book*, 1:120–21 [section 102]; McKinney, *The Pillow Book*, 113–14 [section 101]).

35. This episode appears in section 22 in Morris's translation; see Ivan Morris, *The Pillow Book*, 1:17–19. See also Tsushima and Nakajima, *Shinpen Makura no sōshi*, 33–38 (section 21), and McKinney, *The Pillow Book*, 17–22 (section 20).

36. See Namura Jōhaku, *Onna chōhōki* (Kyoto: Yoshino-ke Abe Jirōbē, 1692), vol. 2, 4 *ura*–5 *omote*. See also *Onna shoreishū* (Kyoto: Yamada Ichirōbē, 1660), 2:13.

37. Takai Ranzan (text), Katsushika Ōi (pictures), *Onna chōhōki* (Edo: Gyokurandō, 1847), 2:14 *omote*.

38. On publishers' and booksellers' catalogues in the Edo period, see Laura Moretti, "The Japanese Early-Modern Publishing Market Unveiled: A Survey of Edo-Period Booksellers' Catalogues," *East Asian Publishing and Society* 2 (2012): 201–3.

39. Yamamoto Yukari, *Kamigata fūzokuga no kenkyū: Nishikawa Sukenobu, Tsukioka Settei o chūshin ni* (Tokyo: Geika Shoin, 2010), 32–33.

40. Yamamoto, *Kamigata fūzokuga no kenkyū*, 33.

41. It is unclear, however, whether Dōyū was involved in the publication of *Picture Book Mount Asahi* only as a publisher or as an editor as well. For a list of works authored by Dōyū and illustrated by Sukenobu, see Yamamoto, *Kamigata fūzokuga no kenkyū*, 256.

42. *Ehon Asahiyama*, vol. 1, 1 *omote*–1 *ura*.

43. Present-day Kagawa prefecture.

44. Although there are no records indicating Sei Shōnagon visited Sanuki or was in the service of Fujiwara no Shōshi, many legends re-create her life after Empress Teishi's death as wandering in Shikoku, specifically in Sanuki and Awa (present-day Tokushima prefecture). In addition, writers and scholars such as Andō Tameakira commented in *Nenzan kibun* that, according to Keichū (1640–1701), Sei spent her old age in Shikoku. See Shioda Ryōhei, ed., *Shosetsu ichiran Makura no sōshi* (Tokyo: Meiji Shoin, 1970), 42–44.

45. This work has been made accessible to modern readers through a 1966 transcription and a 1980 annotated edition that contains a translation into modern Japanese by Hayashi Yoshikazu. See Hayashi Yoshikazu, *Enpon kenkyū: Shigemasa* (Tokyo: Yūkō Shobō, 1966), and Hayashi Yoshikazu, *Hatsuhana, Ehon Haru no akebono*, Hihon Edo bungakusen 9 (Tokyo: Nichirinkaku, 1980). Hayakawa Monta added notes to the original text in 1999 and published an annotated edition accompanied by a partial English translation in 2004. See Hayakawa Monta, ed., *Ehon Haru no akebono* (Tokyo: Kawade Shobō Shinsha, 1999). See also Hayakawa Monta, ed., *Ehon Haru no akebono*, trans. P. Fister and Kuriyama Shigehisa, Nichibunken shozō kinsei enpon shiryō shūsei 3, Nichibunken sōsho 33 (Kyoto: Kokusai Nihon Bunka Kenkyū Sentā, 2004). Both

Hayashi and Hayakawa provide commentary on the illustrations and draw parallels to *Mount Asahi*.

46. Hayakawa, *Ehon Haru no akebono* (2004), 3.

47. Hayashi, *Hatsuhana*, 18. Other works produced collaboratively include *The Jade-Green Curtains in the Crimson Bedroom: Erotic Book of Unchaste Famous Female Poets* (*Suichōkōkei ehon kaikasen*, 1770), which is a parody of *Picture Book: Shells and Famous Poets* (*Ehon kaikasen*, 1759); *Trendy Spring Book: A True Japanese Mirror of Flowery Elegant Words* (*Imayō shunsatsu fūryū enshi ehon tōwa kagami*, 1774), a parody of *Picture Book: A Mirror of Repartees* (*Ehon tōwa kagami*, 1727); and *Penis Stuffed in a Vagina at Daytime: Erotic Book Hime Komatsu* (*Dankon nyomon hiru irizume ehon Hime Komatsu*, 1774), a parody of *Hime Komatsu* (1742).

48. The three poems are from *Shin shūi wakashū* (1363) and *Shin goshūi wakashū* (1375): the poem in book 1 of *Spring Dawn* is poem 954 from *Shin goshūi wakashū*, the poem in book 2 is poem 1329 from *Shin shūi wakashū*, and the poem in book 3 is poem 1197 from *Shin goshūi wakashū*.

49. Hayashi, *Hatsuhana*, 91–92. The translation is mine except for the last line, which I have borrowed from Hayakawa, *Ehon Haru no akebono* (2004), 8. "Spring" here indicates that the book was published on New Year's Day.

50. The latter translation is from Hayakawa, *Ehon Haru no akebono* (2004), 8.

51. Kornicki, "Unsuitable Books" 171, 180, notes that in the late seventeenth century the words *moteasobi* and *nagusami* (amusement) usually signified female reading.

52. One of the reasons for this may have been the perception that erotica was an auspicious object and thus included in a woman's trousseau, or that women, regardless of class, age, or location, were also consumers of *shunga*—as the large number of early modern literary and visual representations of women viewing erotica suggests. See Hayakawa Monta, "Who Were the Audiences for *Shunga*?" in "Shunga: Sex and Humor in Japanese Art and Literature," ed. C. Andrew Gerstle and Timothy Clark, special issue, *Japan Review* 26 (2013): 19, 20–27.

53. *Ehon Asahiyama*, vol. 1, 2 *ura*–3 *omote*. Tsushima and Nakajima, *Shinpen Makura no sōshi*, 143 (section 112). The translation is from Ivan Morris, *The Pillow Book*, 1:124 (section 109). See also McKinney, *The Pillow Book*, 118–19 (section 110).

54. Depending on the edition of *The Pillow Book*, this passage is usually numbered as 109 or 110, but *Mount Asahi*'s publisher decided to open the work with it. The focus on beginnings in the opening of the work may also be related to the fact that the book was published on New Year's Day.

55. Hayashi, *Hatsuhana*, 94.

56. Hayashi, *Hatsuhana*, 96–98. The translation is from Hayakawa, *Ehon Haru no akebono* (2004), 11. The transcription of this dialogue differs from the base text because in breaking the man's speech into two parts. I have adjusted the translation for any discrepancies with the base text.

57. Hayakawa, *Ehon Haru no akebono* (1999), 16.

58. For more on representations of female masturbation, see Anne Walthall, "Masturbation and Discourse on Female Sexual Practices in Early Modern Japan," *Gender and History* 2, no. 1 (April 2009): 1–18.

59. I have modified the translation in Hayakawa, *Ehon Haru no akebono* (2004), 28. Although there the missing subject in the Japanese original has been substituted with "lovers" in the English translation, I prefer to use the word "couple" because of its wide scope, unlike "lovers," whose meaning is often limited to a union out of wedlock.

60. Hayakawa, *Ehon Haru no akebono* (2004), 64.

61. Hayashi, *Hatsuhana*, 256; the translation is from Hayakawa, *Ehon Haru no akebono* (2004), 101.

62. Nakano, *Kangaeru onnatachi*, 24–25.

63. The name O-Taka means "hawk." It also alludes to streetwalkers in Edo, who were called *yudaka* (nighthawks).

64. Hayashi, *Hatsuhana*, 144.

65. Hayashi, *Hatsuhana*, 203.

66. Haruo Shirane, *The Bridge of Dreams: A Poetics of "The Tale of Genji"* (Stanford, Calif.: Stanford University Press, 1987), 190.

67. The name of the character puns on *tsuya*, "intimacy."

68. Hayashi, *Hatsuhana*, 271. Shikijirō's name means "an amorous second son."

69. Hayashi, *Hatsuhana*, 271.

70. Nakano, *Kangaeru onnatachi*, 94–97.

71. Nakano, *Kangaeru onnatachi*, 124. The title translation is from Sumiko Sekiguchi, "Gender in the Meiji Renovation: Confucian 'Lessons for Women' and the Making of Modern Japan," *Social Science Journal Japan* 11, no. 2 (2008): 201–21.

72. Nakano, *Kangaeru onnatachi*, 125.

73. Nakano, *Kangaeru onnatachi*, 126.

74. Andrew Gerstle, *Edo onna no shungabon: En to shō no fūfu shinan* (Tokyo: Heibonsha, 2011), 21–22. Examples of parodies include *Bag of Secrets for Marriage* (*Konrei hiji bukuro*, ca. 1756) and *Great Pleasures for Women and Their Treasure Boxes* (*Onna dairaku takarabeki*, 1751–1763), which are based, respectively, on the books *Bag of Poppies for Marriage* (*Konrei keshibukuro*, 1750) and *The Treasure Chest of Great Learning for Women* (*Onna daigaku takarabako*, 1716).

75. Gerstle, *Edo onna no shungabon*, 108.

76. Gerstle, *Edo onna no shungabon*, 108.

77. Gerstle, *Edo onna no shungabon*, 109.

78. Gerstle, *Edo onna no shungabon*, 222–23.

79. For a discussion of the impact of censorship on the publication of *shunga* after 1722, see Peter Kornicki, *The Book in Japan: A Cultural History from the Beginnings to the Nineteenth Century* (Leiden: Brill, 1998), 350–52.

80. Walthall, "Masturbation and Discourse," 12. One such example that Walthall provides is Matsuho Zankō's *Comprehensive Mirror on the Way of Love* (*Endō tsugan*, 1715).

81. Yonemoto, "Perils of the 'Unpolished Jewel,'" 40.

82. For a different view of the functions of erotica, see Timon Screech, *Sex and the Floating World: Erotic Images in Japan 1700–1820* (Honolulu: University of Hawai`i Press, 1999), 31–38. Screech has argued that in the eighteenth and the early nineteenth centuries *shunga* were used primarily for masturbation. He discounts the possibility that erotic pictures were intended for collective viewing.

83. A full transcription of the work can be found in Emori Ichirō, ed., *Waka, koten bungaku*, vol. 8 of *Edo jidai josei seikatsu ezu daijiten* (Tokyo: Ōzorasha, 1994), 303–15.

84. On Suharaya Mohei and his publishing firm, see Kornicki, *The Book in Japan*, 61, 69, 210–12.

85. Andreas Marks, *Japanese Woodblock Prints: Artists, Publishers, and Masterworks 1680–1900* (Tokyo: Tuttle, 2010), 66.

86. Emori, *Waka, koten bungaku*, 303.

87. Ivan Morris, *The Pillow Book*, 1:243 (section 278); Tsushima and Nakajima, *Shinpen Makura no sōshi*, 282–83 (section 282); and McKinney, *The Pillow Book*, 238 (section 279).

88. Hanabusa Hideki, trans., *Hakushi monjū no hihanteki kenkyū* (Kyoto: Nakamura Insatsu Shuppanbu, 1960).

89. Emori, *Waka, koten bungaku*, 303.

90. The text appears in Emori Ichirō, ed., *Denki, shinkō, hoka*, vol. 9 of *Edo jidai josei seikatsu ezu daijiten* (Tokyo: Ōzorasha, 1994), 182.

91. Emori, *Denki, shinkō, hoka*, 182.

92. The English translation is from Joshua S. Mostow, "*E no gotoshi*: The Picture Simile and the Feminine Re-guard in Japanese Illustrated Romances," *Word and Image* 11, no. 1 (January–March 1995): 44.

93. Mostow, "*E no gotoshi*," 46.

94. For a discussion of courtesans' talents, see Yasutaka Teruoka, "The Pleasure Quarters and Tokugawa Culture," in *Eighteenth Century Japan: Culture and Society*, ed. C. Andrew Gerstle (Richmond, U.K.: Curzon Press, 1989), 10–16.

See also Gotō Takaki, "Kareinaru oiran no bigaku," in *Yoshiwara yūjo no subete*, ed. Watanabe Kenji, Gakken mukku karuta shirīzu (Tokyo: Gakken, 2014), 24–25. Gotō also shows that by the beginning of the eighteenth century high-ranking courtesans' fashions and artistic accomplishments had turned them into role models for commoner women.

95. Such an approach in the instructional manuals for women evokes the training of Kabuki actors in the staging of the feminine roles of *onnagata*. Maki Morinaga, "The Gender of *Onnagata* as the Imitating Imitated: Its Historicity, Performativity, and Involvement in the Circulation of Femininity," *positions* 10, no. 2 (2002): 245–47, argues that portrayers of females on the Kabuki stage become successful not through "somatic characteristics" but by way of "artistic skills of acting" acquired through gender training.

96. Nakano, *Kangaeru onnatachi*, 88–89.

97. The sixteen lists are included in the following sections: "Common Things That Suddenly Sound Special," "Things That Do Not Linger for a Moment," "Pleasing Things," "Things That Are Distant Though Near," "Things That Are Near Though Distant," "Things That Move the Heart," "Depressing Things," "People Who Look as Though Things Are Difficult for Them," "Startling and Disconcerting Things," "Things of Elegant Beauty," "Things Now Useless That Recall a Glorious Past," "Things That Are Frustrating and Embarrassing to Witness," "Things That Are Unpleasant to See," "Things That Make You Feel Nostalgic," "Things That Are Hard to Say," "Unreliable Things."

98. *Ehon Asahiyama*, vol. 1, *ura* 2–*omote* 3. The translation is adapted from Ivan Morris, *The Pillow Book*, 1:124–25 (section 112). See Tsushima and Nakajima, *Shinpen Makura no sōshi*, 144 (section 116), and McKinney, *The Pillow Book*, 119–20 (section 114). Although modern commentators interpret the phrase *kō aru hito no ko* as meaning either "a child full of filial piety" or "a child dressed in mourning for a parent" or both, to Edo commentators the phrase only meant "a child full of filial piety," and hence my choice.

99. Fujii Otoo, *Otogizōshi*, Yūhōdō bunko (Tokyo: Yūhōdō Shoten, 1915).

100. A similar tendency is observed in the illustrations accompanying Sarumaru's poem in the seventeenth-century commentaries on *One Hundred Poets, One Poem Each*. Although the poem centers on the image of a "stag crying for his mate," the illustrations depict a male and female deer together. See Joshua S. Mostow, *Pictures of the Heart: The "Hyakunin Isshu" in Word and Image* (Honolulu: University of Hawai`i Press, 1996), 115–17.

101. The 1818 illustration depicting the woman reaching out with her hand also recalls poem 60 by Koshikibu in the *Hyakunin isshu*. The poem accompanies an anecdote that demonstrates Koshikibu's literary prowess when challenged by Middle Counselor Sadayori. See Mostow, *Pictures of the Heart*, 319–21.

102. For a detailed discussion of the interrelationship between these two trends, see Nakano, *Kangaeru onnatachi*, 79–109.

103. I follow the argument in Barbara Herrnstein Smith, *Contingencies of Value: Alternative Perspectives for Critical Theory* (Cambridge, Mass.: Harvard University Press, 1988), 51, that a work's endurance is determined by "its effectiveness in performing desired/able functions for some set of subjects."

5. SHAPING THE WOMAN WRITER

1. Some texts include Fujiwara no Kintō's (966–1041) poetry collection known as *Kintōshū*, Akazome Emon's *A Tale of Flowering Fortunes* (*Eiga monogatari*, 1028–1034), and the late-Heian historical tale *The Mirror of the Present* (*Imakagami*, ca. 1072).

2. R. Keller Kimbrough, "Apocryphal Texts and Literary Identity: Sei Shōnagon and *The Matsushima Diary*," *Monumenta Nipponica* 57, no. 2 (summer 2002): 135.

3. This episode is described in Ivan Morris, trans., *The Pillow Book of Sei Shōnagon* (London: Oxford University Press, 1967), 1:199 (section 212); Tsushima Tomoaki and Nakajima Wakako, eds., *Shinpen Makura no sōshi* (Tokyo: Ōfūsha, 2010), 234 (section 224); and Sei Shōnagon, *The Pillow Book*, trans. Meredith McKinney (New York: Penguin Books, 2006), 190 (section 222) (McKinney's translation hereafter in these notes cited as McKinney, *The Pillow Book*).

4. Fujiwara no Teishi was pregnant with Princess Bishi (1000–1008).

5. Some studies include Tsushima Tomoaki, *Dōtai toshite no Makura no sōshi* (Tokyo: Ōfūsha, 2005), and Miyazaki Sōhei, *Sei Shōnagon junan no kindai* (Tokyo: Shintensha, 2009).

6. R. Keller Kimbrough, *Preachers, Poets, Women, and the Way: Izumi Shikibu and the Buddhist Literature of Medieval Japan*, Michigan Monograph Series in Japanese Studies 62 (Ann Arbor: Center for Japanese Studies, University of Michigan, 2008), 2.

7. On women and Buddhism, see Michelle Osterfeld Li, *Ambiguous Bodies: Reading the Grotesque in Japanese* Setsuwa *Tales* (Stanford, Calif.: Stanford University Press, 2009), 154–91.

8. Kimbrough, "Apocryphal Texts," 137.

9. Eileen Kato, trans., *Komachi and the Hundred Nights*, in *Twenty Plays of the Nō Theatre*, ed. Donald Keene (New York: Columbia University Press, 1970), 56.

10. On mid-Heian and Kamakura representations of Ono no Komachi, see Terry Kawashima, *Writing Margins: The Textual Construction of Gender in Heian and*

Kamakura Japan, Harvard East Asian Monographs 201 (Cambridge, Mass.: Harvard University Asia Center, 2001), 123–218.

11. Kimbrough, *Preachers, Poets*, 219–43.

12. Richard Bowring, *Murasaki Shikibu: The Tale of Genji*, Landmarks of World Literature, 2nd ed. (Cambridge: Cambridge University Press, 2004), 80–84. For other presentations of Murasaki Shikibu, see Satoko Naito, "The Making of Murasaki Shikibu: Constructing Authorship, Gendering Readership, and Legitimizing *The Tale of Genji*" (PhD diss., Columbia University, 2010).

13. Present-day Tokushima prefecture.

14. Michele Marra, "*Mumyōzōshi*, Part 3," *Monumenta Nipponica* 39, no. 4 (winter 1984): 422.

15. Marra, "*Mumyōzōshi*, Part 3," 424.

16. For an explanation and translation of the whole episode, see Kimbrough, "Apocryphal Texts," 135–36. Through the allusion to the ancient Chinese story recorded in Liu Xiang's (79–8 B.C.E.) *The Strategies of the Warring States* (J. Sengokusaku, Ch. *Zhanguo ce*), Sei Shōnagon demonstrates her knowledge of Chinese literature and underscores her value though she has passed her prime.

17. For a translation of the whole episode, see Kimbrough, "Apocryphal Texts," 136.

18. For a full translation of and introduction to *Matsushima Diary*, see Kimbrough, "Apocryphal Texts," 133–71.

19. Kimbrough, "Apocryphal Texts," 137. The Japanese text is included in Matsuo Satoshi and Nagai Kazuko, eds., *Makura no sōshi: Nōinbon*, Genbun and gendaigoyaku shirīzu (Tokyo: Kasama Shoin, 2008), 470.

20. Kimbrough, *Preachers, Poets*, 138.

21. Kimbrough, *Preachers, Poets*, 138.

22. Richard Bowring, trans., *Murasaki Shikibu: Her Diary and Poetic Memoirs* (Princeton, N.J.: Princeton Library of Asian Translations, 1982), 131.

23. Kawashima, *Writing Margins*, 129

24. Kawashima, *Writing Margins*, 212–14.

25. Roselee Bundy, "Gendering the Court Woman Poet: Pedigree and Portrayal in *Fukurō zōshi*," *Monumenta Nipponica* 67, no. 2 (2012): 204.

26. Bundy, "Gendering," 219.

27. Lisa Raphals, *Sharing the Light: Representations of Women and Virtue in Early China* (Albany: SUNY Press, 1998), 20.

28. Raphals, *Sharing the Light*, 6. Raphals also emphasizes the need to historicize the reception of didactic texts for women, specifically with regard to Confucian and neo-Confucian ideologies. For example, the former upheld "intellectual and ethical excellences as virtues for women," while the latter was concerned with "training women as mothers and its obsession with chastity" (4).

29. Anne Behnke Kinney, trans., *Exemplary Women of Early China: The "Lienü zhuan" of Liu Xiang* (New York: Columbia University Press, 2014), xlvii.

30. The examples are from, respectively, *Hinazuru hyakunin isshu hana monzen* (1756), *Hyakunin isshu jokyōyasabunko* (1769), *Kokin meifu den* (1860–1864), and *Onna yūshoku mibae bunko* (1866).

31. Nakajima Wakako, "*Makura no sōshi* 'Kōrohō no yuki' no dan no juyō o megutte: Chūsei, kinsei no setsuwashū o chūshin ni," *Kokubun ronsō* 18 (March 1991): 13, examines the reception of this episode in a number of *setsuwa* collections from the medieval and early modern periods, such as *Jikkinshō, Etsumokushō, Waka kimyōdan* (1699), *Waka kitoku monogatari* (1699), *Dai Nihonshi* (1809), and *Hyakunin isshu hitoyo gatari* (1833). Nakajima notes that as early as the thirteenth century, when *Jikkinshō* was completed, Empress Teishi was replaced by Emperor Ichijō as the one who makes the allusion to the Chinese poem during the episode. This tendency continued within the *setsuwa* genre until 1809, when *Dai Nihonshi* corrected the mistake and quoted directly from *The Pillow Book*. Within the genre of instruction manuals for women, however, it was not until the Meiji period that Teishi was restored as the original interlocutor.

32. For a study of the work and a partial translation, see John Van Ward Geddes, "A Study of the *Jikkinshō*" (PhD diss., Washington University in St. Louis, 1976). The ten maxims described are as follows: "Be of consistent temperament in your actions," "One should forsake pride," "Do not despise others," "Do not talk too much of the affairs of others," "One should choose one's friends," "One must have principles of loyalty and integrity," "One must carefully consider everything," "One should endure all things," "One should not bear rancor," "One should seek to develop talent and artistic ability."

33. The account of Empress Teishi precedes the episode about Sei, but Sei is the first Heian woman writer who appears in this text.

34. Adapted from Van Ward Geddes, "Study of the *Jikkinshō*," 160–63, following Asami Kazuhiko, ed., *Jikkinshō*, Shinpen Nihon koten bungaku zenshū 51 (Tokyo: Shōgakukan, 1997), 56.

35. Nakajima, "*Makura no sōshi*," 56.

36. Nakajima, "*Makura no sōshi*," 13.

37. The empress's question, "What does the snow of Kōro Peak look like," in *The Pillow Book* is adapted by the author of *Jikkinshō* as, "What does Kōro Peak look like?" See Nakajima, "*Makura no sōshi*," 4.

38. Van Ward Geddes, "Study of the *Jikkinshō*," 116. Japanese text included in Asami, *Jikkinshō*, 17.

39. Nakajima, "*Makura no sōshi*," 5–6.

40. *Hyakunin isshu jokyōyasabunko.*

41. *Onna kanninki yamatobumi* (1713).

42. Kitamura Kigin, *Ominaeshi monogatari* (1661).

43. A tangram is a Chinese puzzle that consists of a square cut into five triangles, one square, and one rhomboid, which can be put together to form various shapes.

44. Tanaka Jūtarō, *Sei Shōnagon inu makurashū*, Koten bunko 49 (Tokyo: Koten Bunko, 1982), 361.

45. See *Nihon kokugo daijiten* (The great dictionary of the Japanese language), JapanKnowledge, http://japanknowledge.com/lib/display/?lid=200202b2d3ac ou9WHZ79. *Nihon kokugo daijiten* also points out that the game is mentioned in Kinga Baitei's *Yanagi's Hair Comb* (*Yanagi no yokogushi*, 1853) and Higuchi Ichiyō's *Growing Up* (*Takekurabe*, 1895–1896).

46. Paul Gordon Schalow, "Formulating a Theory of Women's Writing in 17th-Century Japan: Kitamura Kigin's *Ominaeshi monogatari* (Tales of the Maiden-flower)," *Early Modern Japan* 5, no. 2 (December 1995): 18.

47. The work features the following Heian poets: Kii of Princess Yūshi's Household (Yūshi Naishinnō-ke no Kii, dates unknown), the Suō Handmaid (Suō no Naishi, d. 1110?), Taira no Nakaki's Daughter (Taira no Nakaki no Musume, dates unknown), Handmaid Koshikibu (Koshikibu Naishi, d. 1025), Prince Yasusuke's Mother (Yasusuke Ō no Haha, dates unknown), Murasaki Shikibu, Lady Koben (Koben, dates unknown), Princess Senshi (Senshi Shinnō, 964–1035), Fujiwara no Toshinari's Daughter (Toshinari-kyō no Musume, dates unknown), Aka-zome Emon, Lady Daibu (Kenreimon'in Ukyō no Daibu, ca. 1157–1233), and Izumi Shikibu. Among the other women included are Yamato Hime, Konoha-nasakuya Hime, Oshisaka Ōnakatsu Hime, the legendary Sotoori Hime, and Tachibana no Kachiko (Empress Danrin, 786–850). Kii of Princess Yūshi's Household served Princess Yūshi (1038–1105). Her poem appears as poem 72 in *One Hundred Poets, One Poem Each*; see Joshua S. Mostow, trans., *Pictures of the Heart: The "Hyakunin Isshu" in Word and Image* (Honolulu: University of Hawai`i Press, 1996), 354–56. The Suō Handmaid's poem appears as poem 67 in *One Hundred Poets, One Poem Each*; see Mostow, *Pictures of the Heart*, 340–42. Taira no Nakaki's Daughter was a poet active in the mid-Heian period. Hand-maid Koshikibu was Izumi Shikibu's daughter. Her poem appears as poem 60 in *One Hundred Poets, One Poem Each*; see Mostow, *Pictures of the Heart*, 319–20. Prince Yasusuke's Mother, also known as Shijōnomiya no Chikuzen, was Ise Tayu's daughter. She was active from the late eleventh to early twelfth century. Lady Koben also served Princess Yūshi. Princess Senshi was Emperor Muraka-mi's daughter and a prolific poet. Konohanasakuya Hime appears in Japanese mythology as the daughter of the mountain deity. Oshisaka Ōnakatsu Hime was an empress to Emperor Ingyō (r. 410–453). Sotoori Hime was a concubine to Emperor Ingyō and Ōnakatsu Hime's younger sister. Tachibana no Kachiko was Emperor Saga's wife.

48. Kigin's defense of the moral value of *The Pillow Book* is discussed in the preceding chapter.

49. Kintō's verse reads as follows:

> And for a moment in my heart
> I feel that spring has come.

Sei responds as follows:

> As though pretending to be blooms
> The snow flakes scatter in the wintry sky.

The translation is from Ivan Morris, *The Pillow Book*, 1:120–21. Both verses allude to Bo Juyi's poem "Snow in the South," included in vol. 14 of *Hakushi monjū*. The poem reads as follows:

> At the third hour a great snow comes tumbling from chilly clouds.
> The second month brings a tiny touch of spring to the mountains.

The translation is from McKinney, *The Pillow Book*, episode 101, 326n2.

50. The officials known as the Four Counselors are Minamoto no Toshikata, Fujiwara no Kintō, Fujiwara no Narinobu, and Fujiwara no Yukinari.

51. On this office, see Joshua S. Mostow, "Mother Tongue and Father Script: The Relationship of Sei Shōnagon and Murasaki Shikibu to Their Fathers and Chinese Letters," in *The Father-Daughter Plot: Japanese Literary Women and the Law of the Father*, ed. Rebecca L. Copeland and Esperanza Ramirez-Christensen (Honolulu: University of Hawai`i Press, 2001), 123.

52. Kitamura Kigin, *Ominaeshi monogatari*, ed. Satō Ritsu, Koten bunko 282 (Tokyo: Koten Bunko, 1975), 220–21.

53. The note in Kigin's commentary reads, "These should be the empress's words. However, in Mototoshi's *Etsumokushō* they appear as the emperor's remark." See Kitamura Kigin, *Makura no sōshi: Shunshoshō*, ed. Ikeda Kikan (Tokyo: Iwanami Shoten, 1951), 3:92.

54. Kigin, *Ominaeshi monogatari* (1975), 221.

55. Kinsei Bungaku Shoshi Kenkyūkai, ed., *Kinsei bungaku shiryō ruijū: Kanazōshi hen 7, Honchō jokan 3* (Tokyo: Benseisha, 1972), 39.

56. Emori Ichirō, ed., *Denki, shinkō, hoka*, vol. 9 of *Edo jidai josei seikatsu ezu daijiten* (Tokyo: Ōzorasha, 1994), 243–45.

57. Ishikawa Matsutarō, ed., "*Jokyō bunshō kagami*," in *Joshi yō ōrai 12*, vol. 92 of *Ōraimono taikei* (Tokyo: Ōzorasha, 1994).

58. This is the standard way of portraying Murasaki Shikibu. Likewise, in some conduct books for women, Murasaki Shikibu is introduced via the episode of the snow of Kōro Peak. This confusion between the images of the two writers

suggests that to the authors of educational books for women, Murasaki and Sei symbolized the talented woman writer of the past rather than being perceived as two different literary women with distinct writing styles.

59. For a detailed study of the images of Sei in Edo-period books for women, see Gergana Ivanova, "Knowing Women: Sei Shōnagon's *Makura no sōshi* in Early-Modern Japan" (PhD diss., University of British Columbia, 2012), 175–221.

60. Haruo Shirane, *Early Modern Japanese Literature: An Anthology, 1600–1900* (New York: Columbia University Press, 2002), 360.

61. Naito, "Making of Murasaki Shikibu," 6.

62. Naito, "Making of Murasaki Shikibu," 194.

63. Miyazaki Sōhei, *Sei Shōnagon to Murasaki Shikibu: Sono taihiron josetsu* (Tokyo: Chōbunsha, 1993), 27.

64. Bowring, *Murasaki Shikibu: Her Diary*, 131–32.

65. Patrick W. Caddeau, *Appraising Genji: Literary Criticism and Cultural Anxiety in the Age of the Last Samurai* (Albany: SUNY Press, 2006), 24–25. Also, Miyazaki, *Sei Shōnagon to Murasaki Shikibu*, 28, notes that only Hagiwara Hiromichi's (1815–1863) *A Critical Appraisal of Genji* (*Genji monogatari hyōshaku*, 1854–1861) in the Edo period affirms Tameakira's view of Sei by quoting directly from *Seven Essays on Murasaki Shikibu*.

66. Sharalyn Orbaugh, "The Problem of the Modern Subject," in *The Columbia Companion to Modern East Asian Literature*, ed. Joshua S. Mostow et al. (New York: Columbia University Press, 2003), 24–35.

67. Sharalyn Orbaugh, "Gender, Family, and Sexualities in Modern Literature," in Mostow, *Columbia Companion*, 43.

68. Rebecca L. Copeland, *Lost Leaves: Women Writers of Meiji Japan* (Honolulu: University of Hawai`i Press, 2000), 11.

69. They include Ueda Kazutoshi's *Kokubungaku* (1890); Haga Yaichi and Tachibana Senzaburō's *Kokubungaku tokuhon* (1890); Ochiai Naobumi, Hagino Yoshiyuki, and Konakamura Yoshikata's *Nihon bungaku zensho* (1890–1892); and Mikami Sanji and Takatsu Kuwasaburō's *Nihon bungakushi* (1890). See Tomi Suzuki, "Gender and Genre: Modern Literary Histories and Women's Diary Literature," in *Inventing the Classics: Modernity, National Identity, and Japanese Literature*, ed. Haruo Shirane and Tomi Suzuki (Stanford, Calif.: Stanford University Press, 2000), 74.

70. Tomi Suzuki, "Gender and Genre," 74.

71. Tomi Suzuki, "Gender and Genre," 74.

72. For a discussion of shifting assessments of Heian literature in the Meiji period, see Tomi Suzuki, "*The Tale of Genji*, National Literature, Language, and Modernism," in *Envisioning "The Tale of Genji": Media, Gender, and Cultural Production*, ed. Haruo Shirane (New York: Columbia University Press, 2008), 266.

73. For discussions of the so-called new woman and Meiji schoolgirl, see, respectively, Jan Bardsley, *The Bluestockings of Japan: New Woman Essays and Fiction from Seitō 1911–1916*, Michigan Monograph Series in Japanese Studies 60 (Ann Arbor: Center for Japanese Studies, University of Michigan, 2007), 1–21, and Rebecca L. Copeland, "Fashioning the Feminine: Images of the Modern Girl Student in Meiji Japan," *U.S.-Japan Women's Journal* 30/31 (2006): 13–35.

74. In the emerging ideology of "good wives and wise mothers" women were to "provide the religious and moral foundations of the home, educating their children and acting as the 'better half' to their husbands"; Sharon L. Sievers, *Flowers in Salt: The Beginnings of Feminist Consciousness in Modern Japan* (Stanford, Calif.: Stanford University Press, 1983), 22.

75. Tomiko Yoda, *Gender and National Literature: Heian Texts in the Constructions of Japanese Modernity* (Durham, N.C.: Duke University Press, 2004), 42.

76. Mikami Sanji and Takatsu Kuwasaburō, *Nihon bungakushi* (Tokyo: Kinkōdō, 1890), 1:322.

77. Mikami and Takatsu, *Nihon bungakushi*, 1:322.

78. Mikami and Takatsu, *Nihon bungakushi*, 1:322.

79. Haga Yaichi, *Kokubungakushi jikkō* (Tokyo: Fuzanbō, 1899), 120.

80. Haga, *Kokubungakushi jikkō*, 121.

81. Haga, *Kokubungakushi jikkō*, 121, also describes *The Pillow Book* as concise, original, and powerful.

82. Despite his negative view of Sei, Haga praises Sei's and Murasaki's ability to read Chinese and thinks highly of the fact that both women grew up in families of scholars and had access to education.

83. Umezawa Waken, *Sei Shōnagon to Murasaki Shikibu* (Tokyo: Kokkōsha, 1902). Among the many titles, some examples include Miyazaki Sōhei, *Sei Shōnagon to Murasaki Shikibu: Sono taihiron josetsu* (Tokyo: Chōbunsha, 1993); Suzuki Hideo, *Sei Shōnagon to Murasaki Shikibu: Ōchō joryū bungaku no sekai* (Tokyo: Hōsō Daigaku Kyōiku Shinkōkai, 1998); Konishi Seiichi, *Murasaki Shikibu to Sei Shōnagon: Kizoku ga sakaeta jidai ni*, NHK Ningen Nihonshi (Tokyo: Rironsha, 2003); Uchida Seiko, *Sei Shōnagon Murasaki Shikibu: Ōchō inuha onna vs nekoha onna* (Tokyo: Nihon Bungakukan, 2008); Okuyama Kyōko, *Sei Shōnagon to Murasaki Shikibu: Sennen mae kara ninki sakka*, Denki shirīzu (Tokyo: Shūeisha Mirai Bunko, 2014); Maruyama Yumiko, *Sei Shōnagon to Murasaki Shikibu: Wakan konkō no jidai no miya no nyōbō* (Tokyo: Yamakawa Shuppansha, 2015). In addition, a large number of articles with this same title have been published.

84. Umezawa, *Sei Shōnagon to Murasaki Shikibu*, 153.

85. Umezawa, *Sei Shōnagon to Murasaki Shikibu*, 382.

86. For a discussion of the representation of the "bad" schoolgirl in Meiji print media, see Melanie Czarnecki, "Bad Girls from Good Families: The Degenerate Meiji Schoolgirl," in *Bad Girls of Japan*, ed. Laura Miller and Jan Bardsley, 49–63 (New York: Palgrave Macmillan, 2005).

87. Umezawa, *Sei Shōnagon to Murasaki Shikibu*, 27, 381.

88. Umezawa, *Sei Shōnagon to Murasaki Shikibu*, 93. Although Umezawa draws his examples from passages in which Sei deflects the advances of elite male courtiers, his reading of these passages presents her as promiscuous and amorous.

89. Umezawa, *Sei Shōnagon to Murasaki Shikibu*, 203.

90. Umezawa, *Sei Shōnagon to Murasaki Shikibu*, 200.

91. Fujioka Sakutarō, "Makura no sōshi," in *Kokubungaku zenshi: Heianchō hen*, ed. Akiyama Ken, Tōyō bunko 247 (Tokyo: Heibonsha, 1974), 2:77–78.

92. See a reading of *The Pillow Book* as a political memoir in Joshua Mostow, "Japanese *Nikki* as Political Memoirs," in *Political Memoir: Essays on the Politics of Memory*, ed. George Egerton (London: Cass, 1994), 112. Fujioka Sakutarō, "Genji monogatari 3: Murasaki shikibu," in *Kokubungaku zenshi: Heianchō hen*, ed. Akiyama Ken, Tōyō bunko 247 (Tokyo: Heibonsha, 1974), 2:133, takes a different approach to introducing *The Tale of Genji*, devoting three chapters to it. In the chapter describing Murasaki Shikibu's life, he asserts that although she had extraordinary knowledge of Chinese, she did not show off and commends her for trying to hide it. He states that she was not boastful like Sei and not amorous like Izumi Shikibu but chaste and righteous.

93. Fujimoto Munetoshi, "Kenkyū, hyōronshi," in *Makura no sōshi daijiten*, ed. Makura no Sōshi Kenkyūkai, 823–35 (Tokyo: Bensei Shuppan, 2001).

94. Kaigo Tokiomi, ed., *Nihon kyōkasho taikei: Kindai-hen 7, Kokugo 4* (Tokyo: Kōdansha, 1963), 172–73.

95. Kaigo, *Nihon kyōkasho taikei*, 172–73.

96. Kaigo, *Nihon kyōkasho taikei*, 172–73.

97. Gregory M. Pflugfelder, *Cartographies of Desire: Male-Male Sexuality in Japanese Discourse, 1600–1950* (Berkeley: University of California Press, 1999), 193.

98. Copeland, *Lost Leaves*, 3.

99. *Jogaku zasshi*, August 8, 1885, 22–23.

100. *Jogaku zasshi*, November 10, 1885, 151–52.

101. *Jogaku zasshi*, February 15, 1886, 54–55.

102. Hebizō and Umino Nagiko, *Nihonjin nara shitte okitai Nihon bungaku: Yamato Takeru kara Kenkō made jinbutsu de yomu koten* (Tokyo: Gentōsha, 2011), 8. This comic book introduces nine Japanese literary works from the eighth to the fourteenth century, including *The Pillow Book*, *Murasaki Shikibu's Diary*, *Essays in Idleness*, *Tales of Now and Then* (*Konjaku monogatari*, twelfth century), presenting them as autobiographies or narratives based on historical

facts. In a fashion similar to the approach of Meiji and Taishō scholars, the work creates images of the authors of the featured texts based on their writing.

103. Komukai Yumiko, *Honjitsu mo ito okashi Makura no sōshi* (Tokyo: Kadokawa Shoten, 2014). This comic book addresses the fact that *The Pillow Book* is widely known merely for its opening words, "In spring, the dawn," and introduces diary-like passages from it to convince readers of the work's rich and intriguing content. These passages draw attention to Sei's personality, presenting her not as a woman who lived a thousand years ago but in a way contemporary readers can easily relate to.

104. This program, intended for elementary school students, features Kabuki and film actor Nakamura Shidō II introducing famous figures from Japanese history.

6. NEW MARKETS FOR JAPANESE CLASSICS

1. One example is the amulets associated with Sei Shōnagon Shrine on the grounds of Kurumazaki Shrine in Kyoto. The amulets feature a woman against a pink background dressed in a loose garment reminiscent of the Heian period.

2. Bandō Tomoko, "Kokugoka kyōin yōsei katei de deau *Makura no sōshi* 3," *Yamaguchi Daigaku Kyōiku Gakubu Fuzoku Kyōiku Jissen Sōgō Sentā kenkyū kiyō* 39 (2015): 63.

3. Ministry of Education, Culture, Sports, Science and Technology, http://www .mext.go.jp/a_menu/shotou/new-cs/qa/__icsFiles/afieldfile/2011/03/30 /1304463_001.pdf.

4. Komori Kiyoshi, "Kokugo kyōiku no naka no *Makura no sōshi*," in *Makura no sōshi: Sōzō to shinsei*, ed. Tsushima Tomoaki and Komori Kiyoshi (Tokyo: Kanrin Shobō, 2011), 268.

5. Hashimoto Osamu, *Momojiri goyaku Makura no sōshi*, 3 vols. (Tokyo: Kawade Bunko, 2007).

6. Hashimoto, *Momojiri goyaku*, 1:13–14.

7. Hashimoto, *Momojiri goyaku*, 1:17–18.

8. Hashimoto, *Momojiri goyaku*, 1:18.

9. Hashimoto, *Momojiri goyaku*, 1:17.

10. Hashimoto, *Momojiri goyaku*, 1:20.

11. Mendō Kazuki, *Makura no sōshi*, NHK Manga de yomu koten 1 (Tokyo: Hōmusha, 2006), 352.

12. Variety Art Works, *Makura no sōshi*, Manga de dokuha 77 (Tokyo: Īsuto Puresu, 2014).

13. Akatsuka Fujio, *Makura no sōshi*, Akatsuka Fujio no koten nyūmon (Tokyo: Gakushū Kenkyūsha, 2001).

14. Variety Art Works, *Makura no sōshi*.

15. Komukai Yumiko, *Honjitsu mo ito okashi!! Makura no sōshi* (Tokyo: Kadokawa Shoten, 2014).

16. Akatsuka, *Makura no sōshi*.

17. Hebizō and Umino Nagiko, *Nihonjin nara shitte okitai Nihon bungaku: Yamato Takeru kara Kenkō made jinbutsu de yomu koten* (Tokyo: Gentōsha, 2011), 8.

18. The television hosts and guest speaker frequently exclaim, "Just like us!" (*watashitachi to onaji yō ni*) while discussing *The Pillow Book*.

19. Examples include Carol Tinker, *The Pillow Book of Carol Tinker* (Santa Barbara, Calif.: Cadmus, 1980); Barry Gifford, *Landscape with Traveler: The Pillow Book of Francis Reeves* (New York: Dutton, 1980); Judith Copithorne, *Miss Tree's Pillowbook: Images, Poem Drawings* (Vancouver, Can.: Intermedia, 1971); and Rosellen Brown, *Cora Fry's Pillow Book* (New York: Farrar, Straus and Giroux, 1995). Alison Fell, *The Pillow Boy of the Lady Onogoro* (New York: Harcourt Brace, 1994), is the only exception in being staged in Japan's past.

20. Works of historical fiction include Barrie Sherwood, *The Pillow Book of Lady Kasa* (Montreal: DC Books, 2000); Laura Joh Rowland, *The Pillow Book of Lady Wisteria* (New York: St. Martin's Press, 2002); and Barbara Lazar, *The Pillow Book of the Flower Samurai* (London: Headline, 2013).

21. Anne Allison, "Memoirs of the Orient," *Journal of Japanese Studies* 27, no. 2 (summer 2001): 381–98. See also Jan Bardsley, "Maiko Boom: The Revival of Kyoto's Novice Geisha," *Japan Studies Review* 15 (2011): 35–60. I am indebted to Laura Miller for suggesting that geisha orientalism may also have shaped representations of Heian women outside Japan.

22. Among some of the awards are the Golden Space Needle Award for Best Director (Seattle International Film Festival, 1996); Best Film and Best Cinematography (Sitges, Catalonian International Film Festival, 1996); and London Critics' Circle Film Award for Best Actor of the Year (1997).

23. Ō Aimi, *Pītā Gurīnawē no Makura no sōshi: Za pirōbukku satsuei nisshi* (Tokyo: Shimizu Shoin, 1997), 169. When Greenaway read *The Pillow Book* in the late 1950s, Arthur Waley's was the only English translation of the work.

24. Arthur Waley, *The Pillow Book of Sei Shōnagon* (Tokyo: Tuttle, 2011), 21.

25. Waley, *The Pillow Book*, 21.

26. Tsushima Tomoaki, *Weirī de yomu Makura no sōshi* (Tokyo: Kanae Shobō, 2002), 141–42.

27. Waley, *The Pillow Book*, 32.

28. Waley, *The Pillow Book*, 19.

29. Waley, *The Pillow Book*, 31.

30. Ivan Morris, trans., *The Pillow Book of Sei Shōnagon*, 2 vols. (London: Oxford University Press, 1967); Sei Shōnagon, *The Pillow Book*, trans. Meredith McKinney (New York: Penguin Books, 2006).

31. For example, their names and their fathers' names are identical. Sei Shōnagon is a sobriquet made up of the first character of her family name and characters corresponding to "lesser captain," a position probably held by one of her male relatives. This name was given to her upon commencement of court service. Some scholars have suggested the name Nagiko as her real name, although there is no convincing evidence. In addition, Nagiko's father is named Kiyohara no Motosuke, exactly as for Sei's father. Just as Sei Shōnagon's father was a prominent literary scholar, Nagiko's father is a calligrapher and writer. Both women hold elite employment—one as an attendant in court, the other as a high-end fashion model. Moreover, both women are fascinated by literature, and just as Sei Shōnagon is well versed in classical Chinese, Nagiko speaks Mandarin and English in addition to Japanese.

32. "Elegant Things" and "Splendid Things" are among the very few passages authored by Sei that appear in Greenaway's film.

33. The following statement is only one of the many examples of statements falsely ascribed to Sei Shōnagon in order to reinforce her image as a frivolous and hypersexual woman: "The smell of white paper is like the scent of skin of a new lover who has just paid a surprise visit out of a rainy garden. And the black ink is like lacquered hair. And the quill? Well, the quill is like that instrument of pleasure whose purpose is never in doubt but whose surprising efficiency one always, always forgets."

34. For a detailed analysis of the reception of *The Pillow Book* outside Japan, see Gergana Ivanova, "Eiyaku sareta *Makura no sōshi* ga tsukuridashita taishū bunka," *Kaigai Heian bungaku jānaru* 2 (2015): 11–21.

Bibliography

"Ahō makura kotoba." In *Sharebon taisei*, ed. Sharebon Taisei Henshū Iinkai, 1:237–59. Tokyo: Chūō Kōronsha, 1978.

Akatsuka Fujio. *Makura no sōshi*. Akatsuka Fujio no koten nyūmon. Tokyo: Gakushū Kenkyūsha, 2001.

Allison, Anne. "Memoirs of the Orient." *Journal of Japanese Studies* 27, no. 2 (summer 2001): 381–98.

Asada Tōru. "Kagakusho, karonsho." In *Makura no sōshi daijiten*, ed. Makura no Sōshi Kenkyūkai, 714–21. Tokyo: Bensei Shuppan, 2001.

Asami Kazuhiko, ed. *Jikkinshō*. Shinpen Nihon koten bungaku zenshū 51. Tokyo: Shōgakukan, 1997.

Ban Kōkei. "Kanden jihitsu." In *Hyakka setsurin zokuhen ge no ichi*, ed. Yoshikawa Hanshichi, 101–97. Tokyo: Yoshikawa Kōbunkan, 1906.

Bandō Tomoko. "Kokugoka kyōin yōsei katei de deau *Makura no sōshi* 3." *Yamaguchi Daigaku Kyōiku Gakubu Fuzoku Kyōiku Jissen Sōgō Sentā kenkyū kiyō* 39 (2015): 63–72.

Bardsley, Jan. *The Bluestockings of Japan: New Woman Essays and Fiction from Seitō 1911–1916*. Michigan Monograph Series in Japanese Studies 60. Ann Arbor: Center for Japanese Studies, University of Michigan, 2007.

——. "Maiko Boom: The Revival of Kyoto's Novice Geisha." *Japan Studies Review* 15 (2011): 35–60.

——. "*Seitō* and the Resurgence of Writing by Women." In *The Columbia Companion to Modern East Asian Literature*, ed. Joshua S. Mostow, 93–97. New York: Columbia University Press, 2003.

Berry, Mary Elizabeth. *Japan in Print: Information and Nation in the Early Modern Period*. Berkeley: University of California Press, 2007.

Bhabha, Homi K. *The Location of Culture*. New York: Routledge, 1994.

Bowring, Richard, trans. *Murasaki Shikibu: Her Diary and Poetic Memoirs*. Princeton, N.J.: Princeton Library of Asian Translations, 1982.

——. *Murasaki Shikibu: The Tale of Genji*. Landmarks of World Literature. 2nd ed. Cambridge: Cambridge University Press, 2004.

Brower, Robert H., and Steven D. Carter, trans. *Conversations with Shōtetsu (Shōtetsu monogatari)*. Michigan Monograph Series in Japanese Studies 7. Ann Arbor: Center for Japanese Studies, University of Michigan, 1992.

Bundy, Roselee. "Gendering the Court Woman Poet: Pedigree and Portrayal in *Fukurō zōshi*." *Monumenta Nipponica* 67, no. 2 (2012): 201–38.

Burns, Susan. *Before the Nation: Kokugaku and the Imagining of Community in Early Modern Japan*. Durham, N.C.: Duke University Press, 2003.

Caddeau, Patrick W. *Appraising Genji: Literary Criticism and Cultural Anxiety in the Age of the Last Samurai*. Albany: SUNY Press, 2006.

Carter, Steven D. ed. and trans. *The Columbia Anthology of Japanese Essays: Zuihitsu from the Tenth to the Twenty-First Century*. New York: Columbia University Press, 2014.

Chance, Linda H. "Constructing the Classic: *Tsurezuregusa* in Tokugawa Readings." *Journal of the American Oriental Society* 117, no. 1 (January–March 1997).

——. *Formless in Form: Kenkō, "Tsurezuregusa," and the Rhetoric of Japanese Fragmentary Prose*. Stanford, Calif.: Stanford University Press, 1997.

——. "Japanese Essay." In *Encyclopedia of the Essay*, ed. Tracy Chevalier, 428–31. London: Fitzroy Dearborn, 1997.

——. "*Zuihitsu* and Gender: *Tsurezuregusa* and *The Pillow Book*." In *Inventing the Classics: Modernity, National Identity, and Japanese Literature*, ed. Haruo Shirane and Tomi Suzuki, 120–47. Stanford, Calif.: Stanford University Press, 2000.

Chaves, Jonathan. "Chinese Poems in *Wakan rōei shū*." In *Japanese and Chinese Poems to Sing: The "Wakan rōei shū*," translated and annotated by J. Thomas Rimer and Jonathan Chaves, 15–28. New York: Columbia University Press, 1997.

Childs, Margaret H. "*Chigo Monogatari*: Love Stories or Buddhist Sermons?" *Monumenta Nipponica* 35, no. 2 (summer 1980): 127–51.

Cook, Lewis Edwin. "The Discipline of Poetry: Authority and Invention in the *Kokindenju*." PhD diss., Cornell University, 2000.

——. "Genre Trouble: Medieval Commentaries and Canonization of *The Tale of Genji*." In *Envisioning "The Tale of Genji": Media, Gender, and Cultural Production*, ed. Haruo Shirane, 129–53. New York: Columbia University Press, 2008.

Copeland, Rebecca L. "Fashioning the Feminine: Images of the Modern Girl Student in Meiji Japan." *U.S.-Japan Women's Journal* 30/31 (2006): 13–35.

——. *Lost Leaves: Women Writers of Meiji Japan*. Honolulu: University of Hawai'i Press, 2000.

Czarnecki, Melanie. "Bad Girls from Good Families: The Degenerate Meiji Schoolgirl." In *Bad Girls of Japan*, ed. Laura Miller and Jan Bardsley, 49–63. New York: Palgrave Macmillan, 2005.

DiNitto, Rachel. "Return of the *Zuihitsu*: Print Culture, Modern Life, and Heterogeneous Narrative in Prewar Japan." *Harvard Journal of Asiatic Studies* 64, no. 2 (December 2004): 251–90.

Emmerich, Michael. *The Tale of Genji: Translation, Canonization, and World Literature*. New York: Columbia University Press, 2013.

Emori Ichirō, ed. *Denki, shinkō, hoka*. Vol. 9 of *Edo jidai josei seikatsu ezu daijiten*. Tokyo: Ōzorasha, 1994.

——, ed. *Waka, koten bungaku*. Vol. 8 of *Edo jidai josei seikatsu ezu daijiten*. Tokyo: Ōzorasha, 1994.

Faure, Bernard. *The Power of Denial: Buddhism, Purity, and Gender*. Princeton, N.J.: Princeton University Press, 2003.

Fish, Stanley. "Interpreting the *Variorum*." In *Is There a Text in This Class? The Authority of Interpretative Communities*, 147–73. Cambridge, Mass.: Harvard University Press, 1982.

Fujii Otoo. *Otogizōshi*. Yūhōdō bunko. Tokyo: Yūhōdō Shoten, 1915.

Fujimoto Kizan. *Shinpan Shikidō ōkagami*. Ed. Shinpan Shikidō Ōkagami Kankōkai. Tokyo: Yagi Shoten, 2006.

Fujimoto Munetoshi. "Kenkyū, hyōronshi." In *Makura no sōshi daijiten*, ed. Makura no Sōshi Kenkyūkai, 823–35. Tokyo: Bensei Shuppan, 2001.

Fujioka Sakutarō. "Genji monogatari 3: Murasaki shikibu." In *Kokubungaku zenshi: Heianchō hen*, ed. Akiyama Ken, 2:125–37. Tōyō bunko 247. Tokyo: Heibonsha, 1974.

——. "Makura no sōshi." In *Kokubungaku zenshi: Heianchō hen*, ed. Akiyama Ken, 2:71–91. Tōyō bunko 247. Tokyo: Heibonsha, 1974.

Fukumori, Naomi. "Sei Shōnagon's *Makura no sōshi*: A Re-visionary History." *Journal of the Association of Teachers of Japanese* 31, no. 1 (April 1997): 1–44.

Gerstle, Andrew. *Edo onna no shungabon: En to shō no fūfu shinan*. Tokyo: Heibonsha, 2011.

Goodwin, Janet R. *Selling Songs and Smiles: The Sex Trade in Heian and Kamakura Japan*. Honolulu: University of Hawai`i Press, 2007.

Gotō Takaki. "Kareinaru oiran no bigaku." In *Yoshiwara yūjo no subete*, ed. Watanabe Kenji, 18–27. Gakken mukku karuta shirīzu. Tokyo: Gakken, 2014.

Guest, Jennifer. "Primers, Commentaries, and Kanbun Literacy in Japanese Literary Culture, 950–1250 CE." PhD diss., Columbia University, 2013.

Haga Yaichi. *Kokubungakushi jikkō*. Tokyo: Fuzanbō, 1899.

Hagitani Boku, ed. *Makura no sōshi*. 2 vols. Shinchō Nihon koten taisei. Tokyo: Shinchōsha, 1977.

——. *Makura no sōshi kaikan*. 4 vols. Tokyo: Dōhōsha Shuppan, 1981–1983.

Hamaguchi Toshihiro. "*Makura no sōshi* chūshakusho kaidai." In *Makura no sōshi daijiten*, ed. Makura no Sōshi Kenkyūkai, 789–822. Tokyo: Bensei Shuppan, 2001.

Hanabusa Hideki, trans. *Hakushi monjū no hihanteki kenkyū*. Kyoto: Nakamura Insatsu Shuppanbu, 1960.

Hanasaki Kazuo. *Senryū shungashi*. Tokyo: Taihei Shooku, 1989.

Hara Masako. "Kamo no Mabuchi no *Makura no sōshi kō*: Mabuchi jihitsu kakiire *Makura no sōshi shunshoshō*." In *Kamo no Mabuchi to sono monryū*, ed. Mabuchi Tanjō Sanbyakunen Kinen Ronbunshū Kankōkai. Tokyo: Heibunsha, 1999.

Harper, Thomas. "*The Moonlit Lake Commentary*." In *Reading "The Tale of Genji": Sources from the First Millennium*, ed. Thomas Harper and Haruo Shirane, 368–81. New York: Columbia University Press, 2015.

——, trans. "*The Tale of Genji: A Little Jeweled Comb*." In *Reading "The Tale of Genji": Sources from the First Millennium*, ed. Thomas Harper and Haruo Shirane, 411–506. New York: Columbia University Press, 2015.

Hashimoto Fumio. *Genten o mezashite: Koten bungaku no tame no shoshi*. Tokyo: Kasama Shoin, 1977.

Hashimoto Osamu. *Momojiri goyaku Makura no sōshi*. 3 vols. Tokyo: Kawade Bunko, 2007.

Hayakawa Monta. *Ehon Haru no akebono*. Tokyo: Kawade Shobō Shinsha, 1999.

——, ed. *Ehon Haru no akebono*. Trans. P. Fister and Kuriyama Shigehisa. Nichibunken shozō kinsei enpon shiryō shūsei 3, Nichibunken sōsho 33. Kyoto: Nichibun Kenkyū Sentā, 2004.

——. "Who Were the Audiences for *Shunga*?" In "Shunga: Sex and Humor in Japanese Art and Literature," ed. C. Andrew Gerstle and Timothy Clark. Special issue, *Japan Review* 26 (2013): 17–36.

Hayami Hiroshi. "Maedakebon." In *Makura no sōshi daijiten*, ed. Makura no Sōshi Kenkyūkai, 86–88. Tokyo: Bensei Shuppan, 2001.

——. "Sakaibon." In *Makura no sōshi daijiten*, ed. Makura no Sōshi Kenkyūkai, 88–102. Tokyo: Bensei Shuppan, 2001.

Hayashi Yoshikazu. *Enpon kenkyū: Shigemasa*. Tokyo: Yūkō Shobō, 1966.

——. *Hatsuhana, Ehon Haru no akebono*. Hihon Edo bungakusen 9. Tokyo: Nichirinkaku, 1980.

Hazama Tetsurō. "*Makura no sōshi* kenkyūshi." In *Gengo, gensen, eikyō, kenkyū*, vol. 4 of *Makura no sōshi kōza*, ed. Yūseidō Henshūbu, 301–24. Tokyo: Yūseidō Shuppan, 1976.

Hebizō and Umino Nagiko. *Nihonjin nara shitte okitai Nihon bungaku: Yamato Takeru kara Kenkō made jinbutsu de yomu koten*. Tokyo: Gentōsha, 2011.

Heldt, Gustav. "Saigyō's Traveling Tale: A Translation of *Saigyō Monogatari*." *Monumenta Nipponica* 52, no. 4 (winter 1997): 467–521.

Henitiuk, Valerie. *Worlding Sei Shōnagon: "The Pillow Book" in Translation*. Ottawa: University of Ottawa Press, 2012.

Huey, Robert N. *Kyōgoku Tamekane: Poetry and Politics in Late Kamakura Japan*. Stanford, Calif.: Stanford University Press, 1989.

Hutcheon, Linda. *Irony's Edge: The Theory and Politics of Irony*. New York: Routledge, 1994.

——. *A Theory of Adaptation*. London: Routledge, 2006.

——. *A Theory of Parody: The Teachings of Twentieth-Century Art Forms*. New York: Methuen, 1985.

Igarashi Chikara. *Shinkokubungakushi*. Tokyo: Waseda Daigaku Shuppanbu, 1912.

Ii Haruki. "Kochūshaku kenkyū no igi." In *Heian bungaku no kochūshaku to juyō*, ed. Jinno Hidenori, Niimi Akihito, and Yokomizo Hiroshi, 1:2–6. Tokyo: Musashino Shoin 2008.

Ijichi Tetsuo et al., eds. *Haikai daijiten*. Rev. 7th ed. Tokyo: Meiji Shoin, 1961.

Ikeda Kikan. *Kenkyū Makura no sōshi*. Tokyo: Shibundō, 1963.

——. "*Sei Shōnagon Makura no sōshi* genson shohon no kaisetsu." In "*Sei Shōnagon Makura no sōshi* no ihon ni kansuru kenkyū." Special issue, *Kokugo to kokubungaku* 5, no. 1 (1928): 83–184.

——. *Zuihitsu bungaku*. Tokyo: Shibundō, 1968.

Ikeda Kikan and Kishigami Shinji, eds. *Makura no sōshi*. Nihon koten bungaku taikei. Tokyo: Iwanami Shoten, 1958.

Ikegami, Eiko. *Bonds of Civility: Aesthetic Networks and the Political Origins of Japanese Culture*. Cambridge: Cambridge University Press, 2005.

Imai Gen'e. *Kazan'in to Sei Shōnagon*. Ed. Koga Noriko. Vol. 9 of *Imai Gen'e chosakushū*. Ed. Imanishi Shūichirō et al. Tokyo: Kasama Shoin, 2007.

Inoue Masami, ed. *Shorin shuppan shoseki mokuroku shūsei*. 3 vols. Tokyo: Inoue Shobō, 1962.

Ishida Jōji, ed. *Makura no sōshi: Fu gendai goyaku*. 2 vols. Tokyo: Kadokawa Shoten, 1979–1980.

Ishihara Masaaki. "Nennen zuihitsu 1." In *Hyakka setsurin zokuhen ge no ichi*, ed. Yoshikawa Hanshichi, 199–215. Tokyo: Yoshikawa Kōbunkan, 1906.

Ishikawa Matsutarō, ed. *Joshi yō ōrai* 12. Vol. 92 of *Ōraimono taikei*. Tokyo: Ōzorasha, 1994.

Ivanova, Gergana. "Eiyaku sareta *Makura no sōshi* ga tsukuridashita taishū bunka." *Kaigai Heian bungaku jānaru* 2 (2015): 11–21.

——. "Knowing Women: Sei Shōnagon's *Makura no sōshi* in Early-Modern Japan." PhD diss., University of British Columbia, 2012.

——. "Re-Gendering a Classic: *The Pillow Book* for Early Modern Female Readers." *Japanese Language and Literature* 50 (2016): 105–53.

——. "Textual Variations of Sei Shōnagon's *Makura no sōshi*: Perception of the Text and the Narratorial Voice." Master's thesis, University of Toronto, 2006.

Jauss, Hans Robert. *Toward an Aesthetic of Reception*. Trans. Timothy Bahti. Minneapolis: University of Minnesota Press, 1982.

"Kagaishō." In *Sharebon taisei*, ed. Sharebon Taisei Henshū Iinkai, 3:287–302. Tokyo: Chūō Kōronsha, 1979.

Kaigo Tokiomi, ed. *Nihon kyōkasho taikei: Kindai-hen 7, Kokugo 4*. Tokyo: Kōdansha, 1963.

Kakitani Yūzō. "Sankanbon." In *Makura no sōshi daijiten*, ed. Makura no Sōshi Kenkyūkai, 62–74. Tokyo: Bensei Shuppan, 2001.

Kamei Shin. "Kinsei kōki *Makura no sōshi* kenkyū ippan." *Gazoku* 11 (June 2012): 30–44.

Katō Bansai. *Makura no sōshishō*. Ed. Kokubun Meicho Kankōkai. Nihon bungaku kochū taisei. Tokyo: Kokubun Meicho Kankōkai, 1934.

Kato, Eileen, trans. *Komachi and the Hundred Nights*. In *Twenty Plays of the Nō Theatre*, ed. Donald Keene, 54–63. New York: Columbia University Press, 1970.

Kawashima, Terry. *Writing Margins: The Textual Construction of Gender in Heian and Kamakura Japan*. Harvard East Asian Monographs 201. Cambridge, Mass.: Harvard University Asia Center, 2001.

Keene, Donald. *Seeds in the Heart: Japanese Literature from Earliest Times to the Late Sixteenth Century*. A History of Japanese Literature 1. New York: Holt, 1993.

Kigoshi Takashi. "Shutten, gensen, senshō." In *Makura no sōshi: Shosetsu ichiran*, ed. Shioda Ryōhei, 133–64. Tokyo: Meiji Shoin, 1970.

Kimbrough, R. Keller. "Apocryphal Texts and Literary Identity: Sei Shōnagon and *The Matsushima Diary*." *Monumenta Nipponica* 57, no. 2 (summer 2002): 133–71.

——. *Preachers, Poets, Women, and the Way: Izumi Shikibu and the Buddhist Literature of Medieval Japan*. Michigan Monograph Series in Japanese Studies 62. Ann Arbor: Center for Japanese Studies, University of Michigan, 2008.

Kinney, Anne Behnke. *Exemplary Women of Early China: "The Lienü zhuan" of Liu Xiang*. New York: Columbia University Press, 2014.

Kinsei Bungaku Shoshi Kenkyūkai, ed. *Kinsei bungaku shiryō ruijū: Kanazōshi hen 7, Honchō jokan 3*. Tokyo: Benseisha, 1972.

Kishigami Shinji et al., eds. *Makura no sōshi, Tsurezuregusa*. Kokugo kokubungaku kenkyūshi taisei 6. Tokyo: Sanseidō, 1977.

Kitamura Kigin. *Makura no sōshi: Shunshoshō*. 3 vols. Ed. Ikeda Kikan. Tokyo: Iwanami Shoten, 1951.

——. *Ominaeshi monogatari*. Ed. Satō Ritsu. Koten bunko 282. Tokyo: Koten Bunko, 1975.

Koizumi Yoshinaga. "Learning to Read and Write: A Study of *Tenaraibon*." In *Listen, Copy, Read: Popular Learning in Early Modern Japan*, ed. Matthias Hayek and Annick Horiuchi, 89–138. Brill's Japanese Studies Library 46. Leiden: Brill, 2014.

Komachiya Teruhiko. "*Inu makura, Mottomo no sōshi, Sei Shōnagon chie no ita*: *Makura no sōshi* no kyōju to rufu." *Kōkō tsūshin tōsho kokugo* 322 (May 1994): 1–3.

Komori Kiyoshi. "Kokugo kyōiku no naka no *Makura no sōshi*." In *Makura no sōshi: Sōzō to shinsei*, ed. Tsushima Tomoaki and Komori Kiyoshi, 268–86. Tokyo: Kanrin Shobō, 2011.

Komukai Yumiko. *Honjitsu mo ito okashi!! Makura no sōshi*. Tokyo: Kadokawa Shoten, 2014.

Konishi Seiichi. *Murasaki Shikibu to Sei Shōnagon: Kizoku ga sakaeta jidai ni*. NHK Ningen Nihonshi. Tokyo: Rironsha, 2003.

Kornicki, Peter. *The Book in Japan: A Cultural History from the Beginnings to the Nineteenth Century*. Leiden: Brill, 1998.

——. "Unsuitable Books for Women? *Genji monogatari* and *Ise monogatari* in Late Seventeenth-Century Japan." *Monumenta Nipponica* 60, no. 2 (summer 2005): 147–193.

Kristeva, Tzvetana. "the pillow hook (*the pillow book* as an 'open work')." *Japan Review* 5 (1994): 15–54.

Kurosawa Hiromitsu and Takeuchi Kaoru. *Kokoro ni gutto kuru Nihon no koten*. Tokyo: NTT Shuppan, 2012.

Kusunoki Michitaka. *Makura no sōshi ihon kenkyū*. Tokyo: Kasama Shoin, 1970.

Lesigne-Audoly, Evelyne. "Du texte à l'œuvre: L'édition commentée du Livre-oreiller de Sei Shōnagon par Kitamura Kigin (1674)." PhD diss., INALCO, 2013.

Li, Michelle Osterfeld. *Ambiguous Bodies: Reading the Grotesque in Japanese* Setsuwa *Tales*. Stanford, Calif.: Stanford University Press, 2009.

Maeda Kingorō and Morita Takeshi. "Inu makura." In *Kanazōshishū*, ed. Maeda Kingorō and Morita Takeshi, 33–48. Nihon koten bungaku taikei 90. Tokyo: Iwanami Shoten, 1965.

Mappira Gomenshi. "*Shūi Makura no sōshi kagaishō* tsūshaku 1." *Kinsei shomin bunka* 11 (1952): 23–29.

——. "*Shūi Makura no sōshi kagaishō* tsūshaku 2." *Kinsei shomin bunka* 12 (1952): 26–29.

——. "*Shūi Makura no sōshi kagaishō* tsūshaku 3." *Kinsei shomin bunka* 14 (1952): 22–26.

Marks, Andreas. *Japanese Woodblock Prints: Artists, Publishers, and Masterworks 1680–1900*. Tokyo: Tuttle, 2010.

Marra, Michele. "*Mumyōzōshi*, Part 3." *Monumenta Nipponica* 39, no. 4 (winter 1984): 409–34.

——. *Representations of Power: The Literary Politics of Medieval Japan.* Honolulu: University of Hawai'i Press, 1993.

Maruyama Yumiko. *Sei Shōnagon to Murasaki Shikibu: Wakan konkō no jidai no miya no nyōbō.* Tokyo: Yamakawa Shuppansha, 2015.

Matsubara Hidee. *Usuyuki monogatari to otogizōshi kanazōshi.* Kenkyū sōsho 202. Osaka: Izumi Shoin, 1997.

Matsuo Satoshi and Nagai Kazuko, eds. *Makura no sōshi: Nōinbon.* Genbun and gendaigoyaku shirīzu. Tokyo: Kasama Shoin, 2008.

Mendō Kazuki. *Makura no sōshi.* NHK Manga de yomu koten 1. Tokyo: Hōmusha, 2006.

Midorikawa, Machiko. "Reading a Heian Blog: A New Translation of *Makura no Sōshi.*" Review of *The Pillow Book,* by Sei Shōnagon, trans. Meredith McKinney. *Monumenta Nipponica* 63, no. 1 (spring 2008): 143–60.

Mikami Sanji and Takatsu Kuwasaburō. *Nihon bungakushi.* Vol. 1. Tokyo: Kinkōdō, 1890.

Miller, J. Scott. "The Hybrid Narrative of Kyōden's *Sharebon.*" *Monumenta Nipponica* 43, no. 2 (summer 1988): 133–52.

Mitamura Masako. *Makura no sōshi: Hyōgen no ronri.* Tokyo: Yūseidō Shuppan, 1995.

——. "*Makura no sōshi* no kenkyū no ashibumi." *Nihon bungaku* 31, no. 2 (February 1982): 58–59.

——. "Tennōsei kara *Makura no sōshi* o yomu." In "*Makura no sōshi*-teki jinsei sekkei." Special issue, *Kokubungaku: Kaishaku to kyōzai no kenkyū* 52, no. 6 (2006): 44–51.

Miyakawa Yōko. "Fujiwara no Teishi." In *Makura no sōshi daijiten,* ed. Makura no Sōshi Kenkyūkai, 538–40. Tokyo: Bensei Shuppan, 2001.

Miyazaki Sōhei. *Sei Shōnagon junan no kindai.* Tokyo: Shintensha, 2009.

——. *Sei Shōnagon to Murasaki Shikibu: Sono taihiron josetsu.* Tokyo: Chōbunsha, 1993.

Moretti, Laura. "The Japanese Early-Modern Publishing Market Unveiled: A Survey of Edo-Period Booksellers' Catalogues." *East Asian Publishing and Society* 2 (2012): 199–308.

Morinaga, Maki. "The Gender of *Onnagata* as the Imitating Imitated: Its Historicity, Performativity, and Involvement in the Circulation of Femininity." *positions: east asia cultures critique* 10, no. 2 (2002): 245–84.

Morris, Ivan, trans. *The Pillow Book of Sei Shōnagon.* 2 vols. London: Oxford University Press, 1967.

Morris, Mark. "Sei Shōnagon's Poetic Catalogues." *Harvard Journal of Asiatic Studies* 40, no. 1 (June 1980): 5–54.

Mostow, Joshua S. *Courtly Visions: "The Ise Stories" and the Politics of Cultural Appropriation.* Japanese Visual Culture 12. Honolulu: University of Hawaiʻi Press, 2014.

——. "*E no gotoshi*: The Picture Simile and the Feminine Re-guard in Japanese Illustrated Romances." *Word and Image* 11, no. 1 (January–March 1995): 37–54.

——. "The Gender of *Wakashu* and the Grammar of Desire." In *Gender and Power in the Japanese Visual Field*, ed. Joshua S. Mostow, Norman Bryson, and Maribeth Graybill, 49–70. Honolulu: University of Hawaiʻi Press, 2003.

——. "Illustrated Classical Texts for Women in the Edo Period." In *The Female as Subject: Reading and Writing in Early Modern Japan*, ed. P. F. Kornicki, Mara Patessio, and G. G. Rowley, 59–86. Michigan Monograph Series in Japanese Studies 70. Ann Arbor: Center for Japanese Studies, University of Michigan, 2010.

——. "Mother Tongue and Father Script: The Relationship of Sei Shōnagon and Murasaki Shikibu to Their Fathers and Chinese Letters." In *The Father-Daughter Plot: Japanese Literary Women and the Law of the Father*, ed. Rebecca L. Copeland and Esperanza Ramirez-Christensen, 115–42. Honolulu: University of Hawaiʻi Press, 2001.

——. *Pictures of the Heart: The "Hyakunin Isshu" in Word and Image.* Honolulu: University of Hawaiʻi Press, 1996.

Mostow, Joshua S., and Royall Tyler, trans. *The Ise Stories: Ise Monogatari.* Honolulu: University of Hawaiʻi Press, 2010.

Mutō Sadao. "'Monohazuke' zakkō: Medetaki mono wa." *Senryū Shinano* 610 (January 1994): 1–6.

Nagai Kazuko. "Dōtai toshite no *Makura no sōshi*: Honmon to sakusha to." *Kokubun* 91 (August 1999): 10–19.

Naito, Satoko. "The Making of Murasaki Shikibu: Constructing Authorship, Gendering Readership, and Legitimizing *The Tale of Genji*." PhD diss., Columbia University, 2010.

Nakajima Wakako. "*Makura no sōshi* 'Kōrohō no yuki' no dan no juyō o megutte: Chūsei, kinsei no setsuwashū o chūshin ni." *Kokubun ronsō* 18 (March 1991): 1–15.

Nakamura Yukihiko. "Kinsei zuihitsu ni tsuite." In *Kinsei yogo*, vol. 13 of *Nakamura Yukihiko chojutsushū*, 287–94. Tokyo: Chūō Kōronsha, 1984.

Nakanishi Kenji. "Den-Nōin-shoji-hon." In *Makura no sōshi daijiten*, ed. Makura no Sōshi Kenkyūkai, 75–85. Tokyo: Bensei Shuppan, 2001.

Nakano Setsuko. *Kangaeru onnatachi: Kanazōshi kara "Onna daigaku."* Tokyo: Ōzorasha, 1997.

Newhard, Jamie L. *Knowing the Amorous Man: A History of Scholarship on "Tales of Ise."* Harvard East Asian Monographs 355. Cambridge, Mass.: Harvard University Press, 2013.

Nishio Mitsuo. "Honkoku: Kunitsufumi yoyo no ato." In *Nihon bungaku sōkō: Nishio Mitsuo Sensei kanreki kinen ronshū*, ed. Nishio Mitsuo Sensei Kanreki Kinenkai, 289–346. Tokyo: Tōyō Hōki Shuppan, 1968.

Niwa Kenji. "Yūri." In *Genji monogatari no hensōkyoku: Edo no shirabe*, ed. Suzuki Ken'ichi, 235–40. Tokyo: Miyai Shoten, 2003.

Noma Kōshin. *Kinsei sakka denkō*. Tokyo: Chūō Kōronsha, 1985.

Numajiri Toshimichi. *Heian bungaku no hassō to seisei*. Kokugaku Daigaku Daigakuin kenkyū sōsho, Bungaku Kenkyūka 17. Tokyo: Kokugakuin Daigaku Daigakuin, 2007.

——. "'Sei Shōnagon Makura no sōshishō' no shōdan kubun hōhō." *Nihon Bungaku* 59, no. 5 (May 2010): 42–56.

Ō Aimi. *Pītā Gurīnawē no Makura no sōshi: Za pirōbukku satsuei nisshi*. Tokyo: Shimizu Shoin, 1997.

Okanishi Ichū and Katō Bansai. *Makura no sōshi bōchū, Makura no sōshishō*. Ed. Muromatsu Iwao et al. Kokubun chūshaku zensho 4. Tokyo: Sumiya Shobō, 1967.

Okuyama Kyōko. *Sei Shōnagon to Murasaki Shikibu: Sennen mae kara ninki sakka*. Denki shirīzu. Tokyo: Shūeisha Mirai Bunko, 2014.

Orbaugh, Sharalyn. "Gender, Family, and Sexualities in Modern Literature." In *The Columbia Companion to Modern East Asian Literature*, ed. Joshua S. Mostow, 43–52. New York: Columbia University Press, 2003.

——. "The Problem of the Modern Subject." In *The Columbia Companion to Modern East Asian Literature*, ed. Joshua S. Mostow, 24–35. New York: Columbia University Press, 2003.

Pflugfelder, Gregory M. *Cartographies of Desire: Male-Male Sexuality in Japanese Discourse, 1600–1950*. Berkeley: University of California Press, 1999.

Putzar, Edward. "Inu Makura: The Dog Pillow." *Harvard Journal of Asiatic Studies* 28 (1968): 98–113.

Ramirez-Christensen, Esperanza. *Emptiness and Temporality: Buddhism and Medieval Japanese Poetics*. Stanford, Calif.: Stanford University Press, 2008.

Raphals, Lisa. *Sharing the Light: Representations of Women and Virtue in Early China*. Albany: SUNY Press, 1998.

Rodd, Laurel Rasplica, and Mary Catherine Henkenius, trans. *Kokinshū: A Collection of Poems Ancient and Modern*. Boston: Cheng and Tsui, 2004.

Saeki Junko. *Yūjo no bunkashi: Hare no onnatachi*. Chūō shinsho 853. Tokyo: Chūō Kōronsha, 1987.

Saitō Kiyoe et al., eds. *Makura no sōshi Tsurezuregusa*. Kokugo kokubungaku kenkyūshi taisei 6. Tokyo: Sanseidō, 1960.

Sarra, Edith. "The Poetics of Voyeurism in *The Pillow Book*." In *Fictions of Femininity: Literary Inventions of Gender in Japanese Court Women's Memoirs*, 222–64. Stanford, Calif.: Stanford University Press, 1999.

Sasaki Takahiro. "Teika-bon toshite no *Makura no sōshi*." In *Nihon koten shoshigakuron*, 403–28. Tokyo: Kasama Shoin, 2016.

Schalow, Paul Gordon. "Formulating a Theory of Women's Writing in 17th-Century Japan: Kitamura Kigin's *Ominaeshi monogatari* (Tales of the Maidenflower)." *Early Modern Japan* 5, no. 2 (December 1995): 14–18.

——. "Spiritual Dimensions of Male Beauty in Japanese Buddhism." In *Religion, Homosexuality, and Literature*, ed. Michael L. Stemmeler and José Ignacio Cabezón, 75–92. Las Colinas, Texas: Monument Press, 1992.

——. "Theorizing Sex/Gender in Early Modern Japan: Kitamura Kigin's *Maidenflowers* and *Wild Azaleas*." *Japanese Studies* 18, no. 3 (1989): 247–63.

Screech, Timon. *Sex and the Floating World: Erotic Images in Japan 1700–1820.* Honolulu: University of Hawai`i Press, 1999.

Sei Shōnagon. *The Pillow Book.* Trans. Meredith McKinney. New York: Penguin Books, 2006.

Sekiguchi, Sumiko. "Gender in the Meiji Renovation: Confucian 'Lessons for Women' and the Making of Modern Japan." *Social Science Journal Japan* 11, no. 2 (2008): 201–21.

Shimizu Yoshinori. *Gakkō de wa oshiete kurenai Nihon bungakushi.* Tokyo: PHP Kenkyūjo, 2013.

Shioda Ryōhei, ed. *Shosetsu ichiran Makura no sōshi.* Tokyo: Meiji Shoin, 1970.

Shirane, Haruo. *The Bridge of Dreams: A Poetics of "The Tale of Genji."* Stanford, Calif.: Stanford University Press, 1987.

——, ed. *Early Modern Japanese Literature: An Anthology, 1600–1900.* New York: Columbia University Press, 2002.

——. *Traces of Dreams: Landscape, Cultural Memory, and the Poetry of Bashō.* Stanford, Calif.: Stanford University Press, 1998.

——, ed. *Traditional Japanese Literature: An Anthology, Beginnings to 1600.* New York: Columbia University Press, 2007.

Sievers, Sharon L. *Flowers in Salt: The Beginnings of Feminist Consciousness in Modern Japan.* Stanford, Calif.: Stanford University Press, 1983.

Smith, Barbara Herrnstein. *Contingencies of Value: Alternative Perspectives for Critical Theory.* Cambridge, Mass.: Harvard University Press, 1988.

Stanley, Amy. *Selling Women: Prostitution, Markets, and the Household in Early Modern Japan.* Berkeley: University of California Press, 2012.

Suzuki Hideo. *Sei Shōnagon to Murasaki Shikibu: Ōchō joryū bungaku no sekai.* Tokyo: Hōsō Daigaku Kyōiku Shinkōkai, 1998.

Suzuki, Tomi. "Gender and Genre: Modern Literary Histories and Women's Diary Literature." In *Inventing the Classics: Modernity, National Identity, and Japanese Literature*, ed. Haruo Shirane and Tomi Suzuki, 71–95. Stanford, Calif.: Stanford University Press, 2000.

———. "*The Tale of Genji*, National Literature, Language, and Modernism." In *Envisioning "The Tale of Genji": Media, Gender, and Cultural Production*, ed. Haruo Shirane, 243–87. New York: Columbia University Press, 2008.

Suzuki Tomotarō. "*Makura no sōshi* shohanpon no honmon no seiritsu: Toku ni Keian hanpon, Bansaishō, Shunshoshō, Bōchūbon ni tsuite." In *Heian jidai bungaku ronsō*, 453–95. Tokyo: Kasama Shoin, 1968.

Taihei Shujin. "Fūfu narabi no oka." In *Nishikawa Sukenobu makurabon issō*, 13–106. Sumizuri ehonsen 2. Tokyo: Taihei Shooku, 2008.

Tanaka Jūtarō. *Kōhon Makura no sōshi*. Tokyo: Koten Bunko, 1953–1957.

———, ed. *Makura no sōshi*. Nihon koten zensho. Tokyo: Asahi Shinbunsha, 1947.

———. *Sei Shōnagon inu makurashū*. Koten bunko 49. Tokyo: Koten Bunko, 1982.

———. *Sei Shōnagon Makura no sōshi kenkyū*. Kasama sōsho 10. Tokyo: Kasama Shoin, 1942.

———. "Shohon no denryū." In *Makura no sōshi hikkei*, ed. Kishigami Shinji, 32–44. Tokyo: Gakutōsha, 1967.

Teruoka Yasutaka. "The Pleasure Quarters and Tokugawa Culture." In *Eighteenth Century Japan: Culture and Society*, ed. C. Andrew Gerstle, 3–32. Richmond, U.K.: Curzon Press, 1989.

Tsushima Tomoaki. *Dōtai toshite no Makura no sōshi*. Tokyo: Ōfūsha, 2005.

———. *Weirī de yomu Makura no sōshi*. Tokyo: Kanae Shobō, 2002.

Tsushima Tomoaki and Nakajima Wakako, eds. *Shinpen Makura no sōshi*. Tokyo: Ōfūsha, 2010.

Tyler, Royall, trans. *The Tale of Genji*. New York: Penguin Books, 2003.

Uchida Seiko. *Sei Shōnagon Murasaki Shikibu: Ōchō inuha onna vs nekoha onna*. Tokyo: Nihon Bungakukan, 2008.

Umezawa Waken. *Sei Shōnagon to Murasaki Shikibu*. Tokyo: Kokkōsha, 1902.

Van Ward Geddes, John. "A Study of the *Jikkinshō*." PhD diss., Washington University in St. Louis, 1976.

Variety Art Works. *Makura no sōshi*. Manga de dokuha 77. Tokyo: Īsuto Puresu, 2014.

Waley, Arthur. *The Pillow Book of Sei Shōnagon*. Tokyo: Tuttle, 2011.

Walthall, Anne. "The Life Cycle of Farm Women in Tokugawa Japan." In *Recreating Japanese Women, 1600–1945*, ed. Gail Lee Bernstein, 42–70. Oakland, Calif.: University of California Press, 1991.

Watanabe Kenji. *Edo sanbyaku nen Yoshiwara no shikitari: Prē bukkusu interijensu*. Tokyo: Seishun Shuppansha, 2004.

———. *Kinsei daimyō bungeiken kenkyū*. Tokyo: Yagi Shoten, 1997.

Watanabe Minoru, ed. *Makura no sōshi*. Shin Nihon koten bungaku taikei 25. Tokyo: Iwanami Shoten, 1991.

Watanabe Morikuni and Watanabe Kenji. "Mottomo no sōshi." In *Kanazōshishū*, ed. Watanabe Morikuni and Watanabe Kenji, 53–138. Shin Nihon koten bungaku taikei 74. Tokyo: Iwanami Shoten, 1991. Watson, Burton, trans. *The Tales of the Heike*. New York: Columbia University Press, 2003.

Yahagi Takeshi. "*Makura no sōshi* to kanseki." In *Makura no sōshi daijiten*, ed. Makura no Sōshi Kenkyūkai, 599–615. Tokyo: Bensei Shuppan, 2001.

Yamagishi Tokuhei, ed. *Sei Shōnagon Makura no sōshi*. In *Nihon bungaku taikei: Kōchū*, vol. 3. Tokyo: Kokumin Tosho, 1926.

Yoda, Tomiko. *Gender and National Literature: Heian Texts in the Constructions of Japanese Modernity*. Durham, N.C.: Duke University Press, 2004.

Yokota Fuyuhiko. "Imagining Working Women in Early Modern Japan." Trans. Mariko Asano Tamanoi. In *Women and Class in Japanese History*, ed. Hitomi Tonomura, Anne Walthall, and Wakita Haruko. Michigan Monograph Series in Japanese Studies 25. Ann Arbor: Center for Japanese Studies, University of Michigan, 1999.

Yokoyama, Toshio. "In Quest of Civility: Conspicuous Uses of Household Encyclopedias in Nineteenth-Century Japan." *Zinbun* 34, no. 1 (1999): 197–222.

Yonemoto, Marcia. *Mapping Early Modern Japan: Space, Place, and Culture in the Tokugawa Period (1603–1868)*. Berkeley: University of California Press, 2003.

——. "The Perils of the 'Unpolished Jewel': Defining Women's Roles in Household Management in Early Modern Japan." *U.S.-Japan Women's Journal* 39 (2010): 38–62.

Index

Page numbers in *italics* indicate illustrations.

Minamoto no Shitagō, 76, 163n4

Minamoto no Toshikata, 133, 194n50

Minamoto no Tsunefusa, 7, 20–21, 164n12, 167n6

Minamoto Sekkō, 91, 98, 184n30

Mirror for Women of Our Country, A (*Honchō jokan* 本朝女鑑), 134

Mirror for Women's Epistolary Education, A (*Jokyō bunshō kagami* 女教文章鑑), 134–35, *135*

Mirror of Womanhood: The Book of Secret Transmissions, A (*Jokyō hidensho* 女鏡秘伝書), 108

miscellany (*zuihitsu*): 13, 45–48; *See also The Pillow Book*

Mistaken Commentaries (*Hekianshō* 僻案抄), 41

Mitamura Masako, 10, 84–85

Miyagi Kōyō, 30

modern girl (*moga*), 138

mono no aware (to be moved with emotion), 43, 51

monochrome (*hakubyō*) style, 84, 182n4

monohazuke (detailing of things), 37, 42, 49–54, 172n83, 173n96

monozukushi. See monohazuke

Moonlit Lake Commentary, The (*Kogetsushō* 湖月抄), 26, 183n21

Moretti, Laura, 185n38

Morris, Ivan, 159, 171n62, 167n6, 178n57, 179n59, 189n98

Morris, Mark, 10, 175n12

Most Secret Teachings of The Tale of Genji (*Genchū saihishō* 原中最秘抄), 24

Mostow, Joshua S., 10, 13, 55, 89–90, 113

motherhood, 92; and sterility, 104

Motoori Norinaga, 43–44, 46–47

Murakami, Emperor, 94, 115, 163n4, 193n47

Murasaki Shikibu's Diary (*Murasaki Shikibu nikki* 紫式部日記), 136–37, 139–40, 143, 167n6, 197n102

Mutō Sadao, 54

Nagasawa Omotoo, 170n42

Naito, Satoko, 136

Nakajima Wakako, 13, 129, 192n31

Nakanishi Tazuki, 170n42

Nakano Setsuko, 90, 103–104, 106, 108

Nameless Tale, A (*Mumyōzōshi* 無名草子), 124

national learning (*kokugaku*), 15, 27, 38, 43–45, 78, 137, 170n42

national literature (*kokubungaku*), 16, 136, 138, 140, 151, 154

nazo-zuke (riddle capping), 51–52

nenja (person [implicitly male] who thinks of a particular youth), 55–56, 177n29

neo-Confucian ideology, 4, 15, 43, 69–70, 78, 88, 191n28

New Collection of Ancient and Modern Poems (*Shinkokin wakashū* 新古今和歌集), 171n55

Newhard, Jamie L., 24, 44, 183n21

New History of National Literature (*Shinkoku bungakushi* 新国文学史; Igarashi), 48

new woman (*atarashii onna*), 138, 196n73; *See also* Sei Shōnagon

NHK for School: Bewildering History (Rekishi ni dokiri 歴史にドキリ, TV show), 147–48

Nishikawa Sukenobu, 99, 100; and *The Twin Mounds of Conjugality*, 80, 82; and *Picture Book Mount Asahi*, 91; and Uemura Gyokushiken, 97–98

Nishiyama Sōin, 26

Noh, 58, 71, 123, 124